Chilis to Chutneys

ALSO BY NEELAM BATRA

The Indian Vegetarian (1994)

Chilis to Chutneys

American Home Cooking
with the Flavors of India

NEELAM BATRA

William Morrow and Company, Inc.   New York

It is the policy of William Morrow and Company, Inc., and its
imprints and affiliates, recognizing the importance of preserving what
has been written, to print the books we publish on acid-free paper,
and we exert our best efforts to that end.

Library of Congress Cataloging–in–Publication Data
Batra, Neelam.
  Chilis to chutneys : American home cooking with the flavors of
India / Neelam Batra. — 1st ed.
     p.   cm.
  Includes index.
  ISBN 0-688-15690-8
  1. Cookery, Indic.   I. Title.
TX724.5.I4B36   1998
641.5954—dc21   97-24366
                                     CIP

Printed in the United States of America

First Edition

1 2 3 4 5 6 7 8 9 10

BOOK DESIGN BY BONNI LEON-BERMAN

WWW.WILLIAMMORROW.COM

Good food knows
no boundaries and
lively recipes find a home
in all cuisines.

Acknowledgments

WRITING THIS BOOK HAS been a fair amount of hard work and a lot of fun. And the fun would not have been possible without my family and friends, who, in their own special ways—with words, ideas, or deeds—gave me a bit of themselves. A million thanks to all of you, but, remember, you'll be hearing from me again.

My husband, Pradeep, for your unflagging confidence, support, and "ooooffs" when I accidentally added extra salt in the food.

My lovely daughters, Sumita and Supriya, for all your observations and compliments—even when the foods didn't meet your expectations. But, I must be doing something right, if you subconsciously copy my style. Sumi, your one sentence said it all, "Mom, I find myself cooking like you—it's pathetic." I love you both.

My parents, Prakash and Rani Bhatla, my mother-in-law, Prakash Batra, my brother and sister-in-law, Rakesh and Renu Bhatla, my husband's sisters and brothers-in-law, Veena and Sushil Dua, Raj and Asha Puri and Amita Batra, for encouraging me every step of the way.

Sunil Vora for your gracious "han ji's" (yesses) in answering my queries and questions any time of the day or night. Your skills are many and your knowledge vast.

Kent and Susan Little for testing and evaluating every recipe I put before them.

Anu, Ravi, and Monti Khatod for being my ever-ready guinea pigs and recipe testers.

Sanjokta Budhraja, my husband's cousin, for sharing your priceless wealth of knowledge.

Billoo and Poonam Bhatla, Mini and Rajan Aneja, Sunita and Romesh Chopra, Upma and Vikram Budhraja, Kiran and Ashok Malik, Reita and Virender Bhalla, Poonam and Lalit Pant, Neelam and Raghu Rai, Anita Vora, Bharti and Ashwani Dhalwala, Anjana and Vivek Gadh, and Moyne Puri for your food-related comments and suggestions and lighthearted jokes during our get-togethers and weekly sessions of "variation" poker. This is what keeps me going.

Madhu and Harish Seth, Anju and Ashok Khanna, Madhu and Anoop Sharma, Ranjana and Ranbir Wasu, Raj and Baljit Ahluwalia, Chitra and Sudesh Arora, Naina and Madhukar Kapadia, Raksha Bhatia, and Sarita and Ashok Kacker for sharing your ideas, knowledge, and, above all, the inspiring foods you feed me.

Maureen and Eric Lasher, my agents, for believing in me and my work.

Pam Hoenig, my editor, adviser, and friend, who by now knows more about Indian cuisine than I do.

Bahut Shukriya aur badi maharabani (many, many thanks).

Contents

CONTENTS

Introduction: The New Indian Cuisine

EVEN BEFORE I WAS tall enough to gaze over the tandoor, I would stand, tip-toed, watching the marinated lamb, chicken, and fish being threaded on skewers and then immersed into the large barrel-shaped container, intensely hot from live charcoals. Plastered to its inside walls was an assortment of spicy flat breads that had been "rolled out" by slapping them back and forth between the hands. Minutes later, mouth-watering savory treats would magically emerge and before I could question the dark mysteries surrounding this fiery clay oven, an amazing feast was laid on the table. Then there was no time to talk. Only to eat, eat, eat.

The human mind subconsciously stores experiences that become vibrant memories lasting a life-time. How can I ever forget my childhood in India—the warm monsoon rains, the cool spring breezes, the sing-song calls of the food vendors, the continuous ebb and flow of friends and relatives, and the scrumptious foods that mysteriously appeared from my mother's twenty-four-hour kitchen.

Our kitchen was where the family gathered to eat, talk, and gossip. Even today, when I close my eyes, I feel the rhythmic vibrations of the mortar and pestle, smell the heady aromas arising from the sizzling *masalas* (spices), and hear the words of advice and wisdom that were uttered in normal every-day conversations—words that were spoken amongst the adults but were meant for us kids. Intu-itively, we absorbed them all, not thinking for a moment that along with our insatiable palates, our characters were being shaped and values instilled.

Mealtimes at home were fun and lively. My mother always prepared extra—she had been sur-prised too many times by my father walking in with a bunch of friends. At the end of a meal, my father would sometimes quietly snap his fingers at my mom to signal, "Let's go to the movies." (Next to China, India has the second largest movie industry in the world.) Before she could respond, my brother, Rakesh, and I would jump out of our chairs and run towards the car. But, of course, we were sent back with a smile and a promise of ice cream the next day. So appeased, we would run to *Mata ji's* (my paternal grandmother) room to disturb her quiet reading. (She was very fond of reading Indian religious books.) With her books set aside, she would talk to us, asking questions, telling us sto-ries of our father, uncles, and aunts, and of her own childhood days in Jhang (now in Pakistan). Some-times she talked sadly about the partition between India and Pakistan, about her home in Lahore, the neighbors and friends she had left behind, and those who were killed. She did feel particularly lucky that all her immediate family had escaped. My paternal grandfather, Daddy ji, was a high official in the Indian railways and he had a private coupe that could be hooked on to any railway train. Before the actual fighting broke out between the two countries, he was able to bring the whole family safely to India.

Like all children, my brother and I looked forward to our birthdays. Each birthday started with a *havan* (a religious ceremony). A small fire was burned, the *pandit* (priest) recited millions of mantras, then everyone sang *bhajans* (hymns) and semolina halvah was distributed as *prashad* (sacred food from the gods). Following this was a huge vegetarian feast. (The Hindus serve only vegetarian food after religious ceremonies.) All the relatives would give us money and would make us feel so special.

These are glimpses of my home in New Delhi. Outside this home was another world, the larger world of India, full of people of all backgrounds and diverse cuisines.* My concept of food "outside" had meant eating dishes that were not generally prepared at home—spicy *chaats* (page 8), *channa-pooris* (garbanzo beans and puffy breads), and *alu-tikkis* (potato cutlets) from roadside food stands, *dosas* (rice and lentil pancakes) and *idlis* (steamed rice cakes) from southern Indian restaurants, or *Gujerati dhokla* (steamed chickpea flour bites) *and Bombay pao-bhaji* (bread rolls and mashed spicy vegetables). Along with these savory delights were the neighborhood vendor's cartful of goodies, especially the saffron and pistachio kulfis (ice cream). On special occasions, my father would take us to gourmet restaurants to enjoy Mughlai food or an Indian version of Chinese cuisine.

My affair with cooking didn't start until I got married and came to Los Angeles in 1973. I loved to eat and I knew what good food was. I knew that my mother was the best cook, but, at the same time, I realized that she was too far away for me to run to for help. I had never cooked a complete meal by myself nor had I single-handedly purchased groceries. With no formal training in any cuisine, I embarked upon a journey that eventually led me to my computer. I mentally transported myself to my mother's kitchen in New Delhi. Tapping on my memory and taste for guidance, I started a set of kitchen experiments—some good, some bad, some successful, and some not quite so—learning something new every time. My husband, Pradeep, adequately praised my culinary efforts, maybe because he felt sorry for me or maybe because he was grateful that whatever I gave him was actually better than frozen pizza—I'll never know!

What I do know is that his encouraging words and bouts of wordless smiles (especially when he did not like the dishes) taught me a great deal, so much so that I started to teach at a local college and then at Montana Mercantile, an upscale cooking school in Los Angeles. Finally, I wrote an Indian vegetarian book, geared for use in every American kitchen.

From that book came requests for more recipes—this time, for foods that people in America were familiar with: hamburgers, pizza, pasta, and nonvegetarian fare. Before I knew it, I was experimenting with an array of international cuisines.

*India contains twenty-six states, each with its own language and possessing a unique cuisine.

The world today is a small place—and people from different cultures and ethnic backgrounds are thrown together in all spheres of life. From their constant mingling and interaction, a new appreciation of global food patterns and preferences has developed. This, in turn, has dramatically altered the course of worldwide food preparation. While health and proper nutrition still top the list, our seasoned palates now demand something more exotic in terms of flavor—even in the foods we eat every day. There is a constant search for a burst of flavor, a touch of spice, a sprinkle of new herbs, or a new technique.

As an Indian living in America, my "curried" palate prompts me to bring a taste of my country to familiar American foods. As I cook them, my hands automatically reach out for some of my favorite Indian seasonings—and every addition brings forth a brand new flavor. Imagine what happens when I make pasta sauce with garden fresh tomatoes, ginger, and mint . . . pizza with green cilantro chutney . . . tossed salad with tandoori grilled chicken . . . hamburgers with scallions and garam masala . . . or a marinade of yogurt and Indian spices for my summer barbecued foods. This innovative swapping of flavors carries into my traditional Indian dishes as well, when I borrow aromatic herbs, spices, and foods (like tortillas, wonton wrappers, premade pizza crusts, and stuffed pastas) from other cuisines to make some of my favorite Indian recipes.

My Indian kitchen in America is truly a give-and-take of ideas and tastes. Recipes from this kitchen are rich in history, easy to follow, and quick to cook. They are low-fat (except for the deep-fried ones), highly nutritious, innovative recipes that capture the heart of today's cooking styles, turning every meal into a gastronomic delight. They offer new insight into traditional Indian cooking techniques and procedures, and endless suggestions for the preparation of all types of foods, ranging from fresh fruits and vegetables to meats, dried beans, lentils, rice, and grains.

Bringing this exotic Indian "aromatherapy" (creative cooking is a powerful stress reliever) to your homes may be simpler than you imagine. Today, a majority of the popular Indian herbs and spices are available in most American supermarkets or can be purchased at ethnic Indian markets, which have sprung up in most large cities in America. For your convenience, I've also included a list of mail-order sources (page 306).

By sharing some of my traditional and innovative nonvegetarian and vegetarian creations, I hope to bring to you a new level of culinary adventure and inspire you with recipes that will elicit rave reviews from even your most discriminating friends.

Have fun!

A Blend of Spices

THE SEDUCTIVE ALLURE OF spices has fascinated mankind from time immemorial. It is because of spices that new continents were discovered, wars were fought, trade routes developed, and the course of history dramatically affected. A similar global change is taking place right at this very moment—and this time it is in the world of cooking.

The intermingling of different cultures throughout the world continually introduces us to many new and wonderful spices and herbs from other countries—and our goal is to incorporate all of them in our everyday meals. What better way is there than to mix and match these exotic seasonings with the different cuisines of the world.

Hand in hand with this "spicy" enlightenment is an awareness of new flavors; our enticed palates crave creative foods and we find ourselves relying more and more on unusual spices. And before we know it, we experience the birth of a new cuisine in our own kitchens.

And that is exactly what happens when I add Italian spices to Indian curries, cilantro and ground coriander to pasta sauces, garam masala to Chinese dishes, chaat masala to Mexican fajitas, and cumin-mint masala to roasted leg of lamb—a cuisine that embraces the world with a smile and open arms.

Here is an introduction to a few popular Indian spices and some intriguing spice and herb blends that will add pizzazz to your culinary experiments.

ASAFETIDA (*Hing*)

Available only in Indian and Middle Eastern markets, this strong and pungent resinous gum can be found in its ground or its lumpy form. Raw asafetida has an unpleasant taste, so should always be sautéed in hot oil (or ghee) before the other ingredients are added. When used sparingly, asafetida imparts a pleasant onion-garlic flavor and offers numerous health benefits—from aiding digestion and relieving flatulence to curing certain respiratory disorders.

BLACK SALT (*Kala Namak*)

Available only in Indian markets, this dull pink salt (it is not black as the name suggests) has quite an unpleasant aroma when tasted raw. Add it to salads, chutneys, and drinks, and the aroma is transformed to something quite attractive. Kala namak is very good for digestion and relieves flatulence—maybe that is the reason it is added to raw vegetable and fruit salads. (It is also an important spice of the chaat masala blend, page 8.) It is much less salty than table salt and the two cannot be used interchangeably.

CARDAMOM PODS (*Illaichi*)

Available only in Indian markets, cardamom pods come in two varieties, green and black. (The bleached green pods are available in most supermarkets, but they are quite expensive and not very good.)

The green ones are called *hari* or *choti illaichi* (green or small). They are ⅓ to ½ inch long and contain eighteen to twenty sticky, highly aromatic seeds (especially when they are crushed) that give off a hint of sweet eucalyptus. Green cardamom pods are used in all types of Indian dishes—from curries to desserts and drinks.

The black variety is called *kali* or *bari illaichi* (black or large). They are ½ to ¾ inch long and contain twenty-five to thirty seeds that are slightly sweet, nuttier, and very fragrant.

Generally the varieties can be used interchangeably—the pods whole or crushed, or the seeds only, whole or ground to a powder. If you need to buy seeds, but can't find them, buy the pods, remove the shells and use the seeds only. Or grind the whole pods until fine, then pass them through a sieve and dicard the fibrous matter. Cardamom pods are excellent digestive stimulants and mouth fresheners. The Indians chew on them all times of the day.

CAROM SEEDS (*Ajwain*)

Available only in Indian markets, *ajwain* seeds are also called lovage, omum, or bishop's weed. These celery seed look-alikes are purple to light brown in color, and are related to caraway and cumin seeds. Whole carom seeds are deceptively fragrance free, but when crushed or ground, they become highly aromatic with a flavor reminiscent of thyme—and rightly so, because both contain thymol oil. And for this reason, they can often be used interchangeably.

The taste of carom seeds, however, is very pungent, bitter, and hot, but it mellows down after they have been cooked. *Ajwain* seeds are an important component of chaat masala (page 8) and are used profusely in Indian parantha breads, pakoras and other appetizers, pickles, seafood, and poultry.

As a home remedy, *ajwain* seeds are highly regarded—they are extremely effective as a cure for indigestion and stomach aches and as relief for flatulence.

CORIANDER (*Sukha Dhania*)

Available in most supermarkets, as well as in Indian, Middle Eastern, Mexican, and Oriental markets, these small, ribbed, round seeds come in two varieties: the pale green Indian kind and the beige-brown Moroccan type. I prefer the Indian variety, which, when ground, has a very pleasant, sweet and spicy, citruslike aroma. (The other is not quite as flavorful.) Coriander seeds can be purchased whole or ground. For maximum flavor, I favor buying the whole seeds and grinding them myself. Ground coriander is an indispensable component of curry powder (page 7) and curry sauces. It is used to flavor all sorts of dishes, from appetizers and soups to side dishes and entrées. Coriander seeds are by far my most favorite spice from the Indian spice closet.

The plant that emerges from the coriander seed is called cilantro—it is also referred to as fresh coriander, Chinese parsley, or *hara dhania* (green coriander). The leaves and the stems from the cilantro plant are very aromatic and flavorful and both should be used in cooking or making fresh ground chutneys. Use the soft stems and discard only the overly fibrous ones.

To store cilantro, wash it well in water, spin dry in a salad spinner, then air dry until most of the moisture clinging to the leaves has evaporated. Transfer to a plastic bag, along with a paper napkin (this further absorbs the moisture), and store in the refrigerator for six to eight days. Or you may chop the cilantro and store it in an airtight container that has been lined with a paper towel. Cilantro does not freeze well and dried cilantro leaves (sold in some supermarkets) have no flavor.

As for health, coriander seeds help digestion, relieve acidity, and have a cooling effect on the body. The leaves are considered beneficial in all the functions of the digestive system.

CURRY LEAVES (*Curry Patta or Meethi Neem*)

Available only in Indian and Asian markets and some farmers' markets, curry leaves are the small (1 to 1½ inches long), oval-shaped green leaves of the curry plant, *Murraya koenigii*, and offer a distinct and very special currylike fragrance to the dishes to which they are added. Contrary to popular belief, curry leaves are not ground to make curry powder. In fact (except in some special cases), they have nothing to do with curry powder.

For maximum flavor, use curry leaves in their fresh form, which can be stored in the refrigerator for fifteen to twenty days in plastic bags. Dried leaves have lost most of their flavor. Frozen leaves are an acceptable substitute.

Curry leaves are an excellent tonic—they strengthen the functions of the stomach, help digestion, are a mild laxative, and are used in India to treat morning sickness, diarrhea, and diabetes.

FENUGREEK SEEDS (*Methi Ka Daana or Methere—pronounce like entrée*)

Available in Indian and Middle Eastern markets and in some farmers' markets (only the greens), these brown-yellow legume-shaped seeds (they actually are a legume, rich in protein and iron) have a strong currylike aroma. The raw seeds are very bitter, but their flavor really shines when they are coarsely ground and stir-fried in a little oil. They are a fragrant addition to curry powder and are used in some special pickles, chutneys, and meat and vegetable preparations.

The slightly bitter and extremely fragrant plants that grow from the fenugreek seeds are called fenugreek greens, *hari methi*. These are generally treated like cooking greens and are popularly combined with potatoes to make a side dish. When the leaves (and the soft stems) are air dried, they are referred to as dried fenugreek, *sukhi* or *kasoori methi*. Dried, they are used as a highly aromatic herb to impart an extraordinary flavor to all sorts of foods, from breads and curries to appetizers and side dishes. Sprouted fenugreek seeds are a nutritious addition to salads and are rated very highly in treating various diseases, especially diabetes.

To dry fresh *methi* at home, wash and spin dry the leaves. Transfer them to kitchen towels and let them air dry until they become crumbly, three to five days. Then crush them with your fingers or grind them in a blender or food processor until almost fine and store in the refrigerator for up to two years. Purchased dried, fenugreek leaves often have fibrous stems included. These should be discarded before using the leaves.

Fenugreek seeds and leaves are considered to promote overall good health. They cleanse the body of toxins, are a mild laxative, and help solve digestive problems. They are popular home remedies for diabetes, fevers, respiratory disorders, and sore throats.

MANGO POWDER (*Amchur*)

Available only in Indian markets, buff-colored mango powder is made from sun-dried, tart, unripe green mangoes. Sour raw mangoes are cut into slices and dried in the scorching heat of the summer sun until they are crisp and dull beige-brown in color. These slices are then ground to a powder.

Mango powder offers a tangy taste and is used in dry-cooked vegetables, drinks, and special spice blends like chaat masala (page 8) and offers a soothing effect on the body.

NIGELLA SEEDS (*Kalonji*)

Available only in Indian markets, nigella seeds look like tiny angular pieces of charcoal. These dull black seeds look very similar to onion seeds and are often referred to by that name. They are almost fragrance free when raw, but as soon as they are roasted or stir-fried, they transform into a super-fragrant spice with a flavor that is reminiscent of oregano. Nigella seeds are used in tandoori and oven-baked breads (see Naan Pizza Bread with Nigella Seeds, page 70) and in various spice blends and pickles.

ROSE WATER AND ROSE ESSENCE (*Gulab Jal* and *Ruh Gulab*)
Made from the petals of highly fragrant deep pink roses, rose water and rose essence (*ruh,* meaning "soul") are frequently used in Indian and Middle Eastern cuisines. Rose water is available in large bottles and the concentrated essence comes in small bottles only. Exercise caution when adding the rose essence—just one or two drops will flavor large amounts of food. Both are indispensable in desserts and certain cold drinks. They are often added to pilafs and nonvegetarian curries and are available in Indian and Middle Eatern markets.

SILVER LEAVES (*Chandi Ke Verk*)
Available only in Indian markets, the delicate edible silver leaves don't really belong with the spices, but, just like the spices, they are almost indispensable to Indian cuisine, especially the desserts. They lend an exotic and elegant visual presentation to foods.

Silver leaves are made from pure silver—just like the name suggests. To make silver leaves, paper-thin sheets of silver are sandwiched between 5- to 6-inch sheets of ordinary paper. They are then pressed or pounded upon until they are thinner than tissue paper and almost weightless. In the process they stick to the sheets of paper. This is how they remain until they are used.

To use, pick up the top sheet of paper with the silver sticking to it and place it on the dish to be garnished, silver side down. The silver will immediately cling to the dish and the paper can then be removed. Sprinkle the silver garnish with chopped or ground mixed nuts and serve.

TAMARIND (*Imli*)
Available in Indian, Oriental, Mexican, and some American supermarkets, brown tamarind pods are about 4 inches long with a brittle outside shell. Inside this brittle (but easy to crack and remove) shell is a sour and slightly sweet pulpy fruit with large seeds. To get this fruit recipe-ready, remove the shell and soak the pulp in hot water to soften. With your fingers, gently rub the softened fruit to release and separate the pulp from the seeds. Then squeeze through a strainer to extract the pulp. Use this pulp to make distinctive sauces that have a delicately sweet and tangy flavor.

Alternately, buy packaged shelled and seeded fruits that are compressed into blocks, soak a 2-inch piece in 1 cup of hot water, and follow the directions above. Bottled tamarind concentrate is also available in some of the markets. Simply dissolve 2 tablespoons in 1 cup of water.

During the hot summer months, tamarind provides a cooling effect on the body. It is good for digestion, nausea, and flatulence, and is also a mild laxative.

TURMERIC (*Haldi*)

Available in Indian, Middle Eastern, and most American supermarkets, turmeric is made from the rhizome (underground root) of the tropical turmeric plant *Curcuma longa*. This rhizome looks like a smaller and thinner version of ginger, has a rough, light brown skin, short "fingers," and bright orange flesh. To make ground turmeric, the rhizomes are boiled, skinned, dried, and then ground to a powder. This yellow-orange powder has a mild peppery-curry aroma. Turmeric is one of the essential components of curry powder (and most curries) and it imparts its familiar yellow color to all types of foods.

Turmeric is especially prized for its medicinal qualities. It is a natural antiinflammatory, antibacterial, antiseptic, and blood purifier. It is a tonic for the body, relieves aches and pains, soothes sore throats, and is an effective home remedy for respiratory and several other disorders.

A Blend of Spices

WHEN SPICES AND HERBS come together in different combinations, they become a very important part of the kitchen scene. Cook with them or use them as last-minute flavor enhancers, add them to curries or stews, sprinkle them over salads or sandwiches, mix them into yogurt, vinegar, or citrus marinades, or just scatter them over pizzas and pastas or cooked casserole dishes.

All these masala blends can do double duty as dry rubs when mixed with a touch of oil and applied directly to pieces of fish, poultry, and meat before being placed on the grill or in the oven or skillet.

Curry Powder (or Masala)

WITH SUCH A LARGE assortment of curry powders available in the markets, selecting the best one seems to be quite a task. What should you look for in a curry powder? How can you tell if it is good or not?

Let me first define the word "curry," a word with essentially two meanings—one for the Indians and the other for the rest of the world. To the Indians, this word means a gravy or a sauce, and subsequently, any dish that has a sauce is a curry. To the world in general, "curry" is a spice (or a mixture of spices) and any dish that is enriched with this spice is a "curry," regardless of whether it has a gravy or not. Imagine my reaction when I was first offered a "curried chicken" which had been roasted in the oven!

Curry powder is a mixture of numerous fragrant spices and herbs. This blend was first put together by the British when they were in India. Their efforts at recreating the much-loved Indian foods on their own were not very successful (there were no recipes or books available), so, with the help of their Indian friends, they put together a bunch of spices and called it curry powder, because that was the mixture they used to prepare all their curries (dishes with a sauce). Today, there are as many curry powders as there are chefs and every person who cooks considers himself a chef. If you are one of the lucky few and find a curry blend you love, please save it for a few special dishes only. If you use it more often, all your dishes will look, smell, and taste the same, and you will soon get tired of it.

To make your everyday curries, follow the customary Indian practice—add two spoons of this, a spoon of that, and a pinch of something else and you'll soon realize that all your curries are uniquely different. (Nowhere in this book have I used curry powder to make a curry.)

All curry powders have three essential ingredients: coriander, cumin, and turmeric. The rest are added at the cook's desire. Choose from fenugreek seeds or dried leaves, peppercorns, dried red chili peppers, cardamom pods, fennel seeds, mustard seeds, poppy seeds, ground ginger, cinnamon, cloves, nutmeg, mace, and asafetida. Of these, my absolute favorites are dried fenugreek leaves and cardamom pods (green and black). Today, I also throw in a variety of American and Italian herbs, along with the Indian ones.

Here is the simplest way of making a curry powder: Start with 3 tablespoons ground coriander, 1 tablespoon ground cumin, 1 teaspoon ground turmeric, and add the others at your own discretion.

Curry powder stays fresh for approximately two months at room temperature and six to eight months in the refrigerator.

Chaat Masala

Makes about 1 cup

THIS IS A SAVORY blend of tangy (mango and tamarind powders) and peppery (black and red pepper) seasonings. Added to these are spices that promote digestion (carom seeds and black salt) and others that are prized therapeutically (ground ginger and cumin). Combined, they make a unique blend that, in my opinion, is essential in every kitchen.

Chaat masala can be made at home or purchased prepackaged in most Indian markets in America. And, unlike garam masala and curry powder, the commercial chaat masala blend is very good and I strongly suggest you purchase some on your next visit to an Indian market.

To make your own:
2 tablespoons cumin seeds
1 tablespoon carom seeds
¼ cup mango powder
¼ cup tamarind powder
1 tablespoon black salt
2 teaspoons ground ginger
1 teaspoon ground dried mint
1 teaspoon freshly ground black pepper
½ teaspoon cayenne pepper, or to your taste

Put the cumin seeds in a small, heavy nonstick skillet and roast over moderately high heat until they are fragrant and turn a few shades darker, 2 to 3 minutes. Remove from the heat and mix in the carom seeds. Set aside for 3 to 5 minutes to cool.

Transfer to a coffee or spice grinder or use a mortar and pestle and grind until fine. Remove to a bowl and mix in remaining spices. (If the mango and tamarind powders are lumpy, pass them through a sieve.)

Store in an airtight container in a cool, dark place. Chaat masala stays fresh for several months at room temperature and 6 to 8 months in the refrigerator.

Garam Masala

THIS BASIC INDIAN SPICE blend is one of the most popular, and perhaps, user-friendly spice mixtures in Indian cooking. Authentic garam masala is a blend of four spices that produce internal heat in the body. (The Hindi word *garam* translates to "heat" in English.) The peppercorns also add a peppery heat to the blend.

Garam masala is traditionally made with whole spices that are first dried in the sun and then ground by hand to a powder in a heavy metal or stone mortar and pestle. In America, I take the easy way out—I mix already ground cinnamon, cloves, and peppercorns with freshly ground black cardamom seeds (only because they are not available in the markets, and I generally do all my grinding in an electric coffee or spice grinder).

Of late, my neighborhood supermarkets have been carrying bottles of garam masala along with other Indian spices and herbs. But most of them contain generous amount of other spices to increase the volume. My suggestion is to make your own garam masala, unless you happen to find one that you especially like.

2 tablespoons black cardamom seeds (from about 20 large pods)
3 tablespoons ground cloves
2 tablespoons ground cinnamon
2 tablespoons freshly ground black pepper

In a coffee or spice grinder or with a mortar and pestle, grind the cardamom seeds to a fine powder. Remove to a small skillet and mix in the cloves, cinnamon, and black pepper. Toast the ground spices, shaking the pan, over moderate heat until they are heated through, 30 to 60 seconds.

Cool and keep some in the kitchen (it will keep for 1 to 2 months), and store the remainder in an airtight container in the refrigerator for 6 months or longer.

Makes about ²/₃ cup

VARIATIONS:

For a change of flavor
• Use green cardamom seeds instead of black, or a mixture of both.
• Crumble and grind 7 to 10 bay leaves, to your taste, with the cardamom seeds.
• Mix in 1 tablespoon ground white or black cumin seeds.
• To make the highly fragrant Kashmiri garam masala, mix in 1 tablespoon ground black cumin seeds, 1 teaspoon ground mace, 1 teaspoon freshly grated nutmeg, and 1 teaspoon pan-toasted and ground saffron threads.

Pan-Roasted Cumin-Mint Masala

Makes about ²/₃ cup

HERE I ROAST GROUND cumin, mango and tamarind powders, and dried mint and thyme leaves and combine them with lemon pepper to make a savory blend that can be used interchangeably with chaat masala.

2 tablespoons ground cumin
1 tablespoon mango powder
1 tablespoon tamarind powder
1 teaspoon ground ginger
1 teaspoon salt
½ teaspoon black salt
1 tablespoon dried mint, ground to a powder
1 tablespoon ground dried thyme
¼ cup lemon pepper blend

Put the cumin, mango, and tamarind powders, ginger, and salts in a small, nonstick saucepan and roast over moderately high heat until fragrant, about 2 minutes. Mix in the mint and thyme and roast for another 30 seconds, shaking the pan. Add the lemon pepper and mix everything together. Cool and store in an airtight container for up to 2 months at room temperature or in the refrigerator for 6 to 8 months.

Pilaf Masala

JUST LIKE BOUQUET GARNI, this combination of whole spices is absolutely incredible in all types of rice and grain preparations. Besides rice, this masala adds tremendous flavor to stews, curries (especially meat and chicken), and special sauces.

For each cup of rice, use:
2 bay leaves
One 1-inch stick cinnamon
2 black cardamom pods, pounded lightly to break the skins
10 cloves
10 black peppercorns
½ teaspoon cumin seeds

To use, stir-fry the whole spices in hot (but not smoking) oil over moderately high heat, then remove the spices from the pan, tie them together in a piece of cheesecloth, if you wish (to avoid accidently biting on them), and proceed with the recipe. Combine fresh with every use.

Roasted Peppercorn Masala

Makes about ½ cup

BEWARE, THIS BLEND IS only for the adventurous. A little bit really goes a long way. Tiny rounds of black, red, green, and white peppercorns and super-hot dried red peppers, all dry-roasted in a pan until fragrant, then coarsely ground and combined with aromatic dried herbs and sour salt.

¼ cup peppercorns of mixed colors (black, green, white, and red)
1 dried red chili peppers, coarsely broken
1 tablespoon dried mint
1 tablespoon sour salt (citric acid)
1 tablespoon salt

Put the peppercorns and chili peppers in a small, nonstick skillet and roast over moderately high heat until the peppercorns start popping, 2 to 3 minutes, and a highly fragrant aroma is released.

Transfer to a dish and set aside to cool. In a spice or coffee grinder or with a mortar and pestle, grind the peppercorns and mint together until almost a fine powder. Remove to a bowl and mix in the salts. Store in an airtight container for 2 to 3 months at room temperature or in the refrigerator for 6 to 8 months.

Spicy Mexican-Style Masala

THIS IS A POWERFUL blend of concentrated flavors provided by smoke-dried chipotle peppers, roasted cumin and coriander seeds, and dried fenugreek, oregano, and rosemary leaves.

Makes about ¾ cup

¼ cup cumin seeds
¼ cup coriander seeds
2 to 4 dried chipotle peppers, to your taste, stems removed
2 tablespoons dried fenugreek leaves
2 tablespoons dried oregano
1 tablespoon dried rosemary

Put the cumin and coriander seeds in a small, nonstick skillet and roast over moderately high heat until fragrant and a few shades darker, 2 to 3 minutes. Add the peppers and roast for 1 more minute (this further dries out the peppers and makes them easier to grind); mix in the fenugreek, oregano, and rosemary and roast for another minute.

Remove to a bowl to stop further cooking and bring to room temperature. Transfer to a spice or coffee grinder or use a mortar and pestle and grind to a fine powder. Cool and store in an airtight container for 2 to 3 months at room temperature or in the refrigerator for 6 to 8 months.

Mixed Dried Italian Herbs

A SIMILAR BLEND IS available in the supermarkets all over the country, but this includes some unusual herbs, and all are fresh.

1½ cups firmly packed basil leaves
1 cup firmly packed oregano leaves
½ cup firmly packed Italian parsley leaves
½ cup lemon verbena leaves (optional)
¼ cup firmly packed rosemary leaves
¼ cup firmly packed mint leaves
¼ cup firmly packed fenugreek leaves
5 to 7 bay leaves, to your taste

Wash all the leaves carefully and spin dry. Line cookie sheets with cheese-cloth or paper towels and spread the leaves over them in a single layer. Leave them in a warm spot in the kitchen (or garage) until they dry completely and become crisp, 3 to 5 days. Turn occasionally.

Process all the leaves together in a food processor or blender in 2 or 3 batches until chopped finely, but not powdered. Transfer to 2 airtight containers. Keep 1 in the kitchen for up to 2 months and store the other in the refrigerator for 6 months or longer.

Comforting Soups

MY FASCINATION WITH SOUPS started when I was very young. My father, who is a physician, was always concerned about his own diet and that of his family. My mother, the ever-gracious wife (and mother), attended to his every need—well, almost. So when my father asked for soup with lunch and dinner, he got his soup with lunch and dinner—and so did the rest of the family. (To this day his request holds good.) Along with the soup came a curry, a dry vegetable dish, yogurt, a simple salad of sliced raw vegetables, and, of course, whole-wheat chapati breads and/or rice. (This, incidentally, is a standard, everyday lunch and dinner menu for most of the Punjabi families in New Delhi and elsewhere in India.) My father religiously drank his soup first (which acted as a filler), so he could eat controlled portions of the rest of the meal, especially the breads and rice. He knew something then that we are learning today.

Most of the soups made by my mother were vegetarian—tomato, tomato-vegetable, mixed vegetable, and dried bean and dal (lentil) soups. They were all very delicious and we loved each one of them. To me soup is comfort food par excellence.

Today, my fascination with soups has taken me many steps further. I find myself making different kinds of soups—some light and others more substantial and robust, some as preludes to a lunch or dinner and others a meal in themselves, vegetarian or with poultry, seafood, and meats, sizzling hot or straight from the refrigerator, all delicious and nutritious, each one made with the freshest ingredients available.

Here are some of my favorite soups—soups that nourish us and comfort us, and are our friends on rainy days and sick days, and on the days we feel like eating healthy and light.

Basic Chicken Stock

Makes 7 to 7¹/₂ cups

Do Ahead:

Can be made 3 to 5 days in advance and stored in the refrigerator. It stays fresh in the freezer for 2 to 3 months.

THIS BASIC STOCK CAN be enhanced with the addition of one or more of the following fragrant spices and herbs: black and green cardamom pods, cinnamon, cloves, fennel seeds, nutmeg, bay leaves, rosemary, cilantro, basil, and dried fenugreek.

One 2½- to 3-pound chicken, skin removed and cut into 8 to 10 pieces
8 cups water
¾ teaspoon salt, or to your taste
2 teaspoons black peppercorns, pounded lightly to bruise them

Put all the ingredients in a pressure cooker. Secure the lid and cook over high heat for 1 minute after the pressure regulator starts rocking. Remove from the heat and let the pressure drop by itself, 15 to 20 minutes.

Open the lid and transfer the chicken pieces to a bowl. Let cool, then remove the chicken from the bones and save for another recipe. Return the bones to the pressure cooker and pressure cook once again for 1 minute after the pressure regulator starts rocking. Remove from the heat, and when the pressure drops, open the lid and pass the broth through a strainer. Discard the bones and peppercorns.

Cool and chill the stock in the refrigerator overnight. Then skim off the solidified fat and refrigerate the stock until required.

To make without a pressure cooker, place the chicken with 9 cups water in a large soup pot and bring it to a boil over high heat. Reduce the heat to moderate, cover, and simmer until the chicken is very soft, 30 to 40 minutes. Transfer the chicken pieces to a bowl. Let them cool, then remove the chicken from the bones. Place the bones in the pot and continue to simmer over moderate heat until you have 7 to 7½ cups of stock, 30 to 40 minutes.

Fragrant Clear Chicken Soup

MADE WITH FRAGRANT SPICES, this simple soup is especially comforting when you are under the weather. Mix in some sautéed shredded greens or microwaved diced vegetables along with some shredded cooked chicken and the soup becomes more substantial—and don't forget to add a drop or four of liquid hot red pepper sauce.

I like to stir-fry the whole spices in clarified butter before making the actual soup. This releases their essence and adds flavor to an otherwise bland soup. The clarified butter will solidify when the soup is chilled and is easily removed before the soup is served.

1 tablespoon clarified butter (page 19)
3 bay leaves, crushed
3 to 5 black cardamom pods, to your taste, pounded lightly to break the skins
1 teaspoon black peppercorns
½ teaspoon fennel seeds
One 1-inch stick cinnamon
8 to 10 cloves
1 small onion, peeled and coarsely chopped
6 cloves garlic, peeled and coarsely chopped
One 1-inch piece fresh ginger, peeled and coarsely chopped
One 2½- to 3-pound chicken, skin removed and cut into 8 to 10 pieces
½ teaspoon salt, or to your taste
8 cups water
Chopped cilantro (fresh coriander) leaves, scallion greens, and freshly ground black
    pepper for garnish

In a pressure cooker, heat the clarified butter over moderately high heat and cook bay leaves, cardamom pods, peppercorns, fennel seeds, cinnamon, and cloves, stirring, until fragrant, 1 to 2 minutes. Add the onion, garlic, and ginger and cook, stirring, another minute or two to roast them slightly. Add the chicken, salt, and water.

Secure the lid of the pressure cooker and cook on high heat for 1 minute after the pressure regulator starts rocking. Remove from the heat and let the pressure drop by itself, 15 to 20 minutes. Open the lid and transfer the chicken pieces to a bowl. Let cool, then remove the chicken from the bones and save for

Makes 4 to 8 servings (depending on whether it is served in a cup or a large bowl)

SERVING IDEAS:
  This light soup has tremendous digestive benefits because of the spices. Serve with crackers or garlic bread, or cook your basmati rice in it.

DO AHEAD:
  Will stay fresh in the refrigerator for 3 to 5 days and in the freezer for about 3 months.

another purpose. Return the bones to the pressure cooker and pressure cook once again on high heat for 1 minute after the pressure regulator starts rocking. When the pressure drops, open the lid and pass the broth through a strainer. Discard the bones and spices. Cool and chill the broth in the refrigerator overnight.

Skim off the solidified fat. Boil the broth once again, garnish with chopped cilantro, scallion greens, and pepper, and serve.

To make without a pressure cooker, cook the spices in a large soup pot, stirring often. Cook until the spices are fragrant. Add all the other ingredients with an extra cup of water and bring to a boil over high heat. Reduce the heat to moderate, cover the pot and simmer until the chicken is very soft, 30 to 40 minutes. Place the chicken pieces in a bowl, and set aside to cool. Separate the meat from the bones and save for another purpose. Return the bones to the soup pot and simmer for another 30 to 40 minutes. Proceed with the original instructions.

Clarified Butter

NOTE:

To make flavored clarified butter, add any of the herbs and spices given under Variations to the pan just prior to melting the butter.

AS THE NAME SUGGESTS, clarified butter is butterfat from which the milk solids have been removed. It is authentically made by churning clotted or heavy cream into fluffy whipped butter and then simmering the butter over low heat until all the milk solids separate from the fat and settle to the bottom of the pan. Once this happens, the clarified fat is passed through a strainer. In India this clarified butterfat is called *desi usli*, *khara ghee*, or just *ghee*.

The shelf life of butter is vastly increased after it is clarified as it is the milk solids in the butter that turn rancid and spoil it. Once these solids are removed, the butter stays fresh for a long time (four to six months) at room temperature. Its shelf life in cool weather is even longer.

To make clarified butter:

Put 1 pound of unsalted sweet butter in a heavy medium-size saucepan and simmer, stirring occasionally, over moderately-low heat until the milk solids turn golden and settle to the bottom of the pan, 15 to 20 minutes. (At first the butter will start to foam, but this will eventually subside.) Once this happens, pass everything through a sieve and save the clarified butter in a clean jar. The milk solids that remain in the sieve should not be discarded. They combine superbly with whole-wheat flour to make one of the most delicious parantha breads (page 58). Just mix into the flour and proceed with any of the parantha recipes.

VARIATIONS:
- ½ cup minced fresh mint leaves
- ½ cup minced fresh basil leaves (or lemon or purple basil)
- 2 tablespoons peeled and minced fresh ginger
- 1 tablespoon coarsely chopped garlic
- 3 to 4 bay leaves (preferably fresh)
- 1 to 2 teaspoons cumin seeds
- 1 teaspoon carom seeds (page 2)

Season this flavored ghee with some fresh lemon juice, salt, and pepper and use it as a dipping sauce with cooked lobster or shrimp, as a final glaze on barbecued meats, poultry, or seafood, or serve it with freshly baked breads.

Cream-Style Chicken Corn Soup with Pickled Jalapeño Peppers

Makes 6 to 8 servings

SERVING IDEAS:

Try pairing this soup with Yogurt-Marinated Grilled Sea Bass and Red Peppers on Baby Greens (page 41).

DO AHEAD:

Will stay fresh in the refrigerator for 3 to 5 days; but it does not freeze well because the cornstarch breaks down, causing the soup to become watery.

THIS SOUP OF CHINESE origin is very popular in my home city of New Delhi. There it is always served with a side of fiery-hot pickled green chilies, which some people add to their soup—by the spoonful.

Vegetarians feel that they miss out on this soup, so they often make a vegetarian variation using vegetable broth or milk and water.

Canned chicken broth can be substituted for homemade.

1 recipe Basic Chicken Stock (page 16)
One 15½-ounce can cream-style corn
½ cup cornstarch
⅓ cup plus 2 to 3 tablespoons water
2 large egg whites
Salt and freshly ground black pepper to taste
1 cup finely diced cooked boneless, skinless chicken breasts
1 recipe Soy-Pickled Jalapeño Peppers (page 266)

In a large soup pot, bring the chicken stock to a boil over high heat. Reduce the heat to moderately high, stir in the corn, and simmer for a few minutes. Dissolve the cornstarch in the ⅓ cup water and add it to the soup, stirring constantly to prevent the formation of lumps.

Mix the egg whites with the remaining 2 to 3 tablespoons of water and stir them into the soup slowly. Keep stirring as you add the whites, otherwise they will coagulate into big lumps. Taste and adjust the salt and pepper (remember, the homemade stock already has some), add the diced chicken, and simmer the soup for 3 to 5 minutes.

Transfer to a large bowl, garnish lightly with 1 to 4 tablespoons of the sauce from the pickled jalapeños and serve with the pickled peppers on the side.

A Spicy Chowder of Clams

I GOT THE ORIGINAL recipe for this soup from Carol Berger, who in turn got it from her daughter-in-law, Pernilla. Carol serves the original version in her popular restaurant, The Trail's End, in Portland, Oregon. Carol says, "I use a lot of pepper. I like a peppery chowder."

2 large potatoes, peeled and cut into 1-inch cubes
1 large onion, coarsely chopped
1 tablespoon dried thyme
½ cup dry white wine
Three 6½-ounce cans chopped clams, drained and juice reserved
3 to 4 tablespoons unsalted butter
½ cup all-purpose flour
1 tablespoon peeled and minced fresh ginger
1 tablespoon ground coriander
1 teaspoon ground cumin
½ teaspoon garam masala
1 teaspoon salt, or to taste
½ to 1 teaspoon freshly ground white pepper, to your taste
4 cups nonfat milk, or more to taste

Combine the potatoes, onions, thyme, wine, and clam juice in a large soup pot and bring to a boil over high heat. Reduce the heat to moderate, cover the pot, and cook until the potatoes are fork-tender, 12 to 15 minutes. Mix in the clams and remove from the heat.

To make a roux, melt the butter in a small saucepan over moderate heat, add the flour, and cook, stirring, until a paste is formed. Add the ginger and continue to cook, stirring, until it is fragrant and rich golden in color, 3 to 5 minutes. Add the coriander, cumin, garam masala, salt, and pepper, and mix in 1 cup of the milk and stir until smooth.

Bring the soup to a boil and mix in the roux. Add the remaining 3 cups milk (or more, to the desired thickness) and bring to a boil again. Serve hot.

Makes 6 to 8 servings

SERVING IDEAS:
Carol suggests serving this with a crusty dark bread, sweet butter, and a Northwest microbrew.

DO AHEAD:
Best served fresh. Leftovers will keep for 2 to 3 days in the refrigerator. If the soup thickens too much, add more milk and bring to a boil again.

Gingered Tomato Soup

Makes 8 to 16 servings (depending on whether served in a cup or a large bowl)

SERVING IDEAS:

Present as a light lunch with a salad, Potato and Vegetable Cutlets (page 97), and warm sourdough baguettes.

DO AHEAD:

Stays fresh for 5 to 7 days in the refrigerator and for 3 months in the freezer. Bring to a boil, garnish, and serve.

CREAMY WITHOUT ANY CREAM, this soup is loaded with the wholesome goodness of a multitude of vegetables and herbs. For added flavor, serve with fresh homemade croutons. (To make croutons at home, cut any type of bread into ½-inch cubes and deep-fry until golden. Or apply some butter to slices of bread, toast in an oven on low heat until crispy and golden, then cut into cubes. Or cut the bread into cubes, toss with olive oil, minced garlic, and the herbs of your choice, and bake in a preheated 350°F oven until crispy and golden.)

3 pounds vine-ripened tomatoes, coarsely chopped
1 medium-size potato, unpeeled and coarsely chopped
1 small onion, peeled and quartered
3 to 4 small carrots, quartered
1 stalk celery, coarsely chopped
One 1½-inch piece fresh ginger, peeled and coarsely chopped
1 large clove garlic, peeled
½ cup firmly packed coarsely chopped cilantro (fresh coriander) leaves, soft stems included
1 tablespoon fresh rosemary leaves or 1 teaspoon dried
10 to 15 fresh lemon verbena leaves or 2 stalks lemongrass (optional), coarsely chopped
4 bay leaves
3 cups water
1½ teaspoons salt, or to your taste
1 teaspoon freshly ground black pepper, or to your taste
1 cup low-fat milk (1 percent or 2 percent)
1 tablespoon peanut oil
1 teaspoon cumin seeds
Minced scallion greens or fresh chives for garnish
Dollops of nonfat sour cream for garnish

Put all the vegetables, herbs, and 2 cups of the water in a pressure cooker and cook for 20 to 30 seconds after the pressure regulator starts rocking. Remove from the heat and let the pressure drop by itself, 12 to 15 minutes.

Remove the lid, cool, and process everything in a blender or food processor in 3 or 4 batches until smooth. Pass through a food mill (optional). Rinse the blender and food mill with the remaining cup water and add it to the soup.

Return the soup to the pressure cooker, add the salt and pepper, and bring to a boil over high heat. Add the milk in a slow stream, stirring constantly until the soup boils again. (Stir in more water if you prefer a thinner soup.) Adjust the salt and pepper and set aside.

Before serving, bring to a boil again over high heat. Heat the oil in a small saucepan over moderately high heat until hot. Remove from the heat and stir in the cumin seeds. They should sizzle upon contact.

Immediately add them to the soup. (You have to work fast, or the cumin will become bitter).

To make without a pressure cooker, place all the vegetables, herbs, and water in a large soup pot. Cover the pot, and bring to a boil over high heat. Reduce the heat to moderate, and let the soup simmer until the tomatoes are very soft. Proceed with the original instructions. You will need ½ to 1 cup additional water.

Transfer to individual bowls, garnish with minced scallion greens and sour cream, and serve.

Chilled Roasted Tomato and Red Bell Pepper Soup

Makes 4 to 6 servings

SERVING IDEAS

Perfect on a hot summer day with a salad and the sandwich of your choice.

DO AHEAD:

Stays fresh for 5 to 7 days in the refrigerator and about 3 months in the freezer.

TOMATOES, BELL PEPPERS, BASIL, cilantro, and yogurt all come together in this exciting soup that is served chilled with lots of freshly ground black pepper.

I sometimes throw in one (or part of one) chipotle pepper in adobo sauce to enhance the smoky aroma of this soup.

1 large red bell pepper, halved lengthwise and seeded
3 to 4 medium-size, vine-ripened tomatoes (about 1 pound)
1 large red onion, peeled and quartered
4 to 5 large cloves garlic, to your taste, peeled
½ cup water
One ½- to 1-inch piece fresh ginger, peeled and cut into 3 to 5 thin slices
½ cup loosely packed cilantro (fresh coriander) leaves, soft stems included
½ cup lightly packed fresh basil leaves
1 cup nonfat plain yogurt
2 cups canned tomato juice
Freshly ground black pepper for garnish

Put the bell pepper halves (skin side up), tomatoes, onion, and garlic on a small cookie sheet or a pie dish and roast on the center rack of the oven broiler until the peppers and tomatoes are charred and the onion and garlic are golden. (The tomatoes and onion will have to be turned a few times.) Remove the garlic and onions as they turn golden.

Remove the cookie sheet from the oven and cover with a sheet of aluminum foil for 5 to 7 minutes. (This allows the peppers to sweat and cool down, making them easy to peel.) Peel the tomatoes and pepper halves, removing as much of the charred skin as possible. Do not wash them because this leaches most of the juices and flavor from the peppers. Rinsing your hands as you go along is adequate.

Transfer the tomatoes, peppers, garlic, and onion to a blender or food processor with any juices that have accumulated on the cookie sheet. Deglaze the cookie sheet with the water, taking care to dissolve the browned juices, and add this to the blender also. Add the ginger, cilantro, and basil and blend until everything is smooth. Remove to a large serving bowl.

In the same container, blend the yogurt and tomato juice, transfer to the serving bowl, and mix everything together. Garnish with black pepper and serve chilled.

Pureed Soup of Beets, Carrots, and Other Vegetables

"IT LOOKS LIKE PUNCH, I'm not going to like it," said my daughter Supriya when I offered her this soup. After one spoonful, she grudgingly conceded, "It's quite good, tastes just like tomato soup."

Loaded with some of the best nutrients offered by the vegetable kingdom, this deep burgundy, citrusy soup is a great way to use up bits and pieces of left-over vegetables. I also add sprouts and greens along with an array of fresh herbs.

2 medium-size beets, thoroughly rinsed
2 large carrots, thoroughly rinsed
1 large potato, unpeeled
2 large, vine-ripened tomatoes
1 small fennel bulb, trimmed and thoroughly washed
Broccoli stem from 1 large head
A few red radishes
2 stalks lemongrass (optional)
2 to 4 sprigs fresh rosemary, to your taste
1 cup loosely packed cilantro (fresh coriander) leaves, soft stems included
3 cups water
1 teaspoon salt, or to taste
½ teaspoon freshly ground black pepper, or to your taste
½ to 1 cup fresh orange juice, to your taste
1 to 2 tablespoons fresh lime or lemon juice, to your taste
1 tablespoon extra-virgin olive oil
½ cup minced fresh green garlic or 1 large clove garlic, minced
1 teaspoon dried basil
1 teaspoon dried oregano
1 teaspoon dried parsley

Coarsely chop the beets, carrots, potato, tomatoes, fennel, broccoli stem, radishes, lemongrass, rosemary, and cilantro and place them in a pressure cooker with the water. Secure the lid of the pressure cooker and cook over high heat for 1 minute after the pressure regulator starts rocking. Remove from the heat and let the pressure drop by itself, 15 to 20 minutes.

continued

Makes 8 generous servings

SERVINGS IDEAS

Great with Garbanzo Bean and Potato Salad with Yogurt-Cilantro Chutney (page 53) and rolls. Or pair with Chicken Chili with Black Beans (page 166) and warmed pita pockets.

DO AHEAD:

Stays fresh for about 5 days in the refrigerator and about 3 months in the freezer.

Open the lid and cool for another 15 to 20 minutes. Transfer the contents to a blender or food processor and process in 4 or 5 batches until smooth. Pass the blended soup through a food mill (or a sieve with large holes). This will remove all the fibrous material and leave a pulpy and smooth soup. (Use more water if you need to extract maximum pulp.)

Return the soup to the pressure cooker, add the salt, pepper, and orange and lemon juices and bring to a boil again over high heat. Meanwhile, heat the oil in a small saucepan over moderately high heat and cook the garlic, stirring, until golden. Add the basil, oregano, and parsley and transfer the contents of the pan to the soup. Continue to boil for another minute. Taste and adjust the seasonings before serving.

To make without a pressure cooker, place the first 11 ingredients, with an additional ½ cup of water, in a soup pot. Bring the contents to a boil over high heat. Reduce the heat to moderate, cover the pot, and simmer until the vegetables are very soft, 25 to 30 minutes. Then proceed with the original instructions.

Vegetarian-Style Chunky Vegetable Soup

THIS SOUP HAS IT all—vegetables, greens, dried beans, and rice and a taste that lingers long after the last bite.

Fresh ginger provides a spicy touch, especially if it is added in the last stages of cooking. If you want your soup less "gingery," add it in the beginning with the vegetables; prolonged cooking mellows its bite.

4 cups mixed vegetables chopped into 1-inch pieces (green beans, carrots, celery (with some greens included), red bell peppers, fresh or frozen peas, broccoli, unpeeled potatoes, etc.)

½ cup yellow mung beans, picked over and washed

½ cup basmati rice, picked over and washed in several changes of water until clear

7 to 8 cups water

1 teaspoon salt, or to your taste

2 tablespoons peanut oil

3 tablespoons all-purpose flour

1 tablespoon peeled and minced fresh ginger

2 cups firmly packed coarsely chopped fresh spinach, trimmed of tough stems and thoroughly washed

½ cup firmly packed finely chopped cilantro (fresh coriander) leaves, soft stems included

½ teaspoon roasted (page 12) coarsely ground black peppercorns

3 to 4 tablespoons fresh lemon or lime juice, to your taste

Place the vegetables, mung beans, rice, 7 cups of the water, and the salt in a large pot. Cover and bring to a boil over high heat, then reduce the heat to moderate and continue to cook until the vegetables are soft, 25 to 30 minutes. Stir occasionally.

In a small, nonstick saucepan, heat the oil over moderately high heat and cook the flour and ginger, stirring, until fragrant and golden brown, 2 to 3 minutes. Immediately add 1 to 2 cups of the soup to the roux and bring to a boil while stirring constantly to prevent the formation of lumps, 1 to 2 minutes.

Transfer to the pot with the remaining soup and add the spinach, cilantro, black pepper, and lemon juice. Bring to a boil again over high heat and serve.

Makes 8 to 16 servings (depending on whether served in a cup or a large bowl)

SERVING IDEAS:
Partner with a salad and sandwich or pizza or as a prelude to a more elaborate meal.

DO AHEAD:
Make 3 to 5 days ahead of time. Add the spinach, cilantro, black pepper, and lemon juice and bring to a boil just prior to serving. This step allows the spinach and cilantro to retain their brilliant green color. The black pepper and lemon juice perk up the flavors, and the soup looks freshly made.

Yogurt Soup with Fresh Coconut and Vegetables

Makes 8 servings

SERVING IDEAS:

Refreshing and tangy, this is best served by itself or with steamed basmati rice.

DO AHEAD:

Will keep in the refrigerator for 4 to 5 days. For a fresh flavor, add the curry leaves topping just prior to serving.

NOTE:

Fresh coconut retains a slight crunch even after being processed in a food processor. To make a smoother soup, use one 14-ounce can of coconut milk instead of fresh coconut.

THIS COMES FROM SOUTHERN India, where fresh curry leaves and coconut, along with mustard seeds and asafetida, offer intriguing flavor accents to many dishes.

8 to 10 cups fresh vegetables (such as eggplant, bell peppers, carrots, zucchini, potatoes, onions, cauliflower, pumpkin, kohlrabi), cut into 1-inch pieces
5 cups water
¾ teaspoon ground turmeric
1 teaspoon salt, or to your taste
½ fresh coconut, shelled, peeled, and coarsely diced
2 jalapeño peppers (optional), stems removed
2 cups nonfat plain yogurt
¼ cup firmly packed finely chopped cilantro (fresh coriander) leaves, soft stems included
1 tablespoon peanut oil
15 to 20 fresh curry leaves, to your taste
1 teaspoon black mustard seeds
½ teaspoon asafetida
¼ teaspoon paprika
Chopped cilantro (fresh coriander) for garnish

Put the vegetables, water, turmeric, and salt in a large soup pot, cover, and bring to a boil over high heat. Reduce the heat to moderate and continue to cook until the vegetables are almost tender, 20 to 25 minutes.

Meanwhile, process the coconut, peppers, and yogurt in a food processor or blender until as smooth as possible. (The coconut will never become completely smooth.)

When the vegetables are ready, add the coconut-yogurt mixture and cilantro to the soup pot. Simmer for a few minutes and remove from the heat.

Heat the oil in a small, nonstick saucepan over moderately high heat and cook the curry leaves, stirring, 10 to 15 seconds. Add the mustard seeds and immediately cover the pan to prevent them from popping and flying out. Once the popping subsides, 3 to 5 seconds, remove the lid and stir in the asafetida and paprika. Immediately pour the contents of the pan into the soup.

Transfer to a large serving bowl (or small individual bowls), garnish with chopped cilantro, and serve.

Cold Potato-Leek Soup

THIS TAKEOFF ON VICHYSSOISE showcases the versatile potato at its soupy best. See how it mingles with Indian seasonings to make this low-fat masterpiece. A dash of turmeric gives this soup an attractive yellow color.

1 tablespoon extra-virgin olive oil
2 small leek whites, thoroughly washed and coarsely chopped
1 tablespoon peeled and minced fresh ginger
1 teaspoon minced garlic
20 to 25 fresh curry leaves (optional), to your taste
¼ cup firmly packed coarsely chopped cilantro (fresh coriander) leaves, soft stems
   included
1 tablespoon ground coriander
1 teaspoon ground cumin
¼ teaspoon ground turmeric
¾ teaspoon salt, or to your taste
Freshly ground white pepper to taste
2 large russet potatoes (about 1 pound)
2 cups water
2 cups nonfat plain yogurt
Freshly ground black pepper to taste
Chopped cilantro (fresh coriander) leaves for garnish

Makes 4 to 6 servings

SERVING IDEAS:
   Present as a starter course with Tandoori Chicken Salad with Ginger Mint Dressing (page 34) and focaccia bread.

DO AHEAD:
   Stays fresh for about 5 days in the refrigerator. Do not freeze; the yogurt becomes watery when thawed.

   In a large saucepan, heat the oil over moderate heat and cook the leeks, stirring, until golden, 3 to 4 minutes. Add the ginger, garlic, curry leaves, and cilantro and cook, stirring, 2 to 3 minutes, and add the coriander, cumin, turmeric, salt, white pepper, and potatoes. Cook, stirring, 3 to 5 minutes, then reduce the heat to low, cover the pan, and cook, stirring occasionally, until the potatoes are soft, 7 to 10 minutes. Add the water and simmer until the potatoes are very soft.

   Remove from the heat, let cool, transfer to a blender or a food processor, and blend until smooth. Add the yogurt and blend again. Remove to a serving bowl, adjust the seasonings, and refrigerate until ready to serve. Garnish with cilantro and serve in one large or several small individual bowls.

Green Lentil Soup

Makes 6 to 8 servings

SERVING IDEAS:

This substantial soup is perfect with a simple basmati rice pilaf or a pilaf enhanced with lots of vegetables. Or present this as an entrée with a side of vegetables and parantha or chapati breads or whole-wheat tortillas.

DO AHEAD:

Stays fresh for about 5 days in the refrigerator and about 3 months in the freezer. It will thicken as it cools, so add more water when reheating.

IN AMERICA, THE DISK-shaped dull-green lentils are always presented as a soup that has been simmered for hours with a ham bone or chicken or beef stock. In India, we make a vegetarian entrée with these lentils and serve it with whole-wheat flat breads or rice. In this recipe, I use the authentic Indian approach and some Western herbs to make a robust vegetarian curry-style soup.

To make without a pressure cooker, add extra water and simmer over moderate to low heat until the lentils are tender and creamy, about 1 hour.

3 tablespoons canola oil
5 to 7 dried red chili peppers, to your taste
1 small onion, peeled and finely chopped
1 tablespoon peeled and minced fresh ginger
1 teaspoon minced garlic
1 tablespoon ground coriander
1 teaspoon ground cumin
1 cup loosely packed finely chopped cilantro (fresh coriander) leaves, soft stems included
¼ cup lightly packed fresh oregano leaves or 2 teaspoon dried
1 tablespoon fresh thyme leaves or 1 teaspoon dried
1½ cups dried green lentils, picked over and rinsed
8 cups water
1 teaspoon salt
½ teaspoon ground turmeric
1 teaspoon paprika
Garam masala and finely sliced scallion whites for garnish

In a pressure cooker, heat 2 tablespoons of the oil over moderate heat and cook the peppers, stirring, for about 1 minute (stand away from the stove as you do this in case the peppers burst and fly toward your face). Add the onion and cook, stirring, until it turns golden brown, 5 to 7 minutes. Add the ginger and garlic and cook, stirring, for another minute, then mix in the coriander, cumin, cilantro, oregano, and thyme. Cook for another minute, then add the washed lentils.

Cook the lentils, stirring, for 3 to 5 minutes to roast them. Add the water, salt, and turmeric. Increase the heat to high, secure the lid of the pressure cooker, and cook for about 3 minutes after the pressure regulator starts rocking. Remove from the heat and let the pressure drop by itself, 15 to 20 minutes. Open the lid, stir the contents, and add more water and boil again if you want a thinner soup.

Heat the remaining tablespoon oil in a small saucepan over moderately high heat and add the cumin seeds; they should sizzle upon contact. Remove from the heat, add the paprika, immediately pour the contents into the soup, and stir to mix.

Transfer to a large serving bowl or several small individual bowls, garnish with garam masala and scallion whites, and serve.

Creamy Garbanzo Bean Soup

Makes 2 to 4 servings

SERVING IDEAS:

This refreshing cold soup is as dynamic with pita bread sandwiches as it is with hamburgers and hot dogs. Add less yogurt and it becomes a dip for chips and crudités. Or use it as a sauce for grilled chicken and seafood, a salad dressing, or a marinade for your next barbecue.

DO AHEAD:

Stays fresh in the refrigerator for 3 to 5 days. To enliven the flavors, garnish just prior to serving.

THIS SIMPLE PUREE OF garbanzo beans and yogurt makes a tangy cold soup that is so good for us. It's packed with loads of health-promoting nutrients and no added fat.

For added spunk, puree some serrano or jalapeño peppers with the other ingredients.

1 large clove garlic, peeled
One ½-inch piece fresh ginger, peeled
One 15½-ounce can garbanzo beans, drained and rinsed
A few sprigs cilantro (fresh coriander)
1½ cups nonfat plain yogurt
½ teaspoon salt, or to your taste
Freshly ground black pepper to taste
½ teaspoon roasted (page 10) ground cumin for garnish

Process the garlic, ginger, garbanzo beans, and cilantro with the yogurt in a food processor or blender until smooth. Season with salt and pepper and remove to a medium bowl. Garnish with the cumin and serve chilled.

A Chaat and a Salad

TELL A NATIVE INDIAN that you are having a salad for lunch, and he'll think you're crazy. Tell him that you are having a chaat, and he'll find an excuse to spend the next couple of hours with you. Salad is of no interest to him, but a chaat—now that's a different story.

What he doesn't understand is that your salad and his chaat are part of the same extended family. The Indian concept of a salad is sliced or finely chopped salad vegetables laid out symmetrically on a large platter or mixed together and packed in a bowl with a sprinkling of salt, pepper, red chilies, chaat masala, and a squeeze of fresh limes. These salads are always a part of the bigger meal, never a substantial course on their own.

On the other hand, the word *chaat* exudes a hypnotic charm. A category of Indian food that has no true synonym in the Western culinary dictionary, it is a mélange of one or more fruits, vegetables, potatoes, dried beans and lentils, *papri* (flour chips), and chicken, meat, or seafood. Tossed into this hotchpotch mixture are a bunch of different herbs, spices, chutneys, and sauces—sour, sweet, spicy, pungent, hot, or mild—all contributing to a unique "chaaty" flavor. We Indians welcome this lively composition with open arms at all times of the day.

Isn't this what salads are all about—tossed potpourris of all sorts of greens, vegetables, meats, and nuts dressed with zippy, tangy, and mildly sweet flavors? The seasonings of chaats and salads may be different, but the concept definitely has a strong correlation. This insight came to me only after sampling a vast array of intriguing and exciting salads. How easy it is to replace one ingredient with another and suddenly a salad transforms into a chaat and a chaat into a salad.

Here is my collection of salads and chaat salads that cross all cultural boundaries—colorful summer salads with an assortment of greens, bean sprouts, and vegetables dressed with a light yogurt and lime juice-based dressings as well as more substantial winter salads made with dried beans, grains, meats, and winter vegetables.

Enjoy!

Tandoori Chicken Salad with Ginger-Mint Dressing

Makes 4 to 6 servings

SERVING IDEAS:

Pair this Indian counterpart of Chinese chicken salad with naan breads, Italian focaccia, or simple garlic toasts and a tall glass of chilled Indian beer or fresh lemonade.

DO AHEAD:

Toast the nuts and seeds 8 to 10 days ahead of time. Prepare all the salad vegetables, grill and shred the chicken, and store separately in plastic zipper bags in the refrigerator up to 2 to 3 days ahead. Assemble the salad closer to serving time.

HOW CAN ANYONE EAT raw leaves and vegetables and call it a meal? They obviously haven't tried tandoori chicken mixed with these wonderful greens and colorful vegetables. This salad can also be made with Chicken Tikka Kebabs (page 181).

6 cups firmly packed mixed baby greens
1 small red bell pepper, seeded and cut into 1-inch-long julienne strips
1 small yellow bell pepper, seeded and cut into 1-inch-long julienne strips
1 cup grated and squeezed pickling or Japanese cucumber
1 cup peeled and grated carrots
½ cup thinly sliced scallion whites, or more to taste
3 cups shredded or diced Chicken Tandoori (page 177), or more to your taste
¼ cup blanched almond slivers, toasted (see NOTE below)
1 cup Ginger-Mint Dressing (page 35)
2 teaspoons sesame seeds, toasted (see NOTE)
Freshly ground black pepper to taste

Wash and dry the greens in a salad spinner or on a kitchen towel, then tear the larger leaves into bite-size pieces. Place them in a salad bowl and add the bell peppers, cucumber, carrots, and scallion whites. Cover and refrigerate until needed.

When ready to serve, mix in the chicken and almond slivers. Add the dressing and toss to mix the salad. Top with the sesame seeds and pepper, and serve with additional dressing on the side.

NOTE:

To pan-toast nuts, seeds, or ground spices, place them in a small nonstick skillet and cook, stirring, over moderate heat until highly fragrant and golden, 2 to 4 minutes, depending on the quantity. Transfer immediately to a bowl or plate to stop further roasting from the heat in the skillet.

Cool and store in airtight containers in the refrigerator for 2 to 3 months.

Ginger-Mint Dressing

One 1-inch piece fresh ginger, peeled and cut into thin slices
1 clove garlic, peeled
⅓ cup firmly packed fresh mint leaves
2 tablespoons fresh lime or lemon juice
1 tablespoon honey
¾ cup nonfat plain yogurt
½ teaspoon salt, or to taste

In the work bowl of a food processor fitted with the metal S-blade and the motor running, process the ginger and garlic until minced by dropping them through the feed tube. Stop the motor, add the remaining ingredients and process again until smooth. Stop the motor and scrape down the sides of the work bowl once or twice. Remove to a bowl and refrigerate until needed.

Makes about 1 cup

SERVING IDEAS:
This slightly sweet and tangy, nonfat dressing is charming as a dip with crudités and chips and all sorts of appetizers. When served with the main meal, it doubles as a soothing raita (page 245) that complements an array of curries and rice dishes.

DO AHEAD:
Stays fresh for 8 to 10 days in the refrigerator.

Marinated Chicken Confetti Salad

Makes 8 servings

SERVING IDEAS:

Turn this substantial salad into a meal with some warm rolls or garlic bread, or serve as part of a large buffet.

DO AHEAD:

Cook the chicken and combine all the chopped vegetables up to a day ahead of time and refrigerate until needed. Closer to serving time, add the chaat masala and lime juice to the vegetables and assemble the salad.

THE COMBINATION OF INDIAN and Chinese flavors gives this salad a brand new identity. Chop the vegetables as finely and uniformly as you can. The chicken pieces should look quite big when compared to the rest of the salad.

1 tablespoon peanut oil

1 teaspoon sesame oil

2 tablespoons dark soy sauce

6 tablespoons fresh lime or lemon juice, or more to your taste

2 teaspoons minced garlic

1 tablespoon peeled and minced fresh ginger

1 tablespoon ground coriander

½ teaspoon Chinese five-spice powder

½ teaspoon freshly ground Szechuan peppercorns, or to taste

¼ teaspoon cayenne pepper (optional)

2 pounds boneless, skinless chicken tenders, tendons removed and cut into 1-inch pieces (30 to 35 pieces)

3 cups finely diced vine-ripened tomatoes

1 cup finely chopped scallions (white and pale green parts)

1 cup peeled and finely diced pickling cucumber (or any other seedless variety)

½ cup finely diced red or white daikon radish

1 cup cored, peeled, and finely diced red apple

½ cup loosely packed finely chopped cilantro (fresh coriander) leaves, soft stems included

1 to 2 jalapeño peppers (optional), to your taste, finely chopped

1 teaspoon chaat masala, or to your taste

Salt to taste

2 to 3 cups finely shredded escarole or curly leaf lettuce

1 cup mixed alfalfa and clover sprouts

In a large bowl, combine the peanut oil, sesame oil, soy sauce, 3 tablespoons of the lime juice, the garlic, ginger, coriander, five-spice powder, Szechuan and cayenne pepper, and 1 cup of the tomatoes. Add the chicken and mix to coat completely with the mixture. Cover with plastic wrap and marinate the chicken in the refrigerator for at least 4 and up to 24 hours.

Combine the remaining 2 cups tomatoes, the scallions, cucumber, radish, apple, cilantro, and peppers in a medium bowl. Mix in the chaat masala and the remaining 3 tablespoons lime juice. Adjust the seasoning with salt and additional pepper and lime juice and set aside.

Put the chicken and the marinade in a large, nonstick skillet and cook, stirring occasionally, over moderately high heat until all the juices evaporate and the pieces turn golden, 5 to 10 minutes. Set aside.

Combine the lettuce and sprouts and spread on a serving platter. Put the chopped tomato-cucumber salad over the shredded lettuce, top with the cooked chicken pieces, and serve immediately.

Chicken Salad with Pineapple and Orange

Makes 6 to 8 servings

SERVING IDEAS:

Present as a one-dish meal with garlic bread and a glass of Chardonnay or as part of a Sunday brunch with A Medley of Roots (page 140) or grilled vegetables and a basmati rice pilaf.

DO AHEAD:

Prepare and store the lettuce, chicken, and fruit separate in the refrigerator for 3 to 5 days and assemble just prior to serving time.

MARINATED PINEAPPLE AND PEELED individual sections of mandarin oranges form a zesty ring around bite-size pieces of chicken that is cooked in sweet and tart citrus juices. This lively salad is delicious hot or cold.

Don't let the long list of ingredients intimidate you—the recipe is really very simple. Lemon pepper blend is available in the spice section of the supermarket.

One 20-ounce can pineapple chunks, packed in pineapple juice
One 11-ounce can mandarin oranges, packed in light syrup
¼ cup safflower oil
2 teaspoons plus 3 tablespoons peeled and minced fresh ginger, or more to your taste
2½ teaspoons chaat masala
1 teaspoon lemon pepper blend
1½ cups loosely packed finely chopped cilantro (fresh coriander) leaves, soft stems included
1 tablespoon fresh lime or lemon juice
6 to 10 dried red chili peppers, to your taste
1½ cups finely chopped onions
2 pounds boneless, skinless chicken tenderloins, tendons removed and each cut into 3 to 4 pieces
½ cup orange juice
½ cup fresh lemon or lime juice
1 teaspoon salt, or to your taste
½ teaspoon freshly ground black pepper, or to your taste
2 to 3 cups finely shredded dark green lettuce leaves of your choice

Put a sieve over a bowl and drain the pineapple chunks; reserve ½ cup of the juice, then drain the orange segments, discarding the syrup. Transfer the drained fruits to a bowl and set aside.

In a small, nonstick saucepan, heat 1 tablespoon of oil over moderately high heat and cook, stirring, 2 teaspoons of the ginger until golden, 30 to 60 seconds. Add 2 teaspoons of the chaat masala, the lemon pepper blend, ½ cup of the cilantro, and the lime juice. Transfer to the fruit bowl and mix to coat all the fruit. Cover with plastic wrap and marinate the fruit for 1 to 4 hours in the refrigerator.

Heat the remaining 3 tablespoons of oil in a large, nonstick pan over moderately high heat and cook the red peppers, stirring, until they turn dark, 45 to 60 seconds. (Stand as far from the pan as you can, in case the peppers burst and fly toward your face.) Add the onions and cook, stirring, until they turn dark brown, 10 to 12 minutes. Add the remaining 3 tablespoons ginger and 1 cup cilantro, then mix in the chicken, reserved pineapple juice, orange and lemon juices, salt, and black pepper. Cover the pan and cook over high heat for 5 to 7 minutes. Then reduce the heat to moderate and continue to cook, turning the pieces occasionally, until they are tender and all the liquid evaporates, 15 to 20 minutes. At this point, the chicken pieces should be rich brown in color and have a shiny glaze.

Transfer to the center of a serving platter and place the lettuce around the chicken. Drizzle the spicy juices from the fruit bowl over the lettuce, and place the marinated fruit over the lettuce. Garnish with the remaining ½ teaspoon chaat masala and serve hot, cold, or at room temperature.

Sautéed Turkey Salad with Ginger and Lemon Pepper

Makes 8 servings

SERVINGS IDEAS:

Serve this chaat salad hot, cold, or at room temperature as an appetizer or with a soup and an array of breads.

DO AHEAD:

Marinate the turkey and cook it up to a day in advance. Chop all the vegetables and store separately for 2 to 3 days. Make the salad closer to serving time, or the vegetables will become soggy.

NOTE:

A word of caution—don't overcook the vegetables or they will become watery.

CALL IT A SALAD or a chaat, this colorful centerpiece is sumptuous to the last bite. Use red and yellow pear-shaped baby tomatoes or multicolored cherry tomatoes for a splash of summer colors.

2 pounds boneless, skinless turkey breasts, cut into ¾-inch cubes
¼ cup nonfat plain yogurt, whisked until smooth
2 tablespoons fresh lime or lemon juice, or more to your taste
1 tablespoon peanut oil
1 teaspoon sesame oil
2 tablespoons peeled and minced fresh ginger
2 teaspoons minced garlic
¾ teaspoon salt, or to your taste
1 teaspoon freshly ground black pepper, or to your taste
1 cup diced pickling cucumber, any seedless variety
16 to 20 cherry tomatoes, cut in half
1 cup thinly sliced scallions
12 medium-size mushrooms, quartered
1 to 3 jalapeño peppers, to your taste, minced
1 teaspoon lemon pepper blend, or more to your taste
1 bunch spinach, trimmed of tough stems, thoroughly washed, and finely shredded

Put the turkey in a large bowl. Combine the yogurt, lime juice, peanut and sesame oils, ginger, garlic, salt, and pepper in a small bowl. Add to the large bowl and mix until the turkey is fully coated. Cover with plastic wrap and marinate for 12 to 24 hours in the refrigerator.

Put the turkey and the marinade in a large, nonstick skillet and cook, stirring occasionally, over moderately high heat until all the juices evaporate and the pieces turn golden, 5 to 10 minutes.

Mix in the cucumber, tomatoes, scallions, mushrooms, and peppers. Cook until heated through, 30 to 60 seconds, then add the lemon pepper. Remove from the heat and adjust the seasonings.

Line a large platter with the spinach, spoon the warm salad over the spinach, and serve. (The heat from the salad will wilt the spinach and the juices will season it.)

Yogurt-Marinated Grilled Sea Bass and Red Bell Peppers on Baby Greens

FLAVORS EXPLODE WHEN A marinated sea bass is grilled and served on a bed of greens.

1½ pounds fillets of sea bass or mahi mahi, cut into 1½-inch pieces

2 to 3 large red bell peppers, to your taste, seeded and cut into 1-inch pieces

2 teaspoons minced garlic

1 tablespoon peeled and minced fresh ginger

½ cup nonfat plain yogurt, whisked until smooth

2 tablespoons fresh lime or lemon juice

2 teaspoons sesame oil

2 teaspoons dried oregano

¼ teaspoon ground turmeric

½ teaspoon salt, or to your taste

Freshly ground black pepper to taste

8 to 10 metal skewers or bamboo skewers soaked at least 30 minutes in water

1 tablespoon extra-virgin olive oil (optional)

4 cups assorted baby greens

1 cup shredded radicchio

1 cup Yogurt and Roasted Cumin-Pepper Sauce (page 246), or more to your taste

Put the fish in one bowl and the bell peppers in another. Combine the garlic, ginger, yogurt, lime juice, sesame oil, oregano, turmeric, salt, and pepper in another bowl. Pour half of it over the fish pieces and half over the bell peppers. Combine to coat each well with the mixture. Cover both the bowls with plastic wrap and refrigerate for at least 2 and up to 24 hours.

Start the barbecue. Thread the fish and peppers on the skewers and grill, turning the skewers, over medium-hot coals until the fish turns golden and flaky, 8 to 10 minutes. Brush occasionally with the marinade from the bell pepper bowl. Discard the marinade from the fish bowl. (Use a spatula to loosen the fish pieces if they stick to the barbecue grill.)

Alternately, place the fish pieces in a large, nonstick skillet with the olive oil and cook over moderately high heat, turning once or twice, until golden and flaky, 5 to 7 minutes. Cook the bell pepper pieces in a similar manner.

Serve on a bed of greens and shredded radicchio. Drizzle some of the yogurt sauce over the fish and pass the remaining sauce on the side.

Makes 8 servings

SERVING IDEAS:
Try with Gingered Tomato Soup or Vegetarian-Style Chunky Vegetable Soup (page 22 or 27) and focaccia bread at your next summer brunch.

DO AHEAD:
Marinate the fish and peppers up to a day in advance. Cook the fish and assemble the salad closer to serving time.

NOTE:
For more variety in your vegetables, marinate and grill some zucchini, mushrooms, pearl onions, and cherry tomatoes along with the red bell peppers.

Marinated Shrimp Salad

Makes 4 to 6 servings

THE SECRET INGREDIENTS IN this cold appetizer salad are carom seeds and chaat masala, the savory spice blend from India.

SERVING IDEAS:

Present as an appetizer salad with a bowl of Yogurt-Cilantro Chutney (page 258) or as part of a salad buffet.

DO AHEAD:

Marinate the shrimp up to a day ahead of time. Assemble the salad up to 2 hours in advance.

2 tablespoons olive oil

3 bay leaves

1 small onion, cut in half lengthwise and thinly sliced

1 tablespoon coarsely chopped garlic

½ teaspoon cracked black peppercorns

½ teaspoon crushed carom seeds

1 teaspoon dry mustard

1 pound jumbo shrimp, shelled and deveined

¼ cup fresh orange juice

¼ cup any herb-flavored vinegar

1 tablespoon fresh lime or lemon juice

½ cup loosely packed finely chopped cilantro (fresh coriander) leaves, soft stems included

1 teaspoon salt, or to your taste

2 to 3 cups baby greens or any other dark green or red lettuce

½ teaspoon chaat masala, or more to your taste

In a large nonreactive saucepan, heat the oil over moderately high heat and cook, the bay leaves, onion, and garlic, stirring until the onion turns golden, 3 to 4 minutes. Stir in the peppercorns, carom seeds, and mustard, then add the shrimp, orange juice, vinegar, lime juice, cilantro, and salt. Bring to a boil over high heat. Reduce the heat to moderately low and simmer the shrimp until they turn pink, 5 to 8 minutes. (Add some water if the liquid dries up too quickly.)

Bring the mixture to room temperature, cover with plastic wrap, and refrigerate until chilled, 12 to 24 hours.

To serve, place the shrimp over a bed of greens, sprinkle the chaat masala on top, and serve.

Pureed Paneer Cheese and Watercress in Crispy Iceberg Leaves

THIS POWER SALAD IS served on a platter, surrounded by a ring of iceberg lettuce leaves. The guests use the lettuce leaves as cups, filling them with as much (or as little) of the salad as they want. These crispy leaves offer a welcome crunch to this fragrant and spicy blend of paneer cheese and watercress leaves. Other lettuce leaves can also be used—you may not get the crispy crunch but your body will love the nutritional bonus.

1 large head iceberg lettuce
One 1¼-inch piece fresh ginger, peeled and cut into thin slices
2 cloves garlic, peeled
1 to 4 serrano peppers, to your taste, stems removed
1 large red onion, peeled and cut into 6 to 8 wedges
1 cup firmly packed cilantro (fresh coriander) leaves, soft stems included
1 bunch watercress (or arugula, dandelion, or spinach) leaves, soft stems included
1 cup loosely packed fresh lemon basil leaves (or any other basil)
1 recipe Homemade Paneer Cheese (page 44), crumbled
2 tablespoons fresh lemon or lime juice
1 teaspoon salt, or to your taste
½ teaspoon freshly ground black pepper, or to your taste
1 teaspoon chaat masala, or to your taste
2 cups seeded and finely diced bell peppers of mixed colors (such as red, yellow, purple, orange)

In the work bowl of a food processor fitted with the metal S-blade and the motor running, process the ginger, garlic, serrano peppers, and onion until minced by dropping them through the feed tube. Add the cilantro, watercress, and basil and process until smooth. Mix in the paneer cheese and process until the cheese is minced. Add the lemon juice, salt, pepper, and chaat masala and process until mixed (don't overmix; there should be a grain in the salad). Remove to a serving platter and gently mix in the bell peppers. Surround the salad with the lettuce leaves and serve.

Makes 8 servings

SERVING IDEAS:
Pair with Gingered Tomato Soup (page 22) and focaccia bread or serve with grilled meat or poultry. Trim the base of the lettuce and very carefully separate the leaves, making sure that they remain as whole as possible. Place in a plastic bag and refrigerate until needed.

DO AHEAD:
Separate the lettuce leaves and store in plastic bags in the refrigerator for 3 to 5 days. Make the salad up to 3 days in advance.

Homemade Paneer Cheese

Makes 8 ounces or about
thirty 1 × ¼-inch pieces

*To make paneer
cheese:*
½ *gallon low-fat milk
(1 percent or 2 per-
cent)*
2 *cups nonfat plain
yogurt, whisked
until smooth*
One 2-*foot-square piece
fine muslin or 4 lay-
ers cheesecloth*

WHEN ASKED BY MY students to describe the flavor of paneer cheese, I stopped to wonder. How *does* one describe such a simple, mild, and fresh taste except by saying that it has a whiff of boiled milk combined with the sweetness of homemade yogurt and a soft and spongy bite, reminiscent of farmer cheese or the freshest mozzarella cheese?

Made with milk to which a souring agent (like yogurt, lemon juice, or vinegar) is added to curdle it, this delicate cheese is a great asset in the kitchen. Its versatility shines at every course of the meal as it readily absorbs the flavors of other ingredients that are paired with it. Scatter it over salads or serve it with a sprinkling of salt, pepper, and minced fresh herbs; add it to pizza, lasagne, and sandwiches or to curries, stews, and rice; or transform it into unusual desserts. Paneer cheese epitomizes purity in its simplest form. It retains its shape, does not melt when heated, and absorbs moisture and flavors.

And all this comes with a booster shot of protein and calcium—with very little fat, especially when you make your paneer cheese with low-fat milk, like all the paneer cheese in this book is. (Some people make theirs with half-and-half and then cook it with additional oil, doing away with all the intrinsic goodness of this wonderful food.)

My mother, who has been a vegetarian all her life, made this cheese at least once a week. Her favorite paneer-making pan was a heavy, tin-coated brass *patilla*, an open pan with lips that doubled as handles. In America, I use a large, heavy aluminum or anodized aluminum pan to make my cheese. Just rinse the pan before adding the milk and keep stirring—this prevents the milk from sticking (and burning) at the bottom of the pan and from spilling over.

Instead of draping the muslin over a pan, my mother would call on the children in the family to hold the corners of the cheesecloth when she poured the curdled milk through it; this way she got us involved in the kitchen and taught us the art of paneer making—and innocently we all thought she couldn't make it without us!

The actual paneer cheese procedure, from beginning to end, takes anywhere from 15 to 45 minutes, depending on the amount of milk you start with. The milk boils, you add a sour curdling agent, the milk separates within seconds, you drain it through cheesecloth, and weigh it down with something heavy (a pot of water) for 5 to 10 minutes. The paneer cheese is ready. When they see me make paneer cheese in class, my students realize that cheesecloth can actually be used to make cheese and not just to clean furniture.

Whey—the dull green, semitransparent liquid that separates from the milk curds—has many uses. It is easy to digest and is a good tonic for upset stomachs. I use it to make dough for various breads (even the ones I make in my bread machine), add it to soups, curries, and rice and, if all else fails, I give it to my plants.

Put the milk in a large, heavy pan and bring to a boil, stirring gently, over high heat. Just seconds before the milk actually boils and the bubbles spill over, mix in the yogurt and continue to stir until the milk curdles and separates into curds and whey, 1 to 2 minutes. Remove from the heat.

Drape the muslin or cheesecloth over a large pan and pour the curdled milk over it. As you do this, the whey drains through the muslin into the pan and the curdled cheese remains in the muslin.

With the cheese still inside it, pick up the muslin from the pan and tie it to the kitchen faucet to drain for another 3 to 5 minutes.

Remove the muslin from the faucet and gently twist it around the cheese, then place the cheese between two salad-size plates (or any other flat surfaces) with the twisted muslin on one side. Place a large pan of water on the top plate and let the cheese drain further for 10 to 12 minutes. (Do this close to the sink or you'll have a mess to clean up.)

Remove the pan of water from the cheese (that by now should have compressed into a chunk) and cut the cheese into desired shapes and sizes and use as needed.

Paneer cheese can be stored in airtight containers in the refrigerator for 4 to 5 days or it can be frozen. Since cold paneer is hard to cut, I suggest cutting the cheese into pieces before refrigerating or freezing them.

To freeze: Place the pieces on a plate in a single layer and freeze. When frozen, transfer them to plastic freezer bags and freeze for 3 to 4 months. This allows you to remove only the number of pieces you need for a recipe.

VARIATION: Paneer cheese can also be made with ¼ cup fresh or bottled lemon or lime juice (start with ¼ cup and add more if needed), 3 to 4 tablespoons white vinegar, or 1 quart buttermilk. Lemon juice and vinegar will yield about 6½ ounces of paneer cheese, and the buttermilk will yield about 8 ounces.

Wilted Red Swiss Chard with Sautéed Goat Cheese

Makes 4 to 6 servings

SERVING IDEAS:
Present alongside grilled meats, vegetables, or seafood or as a topping for pasta.

DO AHEAD:
Best when served fresh. However, if you chop everything (up to 2 days ahead of time), the salad doesn't take more than 5 minutes to make.

AS THE CHARD GREENS cook and soften, they absorb a delicate flavor from the stir-fried onion and fresh green garlic. Top these fragrant greens with tangy goat cheese and toasted almonds and you have a charming salad. Cook the leaves until completely wilted and this salad turns into a fascinating side dish. Try it both ways for fun and variety. (Green garlic looks a lot like green onions and is available in Asian, Middle Eastern, and farmers markets.)

2 tablespoons extra-virgin olive oil
1 large onion, cut in half lengthwise and thinly sliced
½ cup finely chopped fresh green garlic (white and pale green parts only) or ½ cup thoroughly washed, finely chopped leek whites and 1 large clove garlic
1 large bunch fresh red Swiss chard leaves, trimmed of stems, washed, spun dry, and cut into ¼-inch shreds (reserve the stems for another purpose)
1 cup coarsely crumbled goat cheese or paneer cheese (page 44), or more to your taste
½ teaspoon salt, or to your taste
½ teaspoon freshly ground black pepper, or to your taste
1 to 2 teaspoons fresh thyme leaves, to your taste
1 to 2 tablespoons fresh lime or lemon juice (optional), to your taste
2 tablespoons sliced almonds, toasted (page 34)

In a large skillet, heat 1½ tablespoons of the oil over moderately high heat and cook the onion, stirring, until it is golden, 3 to 5 minutes. Add the garlic and cook for another 1 to 2 minutes. Add the chard leaves and cook, stirring, until they are barely wilted and glazed with the oil, 2 to 3 minutes. Add the salt and pepper and remove to a serving bowl.

Heat the remaining ½ tablespoon oil in the same skillet and cook the goat cheese, stirring lightly, over moderately high heat, until it starts to turn golden, 1 to 2 minutes. Season with salt and pepper and the thyme, cook for another minute, and mix it with the wilted Swiss chard. Taste and add the lime juice, if you like. Garnish with the toasted almonds and serve.

Indian Coleslaw

EAT AS MUCH OF this as you can, any time of the day. This coleslaw cousin is totally good for you, because it is made with crunchy, anticancerous, nutrient-rich cabbage and nonfat yogurt cheese, and has a taste that is too scrumptious to be true.

2 cups yogurt cheese (page 79)
2 tablespoons fresh lime or lemon juice
½ teaspoon cayenne pepper or paprika
½ teaspoon freshly ground black pepper, or to your taste
½ teaspoon salt, or to your taste
1 small head green cabbage (1 to 1¼ pounds), finely shredded
2 cups seeded and finely diced bell peppers of mixed colors (red, yellow, purple, orange, etc.)
¾ cup minced scallions (white and light green parts; from 10 to 12 scallions)
1 cup loosely packed finely chopped cilantro (fresh coriander) leaves, soft stems included
Tomato wedges or colorful cherry tomatoes for garnish

In a medium bowl, combine the yogurt cheese with the lime juice, cayenne, black pepper, and salt.

In a large bowl, combine the cabbage, bell peppers, scallions, and cilantro, then add the yogurt cheese dressing. Mix with a fork or your fingers until everything is well covered with the dressing.

Transfer to a serving casserole or bowl, garnish with tomato wedges or cherry tomatoes, and serve.

Makes 4 to 6 servings

SERVING IDEAS:
Perfect for a summer barbecue, a winter brunch, or a picnic any time of the year with all sorts of grilled fare.

DO AHEAD:
Make up to 12 hours in advance and store, covered, in the refrigerator. The yogurt cheese can be combined with the lime juice and spices and refrigerated for up to one week.

Chopped Spinach Salad with Cumin-Yogurt Dressing

Makes 8 servings

THIS SALAD WAS INSPIRED by the one prepared by Sunil Vora at his famous Los Angeles restaurant, The Clay Pit.

SERVING IDEAS:

Pair with Silky Turkey Kebab Rolls or Chicken Tikka Kebabs (page 182 or 181) and garlicky focaccia bread.

2 teaspoons cumin seeds
½ to 1 teaspoon black peppercorns, to your taste
1 teaspoon sesame seeds
1½ cups nonfat plain yogurt
2 to 4 tablespoons low-fat milk (1 percent or 2 percent), to your taste
½ teaspoon salt, or to taste
2 to 3 bunches fresh spinach (1¼ to 1½ pounds), trimmed of tough stems, thoroughly washed, and coarsely chopped
½ teaspoon paprika, or to your taste

DO AHEAD:

Make the dressing up to 5 days ahead of time. Wash and chop the spinach up to 3 days ahead. Assemble the salad just prior to serving; if assembled ahead, the spinach leaves become soggy.

Put the cumin seeds and peppercorns in a small, nonstick skillet over moderately high heat and toast, shaking the pan, until they turn a few shades darker and start to pop, 1 to 2 minutes. Cool and coarsely grind them in a spice grinder or with a mortar and pestle. Set aside. Toast the sesame seeds and set aside, without grinding them.

In a small bowl, combine the yogurt and milk and beat with a fork or whisk until smooth. Season with the salt and half of the cumin-peppercorn mixture. Set aside. Place the spinach in a serving bowl, toss with the yogurt dressing, and sprinkle the remaining cumin and peppercorns on top. Garnish with the paprika and sesame seeds and serve.

VARIATION: For a variation, sprinkle some toasted pine nuts and almond slivers on top.

Basmati Rice and Spinach "Tabbouleh"

I STARTED TO PROCESS leftover rice and spinach to make patties, and instead ended up with something that looked like tabbouleh—a Middle Eastern salad made with bulgur wheat and fresh parsley.

As I processed, the minced ginger, garlic, spinach, and rice looked so inviting that I stopped to take a bite. One bite led to two and two led to a lot more. I offered some to my husband, Pradeep, and he gave me the green light—"Just spice it a little more," he said.

2 large cloves garlic, peeled
One 1½-inch piece fresh ginger, peeled and coarsely chopped
1 to 2 jalapeño peppers (optional), to your taste, stemmed
3 cups thoroughly washed firmly packed, coarsely chopped spinach
1 cup firmly packed cilantro (fresh coriander) leaves, soft stems included
4 cups Simply Cumin Basmati (page 270) or any other leftover rice
¼ teaspoon salt, or to your taste
¼ teaspoon freshly ground black pepper, or to your taste
1 tablespoon fresh lime or lemon juice
Tomato wedges or cherry tomatoes for garnish

In the work bowl of a food processor fitted with the S-blade, and with the motor running, drop the garlic, ginger, and peppers through the feed tube and process until minced. Add the spinach and cilantro in 1 or 2 batches and process, stopping to scrape down the sides a few times, until minced. Add the cooked rice and processed until minced.

Stir in the salt, pepper, and lime juice. Transfer to a platter, garnish with tomato wedges or cherry tomatoes, and serve at room temperature or chilled.

Makes 4 to 6 servings

SERVING IDEAS:
Present this "grain and green" combination in radicchio cups with an array of grilled entrées or over toasted bread as a quick open-faced sandwich. Mix in some grated tofu-rella cheese substitute (available in the cheese section of the supermarkets) or cheddar cheese and make grilled sandwiches under the broiler.

DO AHEAD:
This can be made up to 3 days in advance and stored in the refrigerator.

Tomatoes and Zucchini Julienne in Balsamic-Basil Dressing

Makes 8 servings

SERVING IDEAS:
Present as an appetizer salad with freshly baked breads or as part of a larger menu.

DO AHEAD:
Marinate the tomatoes and zucchini separately up to a day ahead and assemble the salad only 1 to 2 hours before serving.

MY FAMILY LOVES IT, my friends love it, and I love it even more. For the best flavor, it is crucial to use brilliantly colored and naturally sweet (red, yellow, or orange) vine-ripened tomatoes. Nothing else will do justice to this summer delight.

To present this salad with an Indian meal, substitute the basil with cilantro (fresh coriander) and a touch of fresh mint leaves.

⅓ cup balsamic vinegar
¼ cup extra-virgin olive oil
1½ tablespoons minced garlic
1 teaspoon salt, or to your taste
½ cup firmly packed finely chopped fresh basil leaves
1½ pounds young, firm zucchini (green and yellow included)
2 pounds vine-ripened tomatoes

Mix together the vinegar, oil, garlic, salt, and basil and set aside.

Cut the tomatoes into ½-inch cubes and place in a mixing bowl. Cut each zucchini crosswise into very thin diagonal slices, then cut each slice into thin julienne sticks and place in a separate bowl.

Pour half the dressing over the tomatoes and the other half over the zucchini. Mix lightly, cover with plastic wrap, and marinate the tomatoes and zucchini in the refrigerator for at least 1 and up to 24 hours (prolonged refrigeration may cause the olive oil to solidify, so bring to room temperature before serving).

Transfer the tomatoes to the center of a serving casserole dish, leaving behind the juices. Surround the tomatoes with a ring of zucchini and serve.

Tomato, Jicama, and Scallion Salad on Endive Boats

THE PALE GREEN, BOAT-shaped leaves of Belgian endive are perfect recipients for this piquant salad of finely diced vegetables.

For a dramatic presentation, place a mound of chopped strawberries, seedless grapes, diced melons, and other fruits of contrasting colors in the center of a platter. (Toss them with lemon juice and chaat masala, if you wish.) Then arrange the endive boats around the fruit.

2 cups finely diced firm, vine-ripened tomatoes
½ cup peeled and grated jicama or white daikon or red radishes
½ cup finely chopped scallion whites
½ cup grated and squeezed pickling cucumber (or any other seedless variety)
½ cup loosely packed finely chopped cilantro (fresh coriander) leaves, soft stems
    included
2 tablespoons finely chopped fresh lemon basil leaves (or any other basil)
1 tablespoon finely chopped fresh mint leaves
1 jalapeño pepper, minced, or more to your taste
2 tablespoons fresh lime or lemon juice, or more to your taste
½ teaspoon salt, or to your taste
½ teaspoon freshly ground black pepper, or to your taste
1 teaspoon chaat masala or lemon pepper blend, or to your taste
2 medium heads Belgian endive, separated into leaves

In a medium bowl, combine the tomatoes, jicama, scallions, cucumber, cilantro, basil, mint, and pepper. Mix in the lime juice, salt, pepper, and chaat masala. Set aside.

Place the endive leaves decoratively on a large platter. Put 1 to 2 tablespoons (depending on the size of the leaf) of the mixed salad on each leaf and serve.

Makes 25 to 30 endive boats

SERVING IDEAS.
Little individual servings make it possible to serve this salad as an appetizer or as part of the main meal. I love it with all types of grilled fare, especially Chicken Tandoori and Grilled Saffron Seekh Kebabs (page 177 and 183).

DO AHEAD:
Combine the vegetables and herbs and refrigerate for up to a day. Mix in the lime juice and spices just prior to serving; otherwise the salt will cause the vegetables to give off water and lose their crispness.

Vibrant Russet and Purple Potato Salad

Present this at your next Fourth of July barbecue with The Indian Hamburger or New Delhi Lamb Burger (page 185 or 186) instead of french fries. It is also charming as a side dish with a variety of curries.

DO AHEAD:

Shred the lettuce, place in plastic bags, and refrigerate for 3 to 5 days. Boil and roast the potatoes up to 5 hours ahead. Assemble the salad just prior serving.

FRESH POMEGRANATE SEEDS OFFER a welcome crunch and color contrast to this lovely salad. If they are not available, use finely diced red bell peppers or extra-firm tomatoes.

This appetizer salad has more potatoes than an Indian yogurt raita and more dressing than a typical Western potato salad.

1½ pounds russet potatoes (peeled or unpeeled), boiled in lightly salted water to cover until tender and cut into ¾-inch cubes
1½ pounds purple potatoes (peeled or unpeeled), boiled in lightly salted water to cover until tender and cut into ¾-inch dice
2 tablespoons peanut oil
2 tablespoons peeled and minced fresh ginger
2 teaspoons minced garlic
½ cup firmly packed finely chopped cilantro (fresh coriander) leaves, soft stems included
2 teaspoons ground cumin
1 teaspoon paprika
1 teaspoon salt, or to your taste
3 to 4 cups washed, spun-dried, and shredded butter lettuce
2 cups Yogurt and Roasted Cumin-Pepper Sauce (page 246)
1 cup fresh pomegranate seeds
Chopped cilantro for garnish

Preheat the oven to 400°F. Lightly grease a baking sheet.

Put the potatoes in a large bowl. Add the oil, ginger, garlic, cilantro, cumin, paprika, and salt and mix everything together very carefully with your hands or a large slotted spoon. Spread evenly over the baking sheet and roast, uncovered, in the center of the oven until golden, 15 to 20 minutes. Occasionally turn the potatoes, very carefully, with a spatula to ensure even browning.

Alternately, mix everything together, cover, and cook in a large, nonstick skillet over moderately high heat (in 2 or 3 batches) until golden, 15 to 20 minutes.

Line a platter with the shredded lettuce and place the potatoes over it. Drizzle about 1 cup of the yogurt sauce over the potatoes and gently fork in the pomegranate seeds. Garnish with chopped cilantro and serve the remaining sauce on the side.

Garbanzo Bean and Potato Salad with Yogurt-Cilantro Chutney

I'VE OFTEN HEARD IT said that the Indians (from India) treat their garbanzo beans like no one else can. Here is a salad made with canned garbanzo beans and potatoes that proves the point. This robust and quick-cooking salad can also double up as a side dish or an entrée.

2 tablespoons peanut oil

2 teaspoons minced garlic

2 tablespoons peeled and minced fresh ginger

2 tablespoons ground coriander

2 teaspoons chaat masala, or more to your taste

3 medium-size russet potatoes, boiled in lightly salted water to cover until tender, peeled, and cut into ¾-inch cubes

Four 15½-ounce cans garbanzo beans (chickpeas), drained and rinsed

¼ cup water

3 tablespoons fresh lime or lemon juice, or more to your taste

½ cup loosely packed, finely chopped cilantro (fresh coriander) leaves, soft stems included

1 large red bell pepper, seeded and cut into ¼-inch dice

2 cups shredded dark green and bronze leaf lettuce

½ teaspoon garam masala for garnish

1½ cups Yogurt-Cilantro Chutney (page 258), or more to your taste

In a large, nonstick skillet, heat the oil over moderately high heat and cook the garlic and ginger, stirring, until golden, 1 to 2 minutes. Stir in the coriander and chaat masala, then add the potatoes and cook, turning once or twice, for 3 to 4 minutes. Mix in the garbanzo beans, water, lime juice, cilantro, and bell peppers. Cook, stirring gently as necessary, until the beans are tender and all the liquid evaporates, 4 to 5 minutes.

Line a large platter with the shredded lettuce. Put the bean salad over the lettuce, making sure that enough lettuce is visible all around the outside. Sprinkle the garam masala over the top and drizzle about ½ cup of the chutney over the salad. Serve the remaining chutney on the side. This salad can be presented warm, at room temperature, or straight from the refrigerator.

Makes 6 to 8 servings

SERVING IDEAS:
Serve by itself as a snack or in combination with other dishes, or stuffed in pita pockets to make quick falafel-type sandwiches.

DO AHEAD:
Stays fresh for 3 to 5 days in the refrigerator. If you do make it in advance, store the cooked garbanzo beans and chutney separately, and assemble the salad closer to serving time.

Crazy Breads and Sandwiches

EVERYONE LOVES BREADS—FLAT breads, leavened breads, light breads, dark breads, robust whole grain breads—whether hot from the oven or just off the stove, fresh from the bakery or the local market, cold in lunch-bag sandwiches, or toasted with butter. They provide sustenance and nourishment and are an integral part of our daily diets. Yet for some reason—along with desserts—breads are the first thing we drop when we go on a diet, not realizing that it is not the actual breads themselves, but the high-fat toppings and fixings that are the true storehouses of calories. When prepared just right, with various whole grains, meats, and vegetables, breads offer valuable complex carbohydrates, protein, and very little fat.

When I was growing up, the word *bread* (called double roti in India, because the dough had risen to double its volume) meant a loaf of white bread that was purchased at the local grocery store. I loved it because it was different from the paranthas, rotis, chapatis, pooris, and naans (different Indian flat breads) that I was so familiar with. It was only after I came to live in America that my rapport with breads grew by leaps and bounds. Very soon, I spotted similarities between the Indian flat-bread dough and the dough used for making loaves of bread; they look alike and contain almost the same ingredients, with one exception—yeast (although some Indian breads like naan and kulchas do contain yeast).

This led to a set of bread and bread-dough experiments. From my Indian kitchen emerged herbs, spices, chutneys, and sauces that added exciting flavor accents to freshly baked loaves and everyday sandwiches. Italian focaccia and pizza breads borrowed popular Indian seasonings, Mexican tortillas and Middle Eastern pita pockets combined famously with Indian spices, and the versatile Indian flat breads subtly merged with Italian and American herbs.

Included in this chapter is a selection of my favorite parantha (griddle-fried) and naan (oven-grilled) breads and some exciting and inspiring adaptations from different cuisines of the world.

A note on Indian parantha and naan breads: Indian cuisine boasts some of the finest flat breads in the world. Though most of the everyday home breads are made with stoneground whole-wheat durum flour, some also incorporate a variety of other flours. These breads are typically made on a concave cast-iron griddle called a *tava*, but they can also be prepared on a pancake griddle or in a skillet. Most of them can also be made in the tandoor (I use the oven instead).

Indian breads are customarily made fresh at every meal (there's always one person in the kitchen turning out bread after bread, while the rest of the family eats them hot, straight off the tava), but today's busy lifestyle doesn't allow us this luxury. So here are some shortcuts and do-ahead hints that will make this luxury a possibility.

DO AHEAD

The dough of all types of parantha and naan breads stays fresh in the refrigerator for 4 to 5 days and can also be frozen. Make a large batch, divide it into small user-friendly portions, place them in plastic zipper bags, keep one in the refrigerator, and freeze the rest. Thaw in the refrigerator or at room temperature—never in the oven or in the microwave oven, as the intense heat hardens the dough from the outside, rendering it useless for cooking purposes.

Parantha and naan breads can be made ahead of time and stacked one on top of the other. Cover with aluminum foil and keep warm in a preheated 200°F oven or in a tortilla warmer for up 2 hours.

To store, lay the breads out on any clean, flat surface and cool them completely (this is very important, or they will sweat and stick to one another). Stack one on top of the other and place them in an airtight container or plastic bag for 4 to 5 days in the refrigerator or freeze for up to 2 months. Bring to room temperature and reheat as directed.

To reheat, place a single layer of the breads on an ungreased cookie sheet and bake in a preheated

450°F oven for 1 to 3 minutes, depending on how cold they were when you started. They can also be toasted in a toaster, a toaster oven until hot, or under the oven broiler.

SERVING SUGGESTIONS

Ideally, parantha breads should be served hot—straight off the stove—but they can also be served warm or at room temperature.

• Place some grilled or stir-fried meat or vegetables over a freshly made parantha bread, roll or fold in half, and eat while it is still hot or wrap in a sheet of aluminum foil and take to work, school, or on a picnic.

• Cut the breads into quarters and pair with frittatas, omelettes, or scrambled eggs and a tall glass of iced tea or coffee.

• Cut into wedges and present as the first course with drinks or serve as a meal in itself with nonfat plain yogurt or a yogurt raita and purchased Indian pickles and chutneys.

• If you feel like indulging, place a dollop of whipped butter in the center of a freshly cooked parantha bread. Break bite-size pieces from the sides, dip into the melting butter, and eat. This really is the best way to enjoy a parantha. Drink a glass of sweetened yogurt *lassi* (a yogurt shake) with your parantha and drift effortlessly to sleep.

As an accompaniment to a meal, allow one to two breads per person. As a complete meal in itself—with yogurt, chutneys, and pickles—allow two to four pieces per person.

Crispy Whole-Wheat Scallion-Rosemary Parantha Bread

Makes 16 to 18 parantha breads

DO AHEAD:

Make the dough up to 2 days ahead of time and hold in the refrigerator. Or partially cook the paranthas—here's how. When the second side is partly cooked, remove the half-cooked paranthas from the griddle. Cool completely and stack one on top of the other. Wrap in aluminum foil and store in the refrigerator for up to 4 days. Remove from the refrigerator, bring to room temperature, and finish cooking on the tava just prior to serving.

I HAVE SEEN ROSEMARY breads in gourmet bakeries all over America, so I decided to add some of this fragrant herb to my parantha bread—with marvelous results. Most Indians, in America and India, are unfamiliar with rosemary. If they only knew what they were missing!

To retain its proper texture, the dough for this bread should be made by hand; the food processor will puree the scallions, rosemary, and serrano peppers, resulting in a bread that is uniformly colored instead of having beautiful flecks of green and white. The bread will, however, still be wonderful.

For the dough:

¾ *cup very thinly sliced scallions (white and light green parts; 6 to 8 scallions)*
¼ *cup minced fresh rosemary leaves*
3 to 4 serrano peppers (optional), to your taste, finely chopped
4 cups stone-ground whole-wheat durum flour
1 teaspoon cracked black peppercorns
1 teaspoon salt, or to taste
¼ *cup vegetable oil*
About 1½ cups water

To cook the bread:

1 cup whole-wheat durum flour in a flat bowl
½ *cup vegetable oil*

Put the scallions, rosemary, peppers, flour, peppercorns, and salt in a large bowl and mix together. Add the oil and mix in with your fingertips, then add the water, about ½ cup or less at a time, mixing as you go along, until the dough gathers into a ball. Add some more flour if the dough seems too sticky and more water if it seems too dry. Cover with plastic wrap and set aside at room temperature for 1 to 4 hours. If holding for a longer period, place the dough in the refrigerator.

Heat a large griddle, skillet, or tava, over moderately high heat until a sprinkling of flour immediately turns dark brown. Wipe off the flour.

Lightly oil your hands and divide the dough into 16 to 18 even, round balls. Cover with a clean kitchen cloth to keep them from drying out and set aside. Working with each ball separately, press lightly to form a disk, then coat completely with flour from the bowl and, with a rolling pin, roll out into a 7- to 8-inch round of even thickness.

Put the parantha bread on the hot griddle. Turn it over when it is dotted with tiny golden spots on the bottom. When the second side is covered with larger brown spots, turn it over again and brush lightly with oil. Turn it over once more and fry the oiled side for about 30 seconds. Brush and fry the second side for about 30 seconds. (There should be a total of 4 turns.) Remove from the griddle and serve hot with any meal.

Minty Cottage Cheese Parantha Bread

Makes 16 to 18 parantha breads

Do Ahead:
See page 56.

THE DOUGH FOR THIS parantha bread is not made with water as is customary—it's made with nonfat cottage cheese. This addition results in soft and silky-smooth parantha breads enriched with a heavy dose of calcium.

Do not add any salt to this recipe because the cottage cheese already contains some.

For the dough:
One 1-inch piece fresh ginger, peeled and cut into thin slices
3 to 4 serrano peppers (optional), to your taste, stems removed
10 to 12 medium-size scallion whites, to your taste
¼ cup firmly packed fresh mint leaves
1 cup firmly packed cilantro (fresh coriander) leaves, soft stems included
3 cups stone-ground whole-wheat durum flour or 2 cups regular whole-wheat flour
*   mixed with 1 cup bread flour*
1 teaspoon freshly ground black pepper
2 tablespoons vegetable oil
2 cups nonfat cottage cheese

To cook the bread:
1 cup whole-wheat durum flour in a flat bowl
½ cup vegetable oil
1 tablespoon ground dried mint leaves

In the work bowl of a food processor fitted with the metal S-blade, drop the ginger, peppers, and scallions through the feed-tube and process until minced. Add the mint and cilantro and process until minced. Add the flours, black pepper, and oil and process for 15 seconds to mix. Add 1¾ cups of the cottage cheese and process until everything is fully mixed and the flour is moist, 10 to 15 seconds. With the motor running, add the remaining cottage cheese by the spoonful through the feed tube, stopping when the dough gathers into a smooth ball and cleans the sides of the work bowl. Add some flour if the dough looks too sticky or more cottage cheese if it looks too dry. Process for another 15 seconds after that.

To make the dough by hand, put the flour in a large bowl and mix in minced ginger, peppers, scallions, mint, cilantro, and oil. Add 1¾ cup cottage cheese and mix with your hands until the dough starts to gather together. Add more cottage cheese as necessary to make a medium-firm dough that does not stick to your fingers (you can oil your hands, but it is not necessary.)

Lightly oil your hands (now it is necessary) and transfer the dough to another bowl. Cover with plastic wrap and let it rest at room temperature for 1 to 4 hours. If holding for a longer period, place in the refrigerator.

Heat a large griddle, skillet, or tava, over moderately high heat until a sprinkling of flour immediately turns dark brown. Wipe off the flour.

Lightly oil your hands and divide the dough into 16 to 18 even, round balls. Cover with a clean kitchen cloth to keep them from drying out and set aside. Working with each ball separately, press lightly to form a disk, coat with flour from the bowl, and, with a rolling pin, roll out into a 7- to 8-inch round of even thickness.

Put the parantha bread on the hot griddle. Turn it over when it is dotted with tiny golden spots on the bottom. When the second side is covered with larger with larger brown spots, turn it over and brush lightly with oil. Turn it over once again and fry the oiled side for about 30 seconds. Brush and fry the second side for about 30 seconds. (There should be a total of 4 turns.) Remove from the griddle, sprinkle with the ground mint leaves, and serve hot with any meal.

Spinach and Potato Parantha Bread

Makes 18 to 20
parantha breads

Do Ahead:
See page 56.

BELONGING TO THE SAME family as Minty Cottage Cheese Parantha Bread (page 60), this green-colored flat bread has an entirely different identity. Like spinach noodles and spinach ravioli, spinach parantha bread offers "green appeal" to the nutritionally minded.

The dough for this bread is best when made in the food processor.

For the dough:

1 large bunch fresh spinach (about ¾ pound) trimmed of tough stems, thoroughly washed, and coarsely chopped

3 to 5 large cloves garlic, to your taste, peeled

One 1½-inch piece fresh ginger, peeled and cut into thin slices

4 to 5 scallions (white and green parts), to your taste, each cut into 3 to 4 pieces

½ cup firmly packed cilantro (fresh coriander) leaves, soft stems included

2 large russet potatoes, boiled in lightly salted water to cover until tender, peeled, and coarsely diced

3 tablespoons vegetable oil

1 teaspoon garam masala

1 tablespoon ground dried fenugreek leaves

1 teaspoon salt, or to your taste

3 cups stone-ground whole-wheat durum flour

1 cup all-purpose or bread flour

¼ cup nonfat plain yogurt or water, or as needed

To cook the bread:

1 cup whole-wheat durum flour in a flat bowl

½ cup vegetable oil

In the work bowl of a food processor fitted with the metal S-blade and with the motor running, drop the garlic, ginger, scallions, and cilantro through the feed tube and process until minced. Add the spinach a little at a time and process, stopping to scrape down the sides a few times, until the spinach is reduced to a smooth puree. Add the potatoes, oil, garam masala, fenugreek leaves, and salt, and process for 30 seconds. Add both the flours, and process until the dough gathers into a smooth ball and the sides of the food processor look clean. (You may need to add a little yogurt if the dough looks too dry or add extra flour if the dough looks too wet). Process for about 30 seconds, then stop the motor.

Lightly oil your hands and transfer the dough to another bowl. Cover with plastic wrap and let it rest at room temperature for 1 to 4 hours. If holding for a longer period, place in the refrigerator.

Heat a large griddle, skillet, or tava, over moderately high heat until a sprinkling of flour immediately turns dark brown. Wipe off the flour.

Lightly oil your hands and divide the dough into 18 to 20 even, round balls. Cover with a clean kitchen cloth to keep them from drying out and set aside. Working with each ball separately, press lightly to form a disk, coat completely with flour from the bowl, and, with a rolling pin, roll out into a 7- to 8-inch round of even thickness.

Put the parantha bread on the hot griddle. Turn it over when it is dotted with tiny golden spots on the bottom. When the second side is covered with larger brown spots, turn it over and brush lightly with oil. Turn it over once again and fry the oiled side for about 30 seconds. Brush and fry the second side for about 30 seconds. (There should be a total of 4 turns.) Remove from the griddle and serve hot with any meal.

Parantha Bread Stuffed with Mashed Potatoes and Peas

Makes 20 stuffed parantha breads

IN THIS BREAD, THE whole-wheat dough forms a shell-like casing, inside of which rests an irresistible combination of spicy mashed potatoes and peas.

Do Ahead:

Make the dough up to 5 days in advance. Make the stuffing up to 2 days in advance. The stuffing can go straight from the refrigerator into the parantha. To partially cook the paranthas, see page 58.

To make the stuffing:

4 to 5 large russet potatoes, boiled in lightly salted water to cover until tender, peeled, and grated or mashed

3 cups frozen green peas, thawed

2 tablespoons peeled and minced fresh ginger

½ cup firmly packed finely chopped cilantro (fresh coriander) leaves, soft stems included

¼ cup minced fresh dill

2 serrano peppers (optional), minced

2 tablespoons fresh lemon juice

2 tablespoons ground coriander

1 teaspoon ground cumin

½ teaspoon garam masala

1 teaspoons salt, or to your taste

To make the dough:

4 cups stone-ground whole-wheat durum flour

About 1⅔ cups water

To cook the bread:

1 cup whole-wheat durum flour in a flat bowl

¼ cup vegetable oil or butter, melted

Put the potatoes in a large bowl.

In a large, nonstick skillet, cook the thawed peas over moderately high heat until all the liquid dries up, 3 to 4 minutes. Transfer to the work bowl of a food processor fitted with a metal S-blade and process until pureed. Remove to the bowl with the potatoes. Add the remaining stuffing ingredients and mix well.

Put the flour in the work bowl, turn the machine on, pour the water in in a thin stream, and process until the dough gathers into a ball. Continue to process until the sides of the bowl look clean, 20 to 30 seconds. (Add 1 or 2 tablespoons extra flour if the dough sticks to the sides of the work bowl, or more water if the dough looks too dry.)

To make the dough by hand, put the flour in a large bowl and add the water, a little at a time, mixing with your fingers until it starts to gather together. Add more water as necessary to make a medium-firm dough that does not stick to your fingers. (Oiling your hands is not necessary, but can be done.)

Remove the dough to a bowl, cover with plastic wrap, and let rest at room temperature for 1 to 4 hours. If holding for a longer period, place in the refrigerator.

Heat a large griddle, skillet, or tava, over moderately high heat until a sprinkling of flour immediately turns dark brown. Wipe off the flour.

While the griddle is heating, lightly oil your hands and divide the dough into 20 even, round balls. Cover with a clean kitchen cloth to keep from drying out and set aside. Working with each ball separately, flatten it with your fingertips, coat with the flour in the bowl and, with a rolling pin, roll it out into a 4- to 5-inch circle. Place 2½ to 3 tablespoons of the stuffing in the center. Bring the edges of the dough circle together, pinch them to seal, and shape into a ball once again, rolling it between the palms of your hands.

Flatten and coat this stuffed ball with flour and roll it out into a 7- to 8-inch circle of even thickness. Keep turning and dusting the parantha with flour while rolling or it may stick to the work surface. If the stuffing *contains* excess moisture, the paranthas may develop tiny holes as you roll them. If that happens, seal them with a pinch of flour.

Place each parantha on the hot griddle skillet, or tava. Turn it over when it is dotted with tiny golden spots on the bottom. When the second side is covered with larger brown spots, turn it over and brush lightly with oil. Turn it over once again and fry the oiled side for about 30 seconds. Repeat the brushing and turning over with the other side. (There should be a total of 4 turns.) Remove from the griddle and serve warm or at room temperature.

Stuffed Parantha Bread with Minced Meat

Makes 20 stuffed
parantha breads

Do Ahead:

The stuffing can be
made 3 to 4 days in
advance and can go
straight from the refrig-
erator into the paran-
tha. (The dough can
also be made ahead of
time, see page 56.) To
partially cook the paran-
thas, see page 58.

STUFFED WITH INTRICATELY FLAVORED ground meat, this elegant parantha bread is made especially for our meat-loving friends. Serve it with non-fat plain yogurt and Green Cilantro Chutney (page 257).

Try this meat stuffing as a filling for puff pastry shells, naan breads, and fresh vegetables (such as tomatoes, bell peppers, zucchini, and potatoes).

For the meat stuffing:

2 pounds extra-lean ground meat (lamb or beef)
2 cups finely chopped onions
1 tablespoon peeled and minced fresh ginger
2 teaspoons minced garlic
*½ cup firmly packed finely chopped cilantro (fresh coriander) leaves, soft stems
  included*
2 tablespoons finely chopped fresh rosemary leaves
1 to 3 serrano peppers (optional), to your taste, finely chopped
1 tablespoon ground coriander
1 teaspoon ground cumin
1 teaspoon garam masala
½ teaspoon ground turmeric
1 teaspoon salt, or to your taste

To make the dough:

4 cups stone-ground whole-wheat durum flour
About 1⅔ cups water

To cook the bread:

1 cup whole-wheat durum flour in a flat bowl
¼ cup vegetable oil

In a large, nonstick saucepan, combine the ground meat, onions, ginger, garlic, cilantro, rosemary, and peppers and cook, stirring, over moderately high heat for 5 to 7 minutes. Reduce the heat to moderately low and cook until the meat browns, 10 to 15 minutes. Stir in the spices and salt and continue to cook for another 2 minutes.

Remove from the stove and push all the meat to one side of the pan. Hold the pan at a slight angle to allow the excess fat from the meat to drain to one side. Remove the fat and discard. Bring the cooked meat to room temperature before using.

To make the dough, put the flour in the work bowl of a food processor fitted with the metal S-blade. Turn the machine on, pour the water in in a thin stream through the feed tube, and process until the dough gathers into a ball. Continue to process until the sides of the bowl look clean, 20 to 30 seconds. (Add 1 or 2 tablespoons extra flour if the dough sticks to the sides of the work bowl, or more water if the dough looks too dry.)

To make the dough by hand, put the flour in a large bowl and add the water, a little at a time, mixing with your fingers until it starts to gather together. Add more water as necessary to make a medium-firm dough that does not stick to your fingers. (Oiling your hands is not necessary, but can be done.)

Transfer the dough to another bowl, cover with plastic wrap, and let it rest at room temperature for 1 to 4 hours. If holding for a longer period, place in the refrigerator.

Heat a large griddle, skillet, or tava, over moderately high heat until a sprinkling of flour immediately turns dark brown. Wipe off the flour.

Lightly oil your hands and divide the dough into 20 even, round balls. Cover with a clean kitchen cloth to keep them from drying out and set aside. Working with each ball separately, flatten it with your fingertips, coat with flour from the bowl, and, with a rolling pin, roll it out into a 4- to 5-inch circle. Place 2½ to 3 tablespoons of the stuffing in the center. Bring the edges of the dough circle together, pinch them to seal, and then shape into a ball once again, rolling the dough between the palms of your hands.

Flatten and coat the stuffed ball with flour from the bowl and roll it out into a 7- to 8-inch circle of even thickness. Keep turning and dusting the parantha with flour while rolling or it may stick to the work surface. If the stuffing contains excess moisture, the paranthas may develop tiny holes as you roll them. If that happens, seal them with a pinch of flour.

Place the parantha on the hot griddle. Turn it over when it is dotted with tiny golden spots on the bottom. When the second side is covered with larger brown spots, turn it over and brush lightly with the oil. Turn it over once again and fry the brushed side for about 30 seconds. Brush the second side with oil, turn the parantha over, and fry that side for about 30 seconds. (There should be a total of 4 turns.) Remove from the tava and serve hot.

Grilled Naan Bread Stuffed with Onions

Makes 16 naan breads

Do Ahead:
See page 56.

USING A DOUGH THAT is similar to that for pizza, we stuff it with minced onions and spices to make a bread that is popular in Indian restaurants. This bread is remarkable when partnered with grilled chicken, seafood, or vegetables.

For the dough:
1 tablespoon dry yeast
1 teaspoon sugar
½ cup warm water (110° to 115°F)
1 large egg (optional)
½ cup nonfat plain yogurt plus 1 additional tablespoon if egg is not used, whisked until smooth
½ cup warm milk (110° to 115°F)
4 cups all-purpose flour
3 tablespoons unsalted butter plus 1 additional tablespoon if making dough by hand, at room temperature
½ teaspoon salt, or to your taste

To fill and cook bread:
1½ to 2 cups minced onions
¼ cup firmly packed minced cilantro (fresh coriander) leaves, soft stems included
1 cup all-purpose flour in a flat bowl
½ cup water
2 tablespoons melted butter, clarified butter, or olive oil (optional)
1 to 2 teaspoons chaat masala, to your taste

Dissolve the yeast and sugar in the warm water in a small bowl and set aside until foamy, 3 to 4 minutes. (If it doesn't foam, that means the yeast is not active. Discard and use new yeast.) Mix the egg, yogurt, and milk together thoroughly and set aside. (Do not worry if the milk curdles.)

To make the dough in a food processor, put the flour, 3 tablespoons of butter, and the salt in the work bowl of a food processor fitted with the metal S-blade and process until mixed. With the motor running, pour the yeast mixture through the feed tube, add the yogurt mixture, and process until the dough gathers into a ball. Continue to process until the sides of the bowl look clean, 20 to 30 seconds. (If the dough looks too sticky, add some more flour through the feed tube; if it looks too dry, add a little more yogurt or milk.)

To make the dough by hand, put the flour, 3 tablespoons of butter, and the salt in a large bowl and mix with your fingers. Add the yeast mixture and three-quarters of the yogurt mixture and mix with your fingers until the dough starts to gather together. Add the remaining yogurt mixture as necessary to make a medium-firm dough that does not stick to your fingers. Apply the 1 tablespoon butter to your fingers as you make the dough; this keeps the dough from sticking to your fingers.

Transfer the dough to a large bowl, cover with plastic wrap, and set aside in a warm, draft-free spot until it doubles in volume, 3 to 4 hours.

Combine the onions and cilantro and set aside.

Using your fist, gently punch down the dough to deflate it and remove the air bubbles. With lightly oiled hands, divide the dough into 16 even, round balls. Keep covered with a clean kitchen cloth to keep them from drying out. Working with each ball separately, flatten it with your fingertips to make a disk and coat completely with flour from the bowl. With a rolling pin, roll out each disk into a 4- to 5-inch circle on a lightly floured work surface. Place 1 to 2 tablespoons of the onion mixture in the center. Bring the edges of the dough circle together, pinch them to seal, then shape into a ball once again by rolling the stuffed dough between the palms of your hands.

Flatten the ball into a disk again and coat completely with flour. Roll it out into a 6- to 7-inch circle of even thickness. Keep turning and dusting with flour while rolling or it may stick to the work surface.

Preheat the broiler. As each bread is rolled out, place it on a cookie sheet (4 to 5 breads per sheet). When all the breads are rolled out, brush the top of each with the water. Place the cookie sheets, one at a time, 4 to 5 inches away from the heat source until brown spots appear and the tops look done, about 1 minute. (You may have to reposition each naan, depending on the heat distribution of the broiler.) Turn each naan over, and cook briefly on the bottom also. Remove the breads to a platter, brush lightly with the butter, sprinkle with a generous pinch of the chaat masala, and serve hot.

Naan Pizza Bread with Nigella Seeds

Makes 2 naan pizza
breads

Do Ahead:

Refrigerate up to 4
hours or freeze for
about 2 months after it
has been rolled out and
allowed to rise the sec-
ond time. The rolled-
out crusts can go
straight from the refrig-
erator or the freezer to
the oven.

THIS SIMPLE BREAD, MADE with Indian naan bread dough, comes with a
splash of butter and a sprinkling of tiny, black nigella seeds. As the bread cooks,
the nigella seeds roast under the broiler, and release a captivating aroma in the
kitchen and in the bread.

Cut into wedges and serve as an appetizer or present it with the main meal.

For the dough:
1 tablespoon dry yeast
1 teaspoon sugar
½ cup warm water (110° to 115°F)
1 large egg (optional)
½ cup nonfat plain yogurt plus 1 additional tablespoon if not using egg, whisked
    until smooth
½ cup warm milk (110° to 115°F)
3 to 4 cloves garlic, to your taste, peeled (mince the garlic if making the dough by
    hand)
4 cups bread flour
3 tablespoons safflower oil plus 1 additional tablespoon oil if making dough by hand
½ teaspoon salt, or to your taste

To roll and cook the bread:
1 cup bread flour in a flat bowl
½ cup freshly grated Parmesan cheese
1 teaspoon nigella seeds
1 tablespoon butter, melted

Dissolve the yeast and sugar in the warm water in a small bowl and set aside
until foamy, 3 to 4 minutes. (If it doesn't foam, that means the yeast is not active.
Discard and use new yeast.) Mix the egg, yogurt, and milk together and set aside.
(Do not worry if the milk curdles.)

To make the dough with a food processor, put the garlic in the work bowl
of a food processor fitted with the metal S-blade and process until minced. Add
the flour, 3 tablespoons of oil, and the salt and process until mixed. With the
motor running, pour the yeast mixture through the feed tube, add the yogurt

mixture, and process until the dough gathers into a ball. Continue to process until the sides of the bowl look clean, 20 to 30 seconds. (If the dough looks too sticky, add some more flour through the feed tube; if it looks too dry, add some more yogurt or milk.)

To make the dough by hand, put the minced garlic, flour, 3 tablespoons of oil, and the salt in a large bowl and mix with your fingers. Add the yeast mixture and three-quarters of the yogurt mixture and mix with your fingers until the dough starts to gather together. Add the remaining yogurt mixture as necessary to make a medium-firm dough that does not stick to your fingers. Apply the 1 tablespoon oil to your fingers as you make the dough; this keeps the dough from sticking to your fingers.

Transfer to a large bowl, cover with plastic wrap, and set aside in a warm, draft-free spot until it doubles in volume, 3 to 4 hours.

Using your fist, gently punch down the dough to deflate it and remove all air bubbles. With lightly oiled hands, divide the dough into 2 round balls. Keep covered with a clean kitchen cloth to keep them from drying out. Working with each ball separately, dust lightly with the flour in the bowl and press it into a flat disk.

Using a rolling pin, roll out into a 12-inch circle on a lightly floured work surface. Place on a well-greased pizza tray. Top first with half the Parmesan cheese and then sprinkle half the nigella seeds over it. Cover with a sheet of aluminum foil and set aside in a warm, draft-free place to rise for 30 to 40 minutes. Repeat with the other ball of dough to make a second pizza.

Preheat the oven to 375°F. Place the pizza trays in the center of the oven and bake until the crusts are golden, 12 to 15 minutes. Reposition the trays midway through baking to ensure even baking. Or bake the pizza breads one at a time.

Remove from the oven, brush lightly with the butter, cut into wedges, and serve hot.

Grilled Gingerbread Naan

DO AHEAD:
See page 56.

THERE ARE GINGERBREADS AND gingerbread cookies—now let's make some gingerbread naan.

For the dough:
1 tablespoon dry yeast
1 teaspoon sugar
½ cup warm water (110° to 115°F)
1 large egg (optional)
½ cup nonfat plain yogurt, plus 1 additional tablespoon if egg is not used, whisked until smooth
½ cup warm milk (110° to 115°F)
One 2-inch piece fresh ginger, peeled and cut into thin slices or minced if making the dough by hand
4 cups all-purpose flour
3 tablespoons vegetable oil plus 1 additional tablespoon if making dough by hand
½ teaspoon salt, or to your taste

To roll and cook the breads:
1 cup all-purpose flour in a flat bowl
½ cup water
2 tablespoons melted unsalted butter or clarified butter
1 tablespoon ground dried fenugreek leaves or mixed Italian herbs

Dissolve the yeast and sugar in the warm water in a small bowl and set aside until foamy, 3 to 4 minutes. (If it doesn't foam, that means the yeast is not active. Discard and use new yeast.) Mix the egg, yogurt, and milk together and set aside. (Do not worry if the milk curdles.)

To make the dough in a food processor, put the ginger in the work bowl of a food processor fitted with the metal S-blade and process until minced. Add the flour, 3 tablespoons of oil, and the salt and process until mixed. With the motor running, pour the yeast mixture through the feed tube, add the yogurt mixture, and process until the dough gathers into a ball. Continue to process until the sides of the bowl look clean, 20 to 30 seconds. (If the dough looks too sticky, add some more flour through the feed tube; if it looks too dry, add a little more yogurt or milk.)

To make the dough by hand, put the ginger, flour, 3 tablespoons of oil, and the salt in a large bowl and mix with your fingers. Add the yeast mixture and three-quarters of the yogurt mixture and mix with your fingers until the dough starts to gather together. Add the remaining yogurt-milk mixture as necessary to make a medium-firm dough that does not stick to your fingers. Apply the 1 tablespoon oil to your fingers as you make the dough; this keeps the dough from sticking to your fingers.

Transfer to a large bowl, cover with plastic wrap, and set aside in a warm, draft-free spot until it doubles in volume, 3 to 4 hours.

Using your fist, gently punch down the dough to deflate it and remove the air bubbles. With lightly oiled hands, divide the dough into 16 even, round balls. Keep covered with a clean kitchen cloth to prevent them from drying out. Working with each ball separately, dust lightly with flour from the bowl and press it into a flat dish. Roll out each disk into a 5- to 6-inch circle on a lightly floured surface. Place on a cookie sheet (4 to 5 breads per cookie sheet).

Preheat the broiler.

When all the breads are on the sheets, baste the top of each with the water. Place the cookie sheets, one at a time, 4 to 5 inches away from the heat source and broil until brown spots appear and the tops look done, about 1 minute. (You may have to reposition each naan, depending on the heat distribution of the broiler.) Turn each naan over and cook until the undersides are golden, 30 to 40 seconds. Remove from the oven, brush lightly with the butter, sprinkle each with a generous pinch of fenugreek leaves, and serve hot with any meal.

Vegetable Focaccia

Makes one 11 × 16-inch
focaccia; 8 servings

SERVING IDEAS:
Present with Chopped
Spinach Salad with
Cumin-Yogurt Dressing
(page 48) and chilled
Saffron Mousse (page
297).

DO AHEAD:
Make the dough,
assemble the focaccia,
and bake for the first 10
minutes. Remove from
the oven, cool, cover
with plastic wrap or alu-
minum foil, and refrig-
erate for up to 4 days. A
few hours before serv-
ing, stir-fry or grill the
vegetables and place
them over the bread,
along with the cheese
and herbs. Finish baking
just prior to serving.

YES, IT'S ITALIAN, BUT it goes so well with Indian food. The dough is very similar to that of Indian naan bread and the vegetables are common to both cuisines. The major differences are the flavorings, the method of preparation, and the final presentation.

2 teaspoons dry yeast
1 teaspoon sugar
½ cup warm water (110° to 115°F)
4 cups bread flour
¾ teaspoon salt, or to your taste
1 teaspoon minced garlic
2 tablespoons dried mixed Italian herbs, crumbled
3 tablespoons vegetable oil plus 1 additional tablespoon if making dough by hand
1 large egg
1 tablespoon extra-virgin olive oil
¼ cup freshly grated Parmesan cheese
1½ cups stir-fried or grilled eggplant or zucchini slices, spinach, broccoli florets, etc.,
    or bite-sized pieces oil-packed sun-dried tomatoes
¾ cup freshly grated part-skim mozzarella cheese
Dried herbs of your choice

Dissolve the yeast and sugar in the warm water in a small bowl and set aside until foamy. (If it doesn't foam, that means the yeast is not active. Discard and use new yeast.)

To make the dough in a food processor, put the flour, salt, garlic, and dried Italian herbs in the work bowl of a food processor fitted with a metal S-blade. With the motor running, pour the 3 tablespoons of vegetable oil in a thin stream through the feed tube until all of it is mixed into the flour. Add the egg and the yeast mixture through the feed tube. Add just enough water to make a medium-firm dough that gathers into a ball. Continue to process until the sides of the bowl look clean, 20 to 30 seconds. (If the dough seems too sticky, add some more flour through the feed tube; if it seems too hard, add a little more water.)

To make the dough by hand, put the flour, salt, garlic, and dried herbs in a large bowl and mix together with your fingers. Mix in the 3 tablespoons of veg-etable oil. Add the egg-and-yeast mixture and mix with your fingers until the dough starts to gather together. Add just enough water as necessary to make a medium-firm dough that does not stick to your fingers. Apply the 1 tablespoon oil to your fingers as you make the dough; this keeps the dough from sticking to your fingers.

Transfer to a large bowl, cover with plastic wrap, and set aside in a warm draft-free spot until it doubles in volume, 3 to 4 hours.

Using your fist, gently punch down the dough to deflate it and remove the air bubbles. With lightly oiled hands, spread the dough over a well-greased round or rectangular pizza sheet or cookie tray. Brush the surface with the olive oil, cover with a clean cloth, and set aside for 30 to 40 minutes in a warm draft-free place for the dough to rise again. Preheat the oven to 400°F. Sprinkle the Parmesan cheese on top and bake in the center of the oven for about 10 minutes. Remove from the oven, add the stir-fried or grilled vegetables, mozzarella cheese, and dried herbs, and return to the oven to bake until the mozzarella is golden and the crust is crisp, 10 to 12 minutes. (Watch the crust; don't let it get too brown—if it happens, reposition the tray in the oven or place another tray under it.)

Bread Machine Bread

WOULDN'T IT BE GREAT to wake up to a new bread every morning? Your own loaf, ready at 6:30 A.M., just in time for a quick bite before the mad rush of the day starts.

Commercial bread machines have made this wish a reality. We can add all the ingredients to a container, set the timer, and then simply wake up to a heavenly aroma, instead of the sudden ring of an alarm clock.

All the bread machines are slightly different, so start with the basic directions provided with your machine and then add different flavorings to create novel breads.

A word of caution: My bread maker calls for adding the extra ingredients at the sound of the first beep (25 minutes), but I am never close enough to my bread maker to hear the beep, so I add all my ingredients at one go. Also, I've noticed that if you add the fresh herbs and vegetables after twenty-five minutes, they tend to remain toward the corners of the bread instead of mixing properly.

Red Bell Pepper, Jalapeño, and Scallion Loaf

Makes 1 large loaf

DO AHEAD:

The bread will keep in a plastic bag at room temperature for 4 to 5 days, in the refrigerator for 10 to 12 days, and in the freezer for up to 2 months.

THIS LUXURIOUS BREAD, CRISPY on the outside and soft on the inside, with specks of red and green and a delightful aroma, will capture your heart at the first bite.

This bread can also be made without a bread machine.

2½ cups bread flour
½ cup regular whole-wheat flour
1½ tablespoons nonfat dry milk
1½ tablespoons sugar
1¼ teaspoons salt, or to taste
1½ tablespoons unsalted butter, cut into small pieces
¾ cup seeded and finely diced red bell pepper
½ cup thinly sliced scallion greens (you'll need 3 to 4 scallions; choose thin ones)
1 to 3 jalapeño peppers, to your taste, finely diced
1 tablespoon minced fresh rosemary leaves
2 teaspoons fresh thyme leaves
1⅛ cups warm water (110° to 115°F)
1¼ teaspoons dry yeast

In a large bowl, combine the flours, dry milk, sugar, salt, and butter and mix together. (Don't worry if the butter does not mix properly.) Add the chopped vegetables and herbs and mix again.

Secure the metal blade in the bread pan and pour the water into it. Then add the flour mixture. Place the yeast on top of the flour and turn the machine on. Sit back and relax, the machine does the rest of the work.

Oatmeal and Zucchini Loaf

THE QUANTITIES OF THE basic ingredients remain the same as in the preceding recipe. The types of flour, vegetables, and herbs change, creating a whole new loaf.

2 cups bread flour
1 cup old-fashioned rolled oats (not the quick-cooking kind), coarsely ground in a
    blender or food processor
1½ tablespoons nonfat dry milk
1½ tablespoons sugar
1¼ teaspoons salt, or to taste
1½ tablespoons unsalted butter, cut into small pieces
¾ cup finely diced zucchini
½ cup finely diced fresh beet stems
1 to 3 jalapeño peppers, to your taste, finely diced
½ cup thinly sliced scallion greens (you'll need 3 to 4 scallions; choose thin ones)
¼ cup firmly packed finely chopped cilantro (fresh coriander) leaves, soft stems
    included
1 teaspoon minced fresh rosemary leaves
2 teaspoons fresh thyme leaves
1 cup warm water (110° to 115°F)
2 teaspoons dry yeast

Makes 1 large loaf

DO AHEAD:
  Store the bread in a plastic bag at room temperature for 4 to 5 days, in the refrigerator for 10 to 12 days, and in the freezer for up to 2 months.

In a large bowl, combine the flours, dry milk, sugar, salt, and butter and mix together. (Don't worry if the butter does not mix properly.) Add the chopped vegetables and herbs and mix again.

Secure the metal blade in the bread pan and pour the water into it. Then add the flour mixture. Place the yeast on top of the flour and turn the machine on. Sit back and relax, the machine does the rest of the work.

Sandwiches with a Touch of India

WHEN I WAS GROWING up, sandwiches were considered exotic snacks, to be served only when you wanted to call attention to your culinary skills. Though what type of skill one needed to slap two slices of well-buttered white bread around paper-thin slices of lightly salted cucumber, tomatoes, or hard-boiled eggs, I do not know. But I actually do understand—sandwiches are part of the legacy left behind by the British when they departed India. It was something new that the Indians had learned and they had to make them to impress their friends, so sandwiches were prepared at birthday parties, evening teas, Sunday brunches, and whenever the occasion called for a celebration. Those sandwiches were wonderful, but after having eaten them for all those years, it's not surprising that the word "sandwich" lost its charm for me.

That is, until I came to America, where sandwiches suddenly had a new meaning. Far from being skimpy one-ingredient snacks, I started seeing sandwiches as wholesome foods well worth their weight in gold. Slowly, I began making different types of sandwiches, some with Indian pickles and chutneys, and others with mayonnaise and mustard, always with a new selection of meats, vegetables, and cheeses, with one important factor guiding my choices—health and good nutrition.

Today, I make lively and satisfying sandwiches with a wide selection of international breads and ingredients. I especially rely on Green Cilantro Chutney and the Yogurt-Cilantro Chutney (pages 257 and 258), using them like Americans use mayonnaise and mustard.

Lunch Bag Sandwiches with Flavored Yogurt Cheese

YOGURT CHEESE, MADE BY draining the liquid whey from the curds, cannot be purchased but rather must be made at home. It is a simple though time-consuming procedure—almost effortless. Once made, yogurt cheese stays fresh for over a week in the refrigerator and can be combined with an endless array of seasonings. It replaces mayonnaise and other sandwich spreads and makes a guilt-free, nutritious dip for chips and vegetables.

To make yogurt cheese, place the yogurt in a piece of muslin or four layers of cheesecloth and tie it to the kitchen faucet for 8 to 10 hours (the longer it hangs, the thicker the cheese) or line a sieve with muslin or cheesecloth, add the yogurt, and allow it to drain in the refrigerator. (Remember to place a bowl under the sieve to catch the draining whey.) The pale green whey trickles out very slowly, leaving behind thick curds in the muslin. This process starts almost as soon as the yogurt is placed in the muslin (depending on how much water there was in the yogurt in the first place) and continues until all that is left is a thick piece of yogurt that looks like soft cream cheese.

Remove the cheese from the muslin and use as you wish. (The whey can be used as broth in soups, curries, or to make the dough for breads. This whey ranges from somewhat to very tangy, depending on how sweet or tangy the yogurt was.) One 32-ounce container of nonfat plain yogurt yields about 2 cups of thick yogurt cheese.

2 teaspoons black peppercorns
2 teaspoons cumin seeds
1 cup thick yogurt cheese (above)
½ cup firmly packed minced fresh mint leaves
½ cup minced scallion whites (10 to 12 scallions)
½ teaspoon salt, or to your taste

For the sandwiches:
16 slices, any variety bread
8 thin slices cheese of your choice, preferably fat free
Cold cuts of your choice
Thin slices bell peppers, zucchini, cucumber, and/or tomatoes
Sunflower, alfalfa, clover, onion, and/or radish sprouts
Deep-green or red lettuce of your choice

Makes 8 sandwiches

DO AHEAD:
Make the flavored yogurt cheese up to 1 week in advance. Prepare all the ingredients—wash, dry, and slice the vegetables and spin-dry the lettuce—place in airtight containers or plastic zipper bags, and store in the refrigerator for 2 to 3 days.

continued

Put the peppercorns and cumin seeds in a small, nonstick skillet and roast over moderate heat until they become fragrant and start to pop, 2 to 3 minutes. In a coffee or spice grinder or with a mortar and pestle, grind them coarsely (you may have to increase the quantity if using a spice grinder because the machine requires a certain minimum to grind properly) and set aside.

Put the yogurt cheese in a bowl and add the mint, scallions, salt, and pepper-cumin mixture. Stir to mix and refrigerate until needed. The yogurt cheese will stay fresh in the refrigerator for more than 1 week.

Spread the yogurt cheese mixture liberally on all 16 slices of bread. Arrange the cheese, meats, vegetables, been sprouts, and lettuce on 8 slices and top with the remaining 8 cheese-smeared slices with the cheese side down.

Store the sandwiches in sandwich bags or cover tightly with plastic wrap or aluminum foil.

VARIATIONS: Add different herbs and seasonings to the yogurt cheese and vary the choice of breads, cheese, and vegetables; there is no end to the sandwiches that can be made in this manner.

Roasted Eggplant Sandwiches

TO ROAST EGGPLANTS, WASH and dry them, then place each one directly over a high flame. Using kitchen tongs, keep turning them around as each side becomes charred, until the whole eggplant is charred and soft, 4 to 5 minutes. (Be aware, some juices will escape and make the stove messy.) This can also be done under the broiler, or on the outdoor grill with a lot less mess.

Set the eggplants aside until they are cool enough to handle. Then peel off the charred skin, but do not wash the eggplants as the charred bits only add to the flavor.

3 to 5 tablespoons nonfat mayonnaise, to your taste
4 to 6 tablespoons Green Cilantro Chutney (page 257), to your taste
8 slices fresh sourdough bread, 7 × 4 inches each
10 to 15 small Japanese eggplants (about 1½ pounds), roasted until tender, peeled, and stems removed
About 1 cup grated cheddarella cheese or a mixture of cheddar and mozzarella
Thin slices wine-ripened red, orange, or yellow tomatoes
Thin slices pickling, Japanese, or English cucumber (cut lengthwise, if possible)
Sunflower, alfalfa, clover, onion, and radish sprouts
Bronze or romaine lettuce leaves

In a small bowl, combine the mayonnaise and chutney and spread evenly on all 8 slices of bread. Top 4 slices evenly with the roasted eggplants, cheese, tomato and cucumber slices, sprouts, and lettuce. Cover with the remaining 4 slices, chutney side down. Cut each large sandwich in half or quarters and serve with slices of fresh fruits and fresh lemonade or café latté.

Makes 8 half or 16 sandwich quarters

DO AHEAD:
Grate the cheese and refrigerate for 7 to 10 days or freeze for up to 2 months. Roast the eggplants up to 5 days in advance and refrigerate. Wash and spin-dry the lettuce and store in the refrigerator in plastic zipper bags for 2 to 3 days.

Grilled Ginger-Fenugreek Toast

Makes 16 toasts

DO AHEAD:

Combine the butter with all the herbs and spices and spread on the bread up to 4 days ahead of time. Place the buttered slices next to each other to reform the original shape of the bread and slide them back into the plastic or wax paper bag the bread came in. Refrigerate until needed.

AS TIMES CHANGE AND cultures intermingle, people's eating habits and taste preferences also undergo change. See what happens to old-fashioned grilled cheese when a new cuisine steps in.

¼ cup (½ stick) butter, or more to taste, at room temperature
1 tablespoon peeled and minced fresh ginger
1 tablespoon ground dried fenugreek leaves
1 teaspoon ground dried mint
½ teaspoon crushed red pepper flakes (optional), or to your taste
½ teaspoon freshly ground black pepper, or to your taste
One 1-pound long French or sourdough bread, cut into 16 diagonal slices
Sprinkling of freshly grated Parmesan cheese and paprika and shredded radicchio
    and clover or onion sprouts for garnish.

In a small bowl, combine the butter, ginger, fenugreek leaves, mint, red pepper flakes, and black pepper.

Spread the mixture evenly on one side of each slice of the bread. Place buttered side down in a griddle or large, nonstick skillet in 2 or 3 batches over moderate heat and cook until golden, 1 to 2 minutes. Turn each piece over and cook the second side for 30 to 40 seconds. (Brush with additional butter if desired.) You can also cook the bread 6 to 8 inches under the broiler.

Transfer to a platter, keeping the buttered side up. Sprinkle Parmesan cheese and paprika on top of each toast, garnish with radicchio and sprouts, and serve.

Sourdough Sandwiches with Sautéed Vegetables

GREEN CILANTRO CHUTNEY AND smoked Tillamook cheese contribute in a big way to the intriguing flavor these sandwiches have.

For special effect and instant attraction, serve them with slices of juicy melons and vine-ripened strawberries placed attractively over curly lettuce leaves.

Makes 2 large sandwiches

1 tablespoon extra-virgin olive oil
2 large extra-firm vine-ripened Italian plum tomatoes, cut into ¼-inch-thick slices
Salt and freshly ground black pepper to taste
4 to 5 small zucchini (3 to 4 inches long), cut into extra-thin slices along the length of each
¾ cup 1-inch or smaller broccoli florets
½ cup 1-inch-long julienne red bell pepper sticks
½ cup chopped fresh Italian parsley leaves
4 slices fresh sourdough bread, 7 × 4 inches each, or 8 smaller ones
¼ cup nonfat mayonnaise, or to your taste
¼ cup Green Cilantro Chutney (page 257), or to your taste
½ cup grated smoked Tillamook cheese, or to your taste
½ cup onion, alfalfa, clover, or radish sprouts

DO AHEAD:

Cut the zucchini, broccoli, peppers, and parsley and grate the cheese up to 2 days in advance. Refrigerate in airtight containers or bags until needed.

Heat the oil in a medium skillet over moderately high heat and add the tomato slices in a single layer. Cook until they turn golden, 1 to 2 minutes. Turn them over, slice by slice, and cook the other side until golden, another 1 to 2 minutes. Sprinkle with salt and pepper and remove to a plate.

Add the vegetables to the same skillet and cook over moderately high heat until they turn golden, 2 to 4 minutes. Mix in the parsley, season with salt and pepper, and set aside.

Lightly toast the bread, then spread all the slices with the mayonnaise. Spread the chutney on half the slices and cheese on the other half. Pile the grilled vegetables, tomatoes, and sprouts over the cheese and cover with the chutney-smeared slices, chutney side down.

Cut in half and serve or butter the outsides lightly, place on a nonstick pancake griddle or skillet, and grill over moderate heat until golden. (Some of the vegetables may slip out, so just pack them back.)

Quesadillas with Chicken Tikka Kebabs and Smoked Gouda Cheese

DO AHEAD:

Make the chutney and cook the chicken up to 4 days in advance. Cut all the vegetables, grate the cheese, and butter the tortillas up to 2 days in advance. Store everything in the refrigerator.

MADE WITH PURCHASED VEGETARIAN-style flour tortillas, grilled chicken, smoked gouda cheese, and yogurt-cilantro chutney, these Mexican sandwiches are deeply satisfying luncheon fare. Pair with freshly squeezed orange juice or a fruity yogurt shake.

Twelve 8-inch flour tortillas, preferably vegetarian style
1 tablespoon unsalted butter, melted, or olive oil
1½ to 2 cups grated smoked gouda cheese
3 to 4 cups coarsely shredded Chicken Tikka Kebabs (page 181), or leftover grilled or sautéed chicken
1½ cups finely chopped vine-ripened tomatoes (about 3 medium tomatoes)
1 cup finely sliced scallions (white and light green parts, about 2 bunches)
1 cup lightly packed finely chopped cilantro (fresh coriander) leaves, soft stems included
Minced serrano peppers (optional), to taste
1 to 2 teaspoons chaat masala, to your taste
1 cup Yogurt-Cilantro Chutney (page 258), or more to your taste

With a basting brush, brush each tortilla very lightly with the melted butter.

Heat a pancake griddle or a large, nonstick skillet over moderately high heat. Working with each tortilla separately, place on the griddle buttered side down. Sprinkle some of the grated cheese evenly over the tortilla and spread the desired amount of chicken, tomatoes, scallions, cilantro, and peppers, along with a sprinkling of chaat masala over half the tortilla. Top with 2 or more tablespoons of the chutney and fold the second half over the chutney. Press lightly with a spatula to seal. (Lower the heat if the underside seems to cook too fast.) Cut in half or into thirds and serve individually as each quesadilla is made or all together with more chutney on the side.

Tortilla and Chicken Rolls

THIS IS A SIMPLE variation of the famous khathi kebab rolls of India. These are made by breaking a whole egg in a warm skillet, covering the egg with a flour chapati (tortilla), and cooking them together. This egg-coated chapati is topped with barbecued lamb or chicken and fixings like marinated onions, ginger, serrano peppers, and chutneys, and is then rolled like a burrito.

In this easy version, I use premade flour tortillas and pan-fry them like French toast. The chicken, of course, has to be marinated and cooked before the actual rolls are made.

Makes 12 rolls

DO AHEAD:
Marinate and cook the chicken up to 3 days in advance. Store in the refrigerator.

To marinate and cook the chicken:
1 tablespoon ground coriander
2 teaspoons garam masala
1 tablespoon ground dried fenugreek leaves
1½ teaspoons paprika
2 tablespoons peanut oil
1 tablespoon minced garlic
1 tablespoon peeled and minced fresh ginger
3 to 4 tablespoons fresh lemon juice, to your taste
1 teaspoon salt, or to your taste
2½ pounds chicken tender or flank steak, cut into thin 2- to 3-inch-long diagonal
    strips
½ cup firmly packed finely chopped cilantro (fresh coriander) leaves, soft stems
    included

To make the sandwiches:
2 large eggs, lightly beaten
2 tablespoons lowfat or regular milk
½ teaspoon salt, or to taste
½ teaspoon freshly ground black pepper, or to your taste
1 to 3 tablespoons peanut oil, to your taste, as needed
Twelve 8-inch flour tortillas, preferably vegetarian style
Chopped lettuce, fresh tomatoes, and scallions (or sweet Maui onions), peeled ginger
    slices, and sliced serrano peppers as desired
½ to 1 cup Yogurt-Cilantro Chutney (page 258), to your taste

continued

Combine the coriander, garam masala, fenugreek leaves, and paprika in a small bowl and set aside.

Heat the oil in a small, nonstick saucepan over moderately high heat and stir-fry the mixed spices for about 30 seconds. Mix in the garlic and ginger, and add the lemon juice and salt. Remove from the heat.

Put the chicken in a nonreactive dish and coat with the garlic mixture. Cover with plastic wrap and marinate in the refrigerator for at least 4 and up to 24 hours.

Put the marinated chicken in a large, nonstick skillet or wok over moderately high heat, add the cilantro, and stir-fry in 2 to 3 batches if necessary until the chicken is golden, 7 to 10 minutes. Remove from the heat and set aside.

Combine the beaten eggs with the milk, salt, and pepper and put in a large flat bowl (one that is slightly bigger than the tortillas).

Heat 1 teaspoon of the oil in a large, nonstick skillet over moderately high heat. Dip each tortilla into the egg batter (as you would for French toast) and put in the hot skillet. When the bottom is golden, turn it over and cook the other side until it turns golden, 30 to 40 seconds.

Remove to a plate and arrange 3 to 4 tablespoons of the cooked chicken down the center. Top with lettuce, tomatoes, scallions, ginger, peppers, and a spoonful of the chutney. Roll as tightly as you can and serve. Repeat with the remaining tortillas. These rolls are best when eaten fresh.

Deep-frying with a Flair

OUR LOVE-HATE RELATIONSHIP with deep-fried foods presents us with a constant dilemma. We love our deep-fried foods with a passion, and fear the fat calories that come with them. Is there a path in the middle that allows us to enjoy our favorite deep-fried specialties—french fries and onion rings (and Indian pakora fritters and samosa pastries, Japanese tempuras, and Chinese egg rolls, to name a few)—without feeling guilty with every bite?

That path is there—and it leads to crispy, crunchy, dry, and almost-free-of-fat deep-fried foods. To get there, you need to learn the proper deep-frying technique—a procedure that turns out delectable, mouthwatering, and lively foods.

The Dos and Don'ts of Deep-frying
• Use a wok if you have one. You will require less oil and will gain a lot more cooking surface because of the concave shape of the wok.
• Use only the poly- and monounsaturated oils, such as peanut, canola, safflower, and olive oil. (Out of these, my preference is peanut oil because it has a higher burning point.) These oils are cholesterol-free and tests have proven that canola and olive oils actually raise the level of the good cholesterol in the body. (In India, most of the commercial deep-frying is done in mustard oil and in homes, peanut, or groundnut, oil.)
• The temperature of the oil plays a crucial part in deep-frying. If foods are added to the oil before it

is properly heated, they tend to absorb more oil. If they are added when the oil is too hot, the outsides burn and the insides remain uncooked. Both result in unpalatable and unappetizing foods. Ideally, the hot oil should cook the outsides of the foods to form a shell-like covering that prevents unnecessary oil absorption and allows proper steaming of the foods inside.

• The wok should be completely dry before any oil is heated in it. Even the slightest bit of moisture will cause splattering and that can be dangerous.

• Check the temperature of the oil before frying. The optimum temperature is somewhere between 350° to 375°F. To test without a thermometer, drop a tiny piece of food (batter, dough, vegetables) into the hot oil. It should immediately start to bubble and rise to the top. The oil is too hot if the outside of the food turns dark brown instantly and not hot enough if the food sinks and sticks to the bottom of the wok.

• Remember not to overcrowd the wok. Adding too much food at one time will lower the temperature of the oil and the foods will be limp and full of oil.

• Proper draining is as, if not more, critical than the temperature of the oil. Using a large slotted spoon, drain the cooked foods as much as you can before removing them from the wok. Hold the food between the slotted spoon and the side of the wok until most of the oil slides back into the wok. Remove the food to paper towels to drain further. Serve on a platter lined with paper doilies (the paper will further absorb more oil).

An interesting fact about deep-frying is that twice-fried foods tend to be less oily than those that have been fried only once. Here's why: The batter or coating absorbs oil as it cooks and forms a shell-like casing around the food inside. If you remove the food before it cooks completely and drain it on paper towels, some of the oil is soaked up by the towels. The second frying (this, by the way, can be done 15 minutes to 4 days after the initial frying) is done in oil that is very hot but not smoking (about 375°F). As the food inside the shell heats up, the steam from the moisture inside actually pushes out some of the oil from the batter, making it even crispier. Drained again on paper towels, these foods lose most of their fat. This twice-frying technique is very common in India. The one and only fact to remember while doing this is, heat the oil to the proper temperature and quick-fry the foods (30 to 60 seconds). The longer they sit in the oil, the more time they have to reabsorb the oil.

Follow these pointers and you will find that your deep-fried foods contain no more fat than if they had been steamed, boiled, or microwaved and then topped with a dollop of butter or margarine.

Now, sit back and enjoy some of world's best bite-size delights.

Batter-Fried Chicken Drumsticks or Tenders

THE INDIAN VERSION OF this global favorite is made with high-protein garbanzo bean flour. Add an egg and some Western herbs for a new twist.

12 to 16 chicken drumsticks (choose the smallest ones you can find), skin removed, or
    24 chicken tenders
½ cup nonfat plain yogurt, whisked until smooth
1 tablespoon fresh lime or lemon juice
1 tablespoon minced garlic
1 tablespoon peeled and minced fresh ginger
1 tablespoon minced fresh rosemary leaves or 1 teaspoon dried
2 tablespoons minced fresh mint leaves
1½ teaspoons garam masala
1 teaspoon salt, or to your taste
1 cup garbanzo bean flour
1 tablespoon minced fresh marjoram leaves
1 teaspoon minced fresh basil leaves
1 large egg white, whisked until smooth
About ½ cup water
2 to 3 cups peanut oil for deep-frying
Sprigs fresh marjoram or rosemary for garnish

Place the chicken in a medium bowl. Whisk together the yogurt, lime juice, garlic, ginger, rosemary, mint, 1 teaspoon of the garam masala, and ½ teaspoon of the salt, add it to the bowl, and combine until the chicken is fully coated. Cover with plastic wrap; marinate in the refrigerator for at least 12 and up to 24 hours.

Sift the garbanzo bean flour into a medium bowl and mix in the marjoram, basil, and the remaining ½ teaspoon each of garam masala and salt. Add the egg white and enough water to make a medium-thick batter. Heat the oil in a wok or a skillet to 350° to 375°F.

Shake off the marinade and dip each marinated chicken drumstick or tenderloin in the batter and remove the excess. Place in the hot oil one at a time without crowding. Fry, turning them once or twice, until light brown, 4 to 5 minutes for the drumsticks and 2 to 3 minutes for the tenders. Drain on paper towels. Refry in hot oil in the same manner until heated through; drain again.

Arrange on a platter, garnish with marjoram, and serve hot.

Makes 4 to 6 servings

SERVING IDEAS:
Pair with Yogurt-Cilantro Chutney or Italian Parsley and Mango Chutney (pages 258 and 260).

DO AHEAD:
Lightly fry, cool completely, and store in the refrigerator for 2 to 3 days. Bring to room temperature and refry in hot oil again before serving.

NOTE:
To see if the oil is ready, drop ⅛ teaspoon batter into the hot oil; if it bubbles and rises to the top immediately, it is ready.

Breaded Chicken Nugget Kebabs

Makes 6 to 8 servings

SERVING IDEAS:

All the pureed green and yogurt chutneys are natural companions to these nugget kebabs. As kids, we loved them with tomato ketchup.

DO AHEAD:

Fry the kebabs until just golden. Drain, cool completely, and store in the refrigerator for 2 to 4 days. Refry in hot oil before serving or place on a cookie sheet in a single layer and bake in a preheated 400°F oven, turning them once or twice, until golden brown, 8 to 10 minutes.

CHICKEN NUGGETS, SO POPULAR in fast-food restaurants all over America, are indeed a type of kebab, and kebabs are very easy to make at home. The homemade versions can be made with selected cuts of ground chicken, meat, or seafood and flavored with a variety of seasonings.

2 pounds ground chicken breast meat
2 tablespoons peeled and minced fresh ginger
2 teaspoons minced garlic
1 tablespoon ground coriander
1 teaspoon ground cumin
2 teaspoons ground dried fenugreek leaves
1 teaspoon garam masala
1 teaspoon salt, or to your taste
2 to 4 tablespoons all-purpose flour, as needed
1 large egg white, beaten until smooth
1 cup finely ground dry bread crumbs
2 to 3 cups peanut oil for deep-frying
Lemon wedges, serrano peppers, and finely chopped scallion greens for garnish

Put the ground chicken in a large bowl and mix in the ginger, garlic, coriander, cumin, fenugreek leaves, garam masala, and salt. This can be done with a large spoon or your hands. If the mixture seems too soft and sticky, add flour as necessary.

Make 30 to 35 round or oval patty-type kebabs. Dip each kebab into the egg white, coat evenly with the bread crumbs, tapping off any excess, and set aside.

In a large wok or skillet, heat the oil over moderately high heat until it reaches 350° to 375°F. (Drop some chicken mixture into the hot oil; if it bubbles and floats to the top immediately, the oil is ready.) Fry the kebabs, as many as the wok can hold at one time without crowding, turning them a few times until they are crispy and golden brown on all sides, 4 to 5 minutes. Remove to paper towels to drain. Transfer to a platter, garnish with lemon wedges, peppers, and scallion greens and serve hot.

Lamb Shami Kebabs

THESE KEBABS ARE MADE with boneless leg of lamb that is first cooked with yellow split peas and spices and then ground and shaped into patties. The texture and flavor are very different from any you've tasted before.

For easy handling of the ground lamb mixture, make sure there is no water remaining in the pan and the lamb pieces are completely dry or the ground mixture will be too moist to handle. It may even disintegrate in the oil as you deep-fry the kebabs. If that happens, add 1 to 2 tablespoons garbanzo bean or all-purpose flour to the unused mixture. The flour will absorb the excess moisture.

2 pounds boneless leg of lamb, all fat removed and cut into 1½-inch cubes
⅔ cup dried yellow split peas, picked over and washed
3 to 5 large cloves garlic, to your taste, peeled
1 small onion, peeled and cut into 4 to 6 wedges
6 green cardamom pods
4 black cardamom pods
One 2-inch stick cinnamon
½ teaspoon cloves
⅓ cup water
One 2-inch piece fresh ginger, peeled and cut into thin slices
2 to 6 serrano or jalapeño peppers (optional), to your taste, stems removed
1 small egg
1 tablespoon ground coriander
Freshly ground black pepper to taste
2 to 3 cups peanut oil for deep-frying
Finely chopped cilantro (fresh coriander) for garnish

Put the lamb, split peas, garlic, onion, cardamom pods, cinnamon, cloves, and water in a pressure cooker. Secure the lid and cook over high heat for 2 minutes after the pressure regulator starts rocking. Remove from the heat and let the pressure drop by itself, 10 to 15 minutes. Open the lid and make sure all the water has dried up and the lamb is completely dry. If not, then cook, uncovered, over moderately high heat until the lamb is completely dry. Set aside to cool. Alternately, put all the ingredients in a large pan, add ¼ cup extra water and cook over moderately high heat for 3 to 5 minutes, reduce the heat to moder-

Makes 16 to 20 kebabs; allow 2 to 3 per person

SERVING IDEAS:
Partner with your favorite green or yogurt chutney. Or present them with hamburger buns and fixings to make Shami kebab burgers. They can also be crumbled and served in salads, tacos, pita pockets, and over pizza.

DO AHEAD:
Can be made a few hours ahead and reheated in a preheated 400°F oven for about 10 minutes. Turn them once or twice. Or they can be made up to 5 days ahead of time and refried.

ately low and cook until the lamb and split peas are soft and no more water remains in the pan, 25 to 30 minutes.

In the work bowl of a food processor fitted with the metal S-blade, process the ginger and peppers together until minced. Add the cooked lamb (first removing the cinnamon stick), egg, coriander, and black pepper and process until minced. Shape the mixture into 16 to 20 two-inch-round patties and set aside.

In a large wok, heat the oil over moderately high heat until it reaches 350° to 375°F. (Drop a pinch of the lamb mixture into the hot oil; if it bubbles and floats to the top immediately, the oil is ready.) Fry the kebabs, as many as the wok can hold at one time without crowding, turning them a few times, until they are crispy and golden on all sides, 4 to 5 minutes. Remove to paper towels to drain. Transfer to a platter, garnish with cilantro, and serve.

Battered Salmon Fillets

FOR A PAN-FRIED VERSION, sprinkle about ½ cup garbanzo bean flour over the marinated fish and mix to coat each piece.

2 pounds 1-inch-thick fillets of salmon, halibut, lingcod, or any other firm fish, cut into 2-inch pieces

1 tablespoon peeled and minced fresh ginger

2 teaspoons cloves garlic, minced

2 to 3 tablespoons fresh lime or lemon juice, to your taste

½ teaspoon coarsely crushed carom seeds

½ teaspoon dried thyme

¼ teaspoon ground turmeric

½ teaspoon salt, or to your taste

1 cup garbanzo bean flour

2 teaspoons gourd coriander

1 teaspoons ground cumin

¼ cup loosely packed finely chopped cilantro (fresh coriander) leaves, soft stems included

Pinch of baking soda

½ teaspoon salt, or to your taste

½ to ⅔ cup water

2 to 3 cups peanut oil for deep-frying

½ teaspoon chaat masala and ½ cup shredded lettuce for garnish

Makes 6 to 8 servings

SERVING IDEAS:

  Present as part of a light lunch with Chopped Spinach Salad with Cumin-Yogurt Dressing or Tomato, Jicama, and Scallion Salad on Endive Boats (page 48 or 51) and Green Cilantro Chutney (page 257).

DO AHEAD:

  Marinate the fish up to a day in advance. Fry the pieces until barely golden. Remove from the wok, drain, and set aside for up to 24 hours in the refrigerator. Refry in hot oil before serving, or place on a cookie sheet in a single layer and bake in a preheated 400°F oven, turning once or twice, until medium brown, 8 to 10 minutes.

Put the fish pieces in a medium bowl. Combine the ginger, garlic, lime juice, carom seeds, thyme, turmeric, and ½ teaspoon of the salt, add to the bowl, and toss together until the salmon is fully coated with the mixture. Cover with plastic wrap and let marinate in the refrigerator for at least 1 and up to 24 hours.

Sift the garbanzo bean flour into a large bowl. Mix in the coriander, cumin, cilantro, baking soda, and the remaining ½ teaspoon salt, and add enough water to make a medium-thick batter.

In a wok or skillet, heat the oil to 350° to 375°F. (Drop ⅛ teaspoon batter into the hot oil; if it bubbles and floats to the top immediately, then oil is ready.)

Transfer the fish pieces and their marinade to the batter and mix gently with your fingers to coat them evenly. Add the pieces to the hot oil one at a time carefully to avoid splattering. Fry the pieces, as many at one time without crowding (page 88), turning them once or twice, until they are rich brown in color, 5 to 7 minutes. Drain on paper towels. Arrange on a serving platter, sprinkle the chaat masala on top, garnish with the shredded lettuce, and serve hot.

Cocktail-Size Wonton Samosa Pastries with Turkey

Makes 50 samosas; allow 3 to 4 per person

SERVING IDEAS:

Superb with Green Cilantro Chutney or Yogurt-Cilantro Chutney (page 257 or 258).

DO AHEAD:

Samosas can be lightly fried, cooled completely, and stored in the refrigerator for 5 to 6 days or frozen for 2 to 3 months. Bring to room temperature and fry again until crisp and golden. Or bake in a preheated 400°F oven for 8 to 10 minutes, turning them once or twice.

CHINESE CUISINE INTRODUCED ME to prerolled wonton wrappers (found in the produce section of the supermarket), a wonderful substitute for the more traditional samosa pastry shells. Now, with minimum effort, I can have tiny homemade samosas at a moment's notice.

Samosas are traditionally made with potatoes, lamb, or chicken, but here I use ground turkey.

1½ pounds extra-lean ground turkey
1 tablespoon minced garlic
1 tablespoon peeled and minced fresh ginger
1 to 3 jalapeño peppers (optional), to your taste, minced
½ cup firmly packed finely chopped cilantro (fresh coriander) leaves, soft stems included
1 tablespoon ground coriander
1 teaspoon ground dried fenugreek leaves
½ teaspoon garam masala
1 teaspoon salt, or to your taste
Freshly ground black pepper to taste
Twenty-five 4-inch wonton wrappers, each cut diagonally in half
A few tablespoons water in a small bowl
2 to 3 cups peanut oil for deep-frying

Put the turkey in a medium bowl. Mix in the garlic, ginger, peppers, cilantro, coriander, fenugreek leaves, garam masala, salt, and pepper.

Working with each half of the wonton wrapper, moisten the edges with water from the bowl. Place 1 to 2 teaspoons of the turkey stuffing in the center of one side of the halved wrapper. Fold the other half over the stuffing to form a triangle. Press to seal the edges. Repeat with the remaining halves until the stuffing is used up.

In a wok or skillet, heat the oil until it reaches 350° to 375°F. (Drop a piece of a wonton wrapper into the hot oil; if it bubbles and floats to the top immediately, the oil is ready). Fry the samosas, as many as the wok can hold at one time without crowding, turning them a few times, until they are crispy and golden on all sides, 4 to 5 minutes. Remove to paper towels to drain. Arrange on a serving platter and serve hot.

Samosa Egg Rolls

WHO SAYS THAT SAMOSAS have to be triangular? In this recipe, I use egg roll wrappers (they are made with flour and water, just like the traditional samosa shells), stuff them with garam masala-accented potatoes, tofu, and morel mushrooms, then shape them into familiar egg rolls. You can find them in the produce section of the supermarket.

8 to 10 dried morel mushrooms, soaked in hot water to cover for 30 minutes
2 tablespoons peanut oil
1 tablespoon peeled and finely minced fresh ginger
1 tablespoon ground coriander
1 teaspoon ground cumin
½ teaspoon garam masala
½ teaspoon paprika
¾ teaspoon salt, or to your taste
2 large russet potatoes, peeled and cut into ¼-inch dice
½ cup firmly packed finely chopped cilantro (fresh coriander) leaves, soft stems included
1 to 3 serrano peppers (optional), to your taste, finely chopped
One 10½-ounce package extra-firm tofu, pressed dry between paper towels and cut into ¼-inch dice
One 1-pound package egg roll wrappers (twenty 6½-inch squares)
A few tablespoons water or beaten egg in a small bowl
2 to 3 cups peanut oil for deep-frying

To make the filling, rinse the reconstituted morel mushrooms under running water to remove all the grit. Squeeze out all the water and cut into small dice. Set aside. (Strain the water in which the morels were soaked through a double layer of cheesecloth and use in another recipe to add flavor.)

In a large, nonstick skillet, heat the oil over moderately high heat and stir-fry the ginger until golden, 30 to 60 seconds. Add the coriander, cumin, garam masala, paprika, and salt, then mix in the potatoes, cilantro, and peppers. Reduce the heat to moderately low, cover the skillet, and cook, stirring as necessary, until the potatoes are soft, 5 to 7 minutes.

Slide the potatoes to one side of the skillet and cook the morel mushrooms on the other side, stirring, for 1 to 2 minutes. Then push the mushrooms toward

Makes 16 to 20 samosa egg rolls

SERVING IDEAS:
Present with salsa, Yogurt-Cilantro Chutney (page 258), or tomato ketchup (add a few drops of liquid hot red pepper sauce). The filling doubles as a delicious side dish with saucy curries.

DO AHEAD:
Lightly fry, cool completely, and store in the refrigerator for 5 to 6 days, or freeze 2 to 3 months. Bring to room temperature and fry again until crisp and golden. Or bake in a preheated 400°F oven for 8 to 10 minutes, turning them once or twice.

the potatoes and add the tofu. Cook the tofu, stirring carefully, for 1 to 2 minutes, then mix everything together. Cook for another minute or 2 to blend the flavors. Remove from the heat and cool.

To make the egg rolls, position one corner of a wrapper sheet pointing toward you and place about ⅓ cup of the filling 2 inches from the corner. Cover the filling with the corner (toward you) and roll halfway up the wrapper, making an elongated roll as you go along. Fold the corners from the two sides of the elongated roll over the filling. Moisten the remaining corner and edges with the water or beaten egg and finish making the roll. Repeat with the remaining wrappers until all the filling and wrappers are used up.

In a wok or skillet, heat the oil until it reaches 350° to 375°F. (Drop a piece of an egg roll wrapper into the hot oil; if it bubbles and floats to the top immediately, the oil is ready.) Fry the egg rolls, as many as the wok can hold at one time without crowding, turning them a few times, until they are crispy and golden on all sides, 4 to 5 minutes. Remove to paper towels to drain.

Transfer to a platter, slice diagonally into halves or thirds, and serve with your favorite chutney.

Potato and Vegetable Cutlets

THIS HAND-ME-DOWN legacy from the British was always a treat to us children who grew up on curries and chapatis.

2 pounds russet potatoes (peeled, boiled in lightly salted water to cover until tender, and drained)
1 to 3 serrano peppers (optional), to your taste, minced
¾ teaspoon salt, or to your taste
½ teaspoon freshly ground white pepper, or to your taste
1 cup finely diced mixed vegetables (carrots, zucchini, cauliflower, and peas)
1 teaspoon peeled and minced fresh ginger
¼ cup minced scallions (white and light green parts)
2 tablespoons finely chopped cilantro (fresh coriander) leaves, soft stems included
1 large egg white, beaten until smooth
1 cup finely ground dry bread crumbs
2 to 3 cups peanut oil for deep-frying
Shredded lettuce and julienned beets and carrots for garnish

Mash the potatoes and mix in the peppers, salt, and pepper.

Put the vegetables in a microwaveable dish, cover, and cook on high power until crisp-tender, 1½ to 2 minutes. Or place in a small pan with 2 tablespoons water, cover, and cook over moderate heat until crisp-tender, 3 to 5 minutes. Mix in the ginger, scallions, and cilantro. Divide into 16 equal portions and set aside.

Divide the mashed potatoes in 16 equal portions, and, with lightly greased hands, shape them into round balls. Flatten the balls into 3- to 4-inch disks. Press each disk in the center with 3 fingers to form a hollow space. Fill the hollow space with the vegetable filling, bring the edges together over the filling, and shape into a ball again. Flatten the ball again to make a disk or oval cutlet. Dip each cutlet into the egg white, coat evenly with the bread crumbs, tap off any excess, and set aside.

In a large wok, heat the oil over moderately high heat until it reaches 350° to 375°F. (Drop a pinch of the potato mixture into the hot oil; if it bubbles and floats to the top immediately, the oil is ready.) Fry the cutlets, as many as the wok can hold at one time without crowding, turning them a few times, until they are crispy and golden on all sides, 4 to 5 minutes. Drain on paper towels. Transfer to a platter, garnish with shredded lettuce and julienned beets and carrots, and serve hot.

Makes 6 to 8 servings

SERVING IDEAS:
These lunchtime favorites are perfect with Yogurt-Cilantro Chutney (page 258). Accompany with Gingered Tomato Soup (page 22) and a tossed green salad.

DO AHEAD:
Fry lightly, cool completely, and refrigerate up to 4 days. Bring to room temperature and fry again in hot oil. Or bake in a preheated 400°F oven for 8 to 10 minutes, turning them once or twice.

French Fries with Chaat Masala

Makes 6 to 8 servings

SERVING IDEAS:

Glorious with hamburgers and hot dogs, as well as with vegetarian sandwiches. Garnish with finely diced colorful bell peppers and shredded dark green lettuce and serve as a snack with Indian beer or a spicy white wine. Or sprinkle some Soy-Pickled Jalapeño Peppers (page 266) over them and serve as a dry-cooked side dish with curries.

DO AHEAD:

These fries are best when served fresh; however, leftovers can be reheated in a skillet over moderate heat or in a preheated 400°F oven for 6 to 8 minutes, turning them once or twice.

IN INDIA WE CALLED them potato chips, finger chips, or potato fingers. Depending on her mood, my mother would spice them with salt, pepper, and dried red chilies or with chaat or other special masalas. Sometimes she garnished them with chopped green chilies and cilantro and at others she would mix them with finely diced tomatoes, scallions, cilantro, mint, and fresh lemon juice. The choice of chutney depended on what she had in her refrigerator—green mint or cilantro chutney, yogurt-scallion sauce, or plain ketchup (the Indians call it sauce). She was always innovative with her "potato chips," probably because they were the quickest snack to make.

2 tablespoons minced fresh garlic chives or scallion greens
2 tablespoons finely chopped cilantro (fresh coriander) leaves, soft stems included
2 teaspoons finely chopped fresh mint leaves
2 teaspoon finely chopped fresh oregano leaves
2 to 3 cups peanut oil for deep-frying
6 to 8 small russet potatoes, peeled and each cut into 8 to 10 wedges
1 teaspoon chaat masala

Put the chives, cilantro, mint, and oregano in a small saucepan and roast, stirring, over moderate heat until dry and crisp, 3 to 5 minutes. Set aside.

In a wok or skillet, heat the oil until it reaches 350° to 375°F. (Drop a small piece of potato into the hot oil; if it bubbles and floats to the top immediately, the oil is ready.) Fry the potato wedges, as many as the wok can hold at one time without crowding, turning them a few times, until they are crispy and golden on all sides and tender inside, 4 to 5 minutes. Remove to paper towels to drain. Transfer to a platter and top with the chaat masala and roasted herbs. Toss with a large spoon or your fingers to mix.

Leftover French Fries

SHOULD WE DUMP THEM or save them is our dilemma every time we have leftover fries. Most of us end up throwing them away, because they don't taste good the next day. Well, here's a delicious way of recycling our fries—after all, french fries are just deep-fried potatoes.

Place leftover fries in a nonstick skillet over moderately high heat and cook, turning a few times, until they are heated through. Then mix in some minced garlic and ginger (optional), chopped tomatoes, scallions, and cilantro (and/or dill, fenugreek leaves, watercress, or others) and cook until the tomatoes are softened. Sprinkle some ground coriander and cumin, salt, and pepper over the top and cook a few minutes longer. Squeeze some fresh lemon juice over it all and serve on the side with any meal.

New Delhi Onion Rings

Makes 6 to 8 servings

DO AHEAD:

Onion rings can be lightly fried, cooled completely, and refrigerated for 4 to 5 days. To reheat, bring to room temperature and refry until crisp and golden, or place on a cookie sheet and bake in a preheated 400°F oven or broil until golden, turning once.

VARIATION: Make onion slices instead of rings. Cut the onions into slices but do not separate into rings. Working very carefully, dip each onion slice in the batter and shake off the excess. Add the batter-coated onion slices, one at a time, to the hot oil without crowding. Fry, turning once or twice, until light brown, 2 to 3 minutes. Drain, garnish, and serve.

ONE LOOK AND I thought that I was getting onion pakora fritters; one bite and I knew that they were different. These are delicious by themselves or with ketchup, salsa, or barbecue sauce. For special occasions, serve with Italian Parsley and Mango Chutney (page 260).

1 cup garbanzo bean flour
2 tablespoons fresh thyme leaves or 1 tablespoon dried
2 tablespoons minced fresh parsley or cilantro (fresh coriander) leaves
1 to 2 serrano peppers (optional), to your taste, finely minced
1 tablespoon ground coriander
⅛ teaspoon baking soda
¾ teaspoon salt, or to your taste
About ¾ cup water
2 to 3 cups peanut oil for deep-frying
5 to 6 small to medium-size onions, cut into thin slices, then separated into rings
Sprigs fresh thyme or parsley for garnish
1 teaspoon chaat masala for garnish

Sift the garbanzo bean flour into a medium bowl and mix in the thyme, parsley, peppers, coriander, baking soda, and salt. Add enough water to make a medium-thick batter.

In a wok or skillet, heat the oil until it reaches to 350° to 375°F. (Drop ⅛ teaspoon batter into the hot oil; if it bubbles and floats to the top immediately, the oil is ready.)

Place all the onion rings in the batter and mix with your fingers to coat completely. Add them individually or in small bunches to the hot oil carefully to avoid splattering. Fry, as many as the wok can hold at one time without crowding, turning them once or twice, until they are crispy and golden brown, 2 to 3 minutes per batch. Remove to paper towels to drain. Arrange on a platter, garnish with sprigs of thyme or parsley, sprinkle the chaat masala on top; serve hot.

Mushroom Fritters in Tomato–Bell Pepper Sauce

SUNIL VORA'S (OF THE Clay Pit restaurant in Los Angeles) stunning creation—batter-fried mushrooms smothered in a bell pepper-onion-tomato sauce—placed gracefully on a bed of lettuce greens, gets rave reviews from every person who tastes it. Sunil combines Indian, Chinese, and American ingredients to make this unusual recipe.

3 tablespoons cornstarch

1½ tablespoons garbanzo bean or all-purpose flour

1 tablespoon ground coriander

½ teaspoon salt

½ cup water

2 to 3 cups peanut oil for deep-frying

1 pound large mushrooms, trimmed and washed

1½ cups finely chopped onions

2 cups finely chopped vine-ripened tomatoes (about 2 large tomatoes)

1 large green bell pepper, seeded and finely diced

½ cup firmly packed finely chopped cilantro (fresh coriander) leaves, soft stems included

¼ to 1 teaspoon liquid hot red pepper sauce, to your taste

¼ cup soy sauce

½ cup ketchup

1 tablespoon cornstarch dissolved in ½ cup water

Lettuce greens to line serving platter

In a small bowl combine the cornstarch, garbanzo bean flour, coriander, and salt. Add the water to make a medium-thick batter.

In a wok or skillet, heat the oil until it reaches 350° to 375°F. (Drop ⅛ teaspoon batter into the hot oil; if it bubbles and floats to the top immediately, the oil is ready.) Dip each mushroom into the batter, shake off the excess batter by slapping it lightly against the bowl, and place in the hot oil carefully to avoid splattering. Fry the mushrooms, as many as the wok can hold at one time without crowding, turning them a few times, until they are crispy and golden on all sides, 4 to 5 minutes. Remove to paper towels to drain. Set aside until needed.

continued

Makes 8 servings

SERVING IDEAS:

These gleaming mushrooms can be served as appetizers (on toothpicks), a side dish, or even as a topping for pizza and open-faced sandwiches.

DO AHEAD:

Best served fresh; however, the mushrooms can be batter fried and refrigerated for 2 to 3 days. The sauce can be made partially (until the juices from the tomatoes evaporate) and refrigerated for 2 to 3 days. Heat the sauce, add the remaining ingredients along with the fried mushrooms, and finish making the dish.

Remove all but 2 tablespoons oil from the wok. Heat the wok over moderately high heat and cook the onions, stirring, until golden, 3 to 5 minutes. Add the tomatoes and cook, stirring, until most of their juices evaporate, 4 to 6 minutes. Add the bell pepper and cilantro, and mix in the liquid hot red pepper sauce, soy sauce, and ketchup, and cook for another minute. Add the mushrooms and stir in the cornstarch dissolved in water to bind the sauce together. Adjust the seasonings with salt and pepper.

Transfer to a serving platter lined with lettuce greens and serve hot.

New World Pizza and Pasta

EMERGING FROM THE CONSTANT intermingling of cultures is a new appreciation of global food patterns and preferences, and this has dramatically altered the course of food preparation all over the world. While health and proper nutrition still top the list, our seasoned palates now demand something more exotic in terms of flavor—even in the foods we routinely eat.

This awareness has also changed our perception of pizza and pasta, the two most popular foods in America (next to hamburgers and french fries). Today, the normal, run-of-the-mill pizzas and pastas that rely heavily on tomato sauce, cheese, and processed meats are no longer considered chic and in style. Instead, we desire lighter, more flavor-laden pizzas and pastas. And when prepared just right, these pizzas and pastas truly are among some of the best foods in the world. They provide us with essential complex carbohydrates, and when teamed with vitamin-rich vegetables and greens, garden-fresh herbs, and exotic spices, they are instantly transformed into heart-friendly super foods.

This is the reason (in addition to the fact that my daughters demanded them every day) that prompted me to bring pizzas and pastas into my Indian kitchen in America. My mix-and-match experiments led to some very interesting interplays of ingredients and ideas. And once I got started, there was no pulling back.

ON MAKING PIZZA

For maximum nutritional benefit, use a variety of whole-grain flours to make your pizza crusts. Or sneak some whole-grain flours in the basic flour crust. When you bake, watch for the heat in the oven. Reduce it if the pizza crust seems to be browning too fast or turn it up if it seems too slow. For best results, use a baking stone or tiles. Preheat these on the center rack of a 450°F oven for about 30 minutes before placing the pizza over them. Be very careful—they are extremely hot. Metal pizza trays and cookie sheets are fine too—make sure they are heavy. Always bake the pizza in the center of the oven and if you make more than one pizza at a time, reposition the trays midway to ensure even baking (the lower tray gets more heat and the pizza tends to brown faster).

Basic Pizza Crust

LOOKING FOR NEW IDEAS for your child's party? Try what I did on my daughter's sixth birthday. I made a whole lot of pizza dough, brought out small cookie sheets, laid out a pizza bar, and let each child make her (or his) own custom pizza. What a riot it was—and I didn't have to worry about anyone going home hungry.

Make sure that all the little hands have been washed before they are allowed to handle this edible Pla-do.

1 teaspoon sugar
1½ tablespoons dry yeast
1¼ cups warm water (110° to 115°F)
3½ cups bread flour
¾ teaspoon salt, or to your taste
1 tablespoon canola, safflower, saffola, or corn oil plus 1 additional tablespoon oil if making dough by hand
1 tablespoon extra-virgin olive oil

Dissolve the sugar and yeast in the warm water in a small bowl and set aside until foamy, 3 to 4 minutes. (If it doesn't foam, that means the yeast is not active. Discard it and use new yeast.)

To make the dough with a food processor, put the flour, salt, and oils in the work bowl fitted with the metal S-blade and process for a few seconds. With the motor running, pour the yeast mixture through the feed tube and process until the flour gathers into a ball. Continue to process until the sides of the bowl look clean, 20 to 30 seconds. (If the dough looks too sticky, add some more flour through the feed tube; if it looks too dry, add some more water.)

To make the dough by hand, put the flour, salt, and oils in a large bowl and mix with your fingers. Add three quarters of the yeast mixture and mix again with your fingers until the dough starts to gather together. Add the remaining yeast mixture as necessary to make a medium-firm dough that does not stick to your fingers. Apply the 1 tablespoon oil to your fingers as you make the dough; this keeps the dough from sticking to your fingers.

Transfer the dough to a well-oiled large bowl, cover with plastic wrap, and set aside in a warm, draft-free spot until it doubles in volume, 3 to 4 hours.

Grease two pizza trays with canola oil and dust liberally with flour. Using your fist, gently punch down the dough to deflate it and remove the air bubbles. With lightly oiled hands, divide the dough in half and place one portion on each tray. Cover with plastic wrap and set aside for about 30 minutes (this makes the dough soft and pliable). Working with each portion separately, spread the dough toward the edges of each tray, making a 12- to 14-inch circle of relatively even thickness. Alternately, with a rolling pin, roll the dough on a lightly floured surface into two 12- to 14-inch circles, put them on the pizza trays, and proceed with the recipe.

Moisten the outer edges of the rolled-out dough and fold over about ½ inch of the dough toward the center, pressing lightly to seal. This makes a raised edge and the cheese and toppings don't spill off. (This step is optional.) Place the trays in a warm spot to rise for 5 to 7 minutes. The crust is ready for a variety of toppings.

Whole-Wheat Pizza Crust

Makes two 12-inch thin pizza crusts

DO AHEAD:
See Basic Pizza Crust, page 104.

THIS CRUST IS MADE with a mixture of whole-wheat and bread flour with some wheat gluten added. Wheat gluten is wheat flour from which the starches have been removed. With the starches gone, whatever remains is all protein. This protein improves the quality of the bread and allows the dough to rise to its optimum capacity. Wheat gluten is available in some grocery stores and health food stores.

1 teaspoon all-purpose flour
1 teaspoon sugar
1½ tablespoons dry yeast
1½ cups warm water (110° to 115°F)
2 cups whole-wheat flour
1½ cups bread flour
3 tablespoons wheat gluten
1 teaspoon salt, or to your taste
2 tablespoons canola, safflower, saffola, or corn oil plus 1 additional tablespoon oil if making dough by hand
1 tablespoon extra-virgin olive oil

Dissolve the all-purpose flour, sugar, and yeast in the warm water and set aside until foamy, 3 to 5 minutes. (If it doesn't foam, that means the yeast is not active. Discard it and use new yeast.)

To make the dough with a food processor, put the flours, wheat gluten, salt, and oils in the work bowl fitted with the metal S-blade and process for a few seconds. With the motor running, pour the yeast mixture through the feed tube and process until the flour gathers into a ball. Continue processing until the sides of the work bowl look clean, 20 to 30 seconds. (If the dough seems too sticky, add some more flour through the feed tube; if it seems too dry, add some more water.)

To make the dough by hand, put the flours, wheat gluten, salt, and oils in a large bowl and mix with your fingers. Add three quarters of the yeast mixture and mix again with your fingers until the dough starts to gather together. Add the remaining yeast mixture as necessary to make a medium-firm dough that does not stick to your fingers. Apply the 1 tablespoon oil to your fingers as you make the dough; this keeps the dough from sticking to your fingers.

Transfer the dough to a well-oiled large bowl, cover with plastic wrap, and set aside in a warm, draft-free spot until it doubles in volume, 3 to 4 hours.

Grease two pizza trays with canola oil and dust liberally with flour. Using your fist, gently punch down the dough to deflate it and remove the air bubbles. With lightly oiled hands, divide the dough in half and place one portion on each tray. Cover with plastic wrap and set aside for about 30 minutes (this makes the dough soft and pliable). Working with each portion separately, spread the dough toward the edges of each tray, making a 12- to 14-inch circle of relatively even thickness. Alternately, with a rolling pin, roll the dough on a lightly floured surface into two 12- to 14-inch circles, put them on the pizza trays, and proceed with the recipe.

Tuck about ½ inch of the dough under the edges, pressing lightly to seal. This makes a raised edge and the cheese and toppings don't spill off. (This step is optional.) Place the trays in a warm spot to rise slightly for 5 to 7 minutes. The crust is now ready for a variety of toppings.

Oat Bran Crust with Jalapeño-Basil Pesto Chutney

Makes one 14-inch-crust pizza

Do Ahead:
  See Basic Pizza Crust, page 104.

THERE IS NOTHING SHY about this wholesome pizza crust that is enhanced with the bold, intense flavors of a heavenly pesto-style chutney. (If your chutney is not hot enough, mince some more jalapeño peppers in the food processor before adding the flour.) Oat bran and fine semolina are available in health food stores and most supermarkets.

1 teaspoon sugar
1 tablespoon dry yeast
About ⅔ cup warm water (110° to 115°F)
⅔ cup Jalapeño and Basil Pesto-Style Chutney (page 259)
1½ cups oat bran
1 cup fine semolina
1 cup all-purpose flour
1 teaspoon salt, or to your taste
1 tablespoon extra-virgin olive oil plus 1 additional tablespoon oil if making dough
    by hand

Dissolve the sugar and yeast in the warm water and set aside until foamy, 3 to 5 minutes. (If it doesn't foam, that means the yeast is not active. Discard it and use new yeast.)

To make the dough with a food processor, put the chutney and the oat bran, semolina, flour, salt, and oil in the work bowl fitted with the metal S-blade and process for a few seconds. With the motor running, pour the yeast mixture through the feed tube and process until the flour gathers into a ball. Continue processing until the sides of the work bowl look clean, 20 to 30 seconds. (If the dough looks too sticky, add some more flour through the feed tube; if it looks too dry, add some water.)

To make the dough by hand, put the chutney and the oat bran, semolina, flour, salt, and oil in a large bowl and mix together with your fingers. Add three quarters of the yeast mixture and mix again with your fingers until the dough starts to gather together. Add the remaining yeast mixture as necessary to make a medium-firm dough that does not stick to your fingers. Apply the 1 tablespoon oil to your fingers as you make the dough; this keeps the dough from sticking to your fingers.

Transfer the dough to a well-oiled large bowl, cover with plastic wrap, and set aside in a warm, draft-free spot until it doubles in volume, 3 to 4 hours.

Grease a pizza tray with canola oil and dust liberally with flour. Using your fist, gently punch down the dough to deflate it and remove the air bubbles. Place it on the tray. Cover with plastic wrap and set aside for about 30 minutes (this makes the dough soft and pliable). Working with your hands, spread the dough toward the edges of the tray, making a 14-inch circle of relatively even thickness. Alternately, with a rolling pin, roll the dough on a lightly floured surface into a 14-inch circle, put it on the pizza tray, and proceed with the recipe.

Tuck about ¼ inch of the dough under the edges, pressing lightly to seal. This makes a raised edge and the cheese and toppings don't spill off. (This step is optional.)

Place the tray in a warm spot to rise for 5 to 7 minutes. The crust is now ready for a variety of toppings.

Thin-Crust Pizza with Garbanzo Beans and Cilantro

Makes 4 to 6 servings

SERVING IDEAS:

Great with a tossed green salad or Indian Coleslaw (page 47). Or cut it into small wedges and present as appetizers with Yogurt-Cilantro Chutney (page 258) on the side.

DO AHEAD:

Cook the garbanzos and refrigerate them for 3 to 5 days. Assemble the pizzas a few hours in advance and cook closer to serving time.

"EEEEW, PIZZA WITH GARBANZO beans. We've never heard of anything like that" was the reaction I got when I served this to my daughters. Thank you, that's exactly the point.

Two 12-inch thin unbaked pizza crusts (pages 104–5)
2 tablespoons canola oil
1 cup finely chopped onions
2 large cloves garlic, minced
2 tablespoons ground coriander
3 cups prepared tomato sauce
3 cups canned garbanzo beans (chickpeas), drained and rinsed
1 cup firmly packed finely chopped cilantro (fresh coriander) leaves, soft stems
    included
1¾ cups grated mild or medium-sharp Cheddar cheese
½ cup minced scallion greens
1 to 4 teaspoons chopped pickled or fresh jalapeño peppers (optional), to your taste
Garam masala for garnish

In a medium nonstick saucepan, heat the oil over moderately high heat and cook the onions, stirring, until golden, 3 to 4 minutes. Mix in the garlic and cook for another minute. Add the coriander and stir for about 30 seconds. Mix in the tomato sauce, garbanzo beans, and cilantro and bring to a boil over high heat. Reduce the heat to moderate, cover, and cook for 8 to 10 minutes until somewhat thickened. Remove from the heat and set aside to cool.

Preheat the oven to 400°F.

Lay out the two unbaked pizza crusts on pizza trays. Spread about ½ cup of the cheese over each crust and cover evenly with the cooked garbanzo beans. Top each with the scallion greens and chopped chilies and sprinkle the remaining ¾ cup cheese evenly on top of both of them.

Transfer the pizzas to the top and center racks of the oven and bake until the crust is crispy and golden, 15 to 18 minutes. Reposition the trays midway through to ensure even baking.

Remove from the oven, garnish with a sprinkling of garam masala, and serve immediately.

Whole-Wheat Pizza with Tofu and Morel Mushrooms

THIS PIZZA GOES GOURMET with morels and tofu.

Two 12-inch thin, unbaked whole-wheat pizza crusts (pages 106–7)
2 tablespoons canola oil
1 cup finely chopped onions
2 large cloves garlic, minced
1 tablespoon peeled and minced fresh ginger
1 tablespoon ground coriander
1 teaspoon ground cumin
1 teaspoon fennel seeds
1 teaspoon dried basil
1 teaspoon dried oregano
1 teaspoon dried parsley
3 cups prepared tomato sauce
½ cup grated low-fat mozzarella cheese
½ cup grated Monterey Jack cheese or Tofu Rella Jalapeño Jack Cheese alternative
One 10-ounce package extra-firm tofu, towel dried and coarsely crumbled
½ cup sliced morel mushrooms (fresh or reconstituted dried), or more to your taste
1 Anaheim pepper, thinly sliced
Garam masala for garnish

Makes 4 to 6 servings

SERVING IDEAS:
For a booster shot of calcium and vitamins, pair with Chopped Spinach Salad with Cumin-Yogurt Dressing (page 48).

DO AHEAD:
Make the sauce up to a week in advance. Assemble the pizzas a few hours ahead and bake closer to serving time.

In a medium, nonstick saucepan, heat the oil over moderate heat and cook the onions, stirring, until golden, 3 to 4 minutes. Mix in the garlic and ginger and cook for another minute. Add the coriander, cumin, and fennel seeds, then mix in the basil, oregano, and parsley. Stir for about 30 seconds, mix in the sauce, and bring to a boil over high heat. Reduce the heat to moderate; cook, stirring, until the sauce is slightly thick, 10 to 15 minutes. (The tomato sauce may splatter; if that happens, cover the pan.) Remove from the heat; set aside to cool. Preheat the oven to 400°F.

Lay out the unbaked pizza crusts on pizza trays. Mix the cheeses and spread about ¼ cup over each crust; cover evenly with the tomato sauce. Top with the crumbled tofu, morels, and peppers and sprinkle the remaining ½ cup cheese evenly on top of them.

Transfer the pizzas to the top and center racks of the oven and bake until crisp and golden, 15 to 18 minutes. Reposition the trays midway through to ensure even baking. Remove from the oven, garnish, and serve hot.

Oat Bran Pizza with Grilled Italian Eggplants and Yellow Pattypan Squash

Makes 4 to 6 servings

SERVING IDEAS:

Chilled melons, grapes, and strawberries are perfect to offset the gutsy flavors of this pizza.

VARIATION:

Add grilled seafood or chicken along with, or instead of, the vegetables.

DO AHEAD:

Assemble the pizza up to 4 hours in advance and store in the refrigerator. Bake just prior to serving.

ON MY FIRST TRY, the dough did not rise much, but, much to my delight, the pizza still turned out to be astonishingly moist and crisp.

1 Oat Bran Crust with Jalapeño and Basil Pesto-Style Chutney (page 259)
2 tablespoons extra-virgin olive oil, or more if needed
1 large clove garlic, minced
3 teaspoons mixed dried Italian herbs
2 extra-large, vine-ripened tomatoes, chopped
½ cup firmly packed fresh basil leaves
½ teaspoon salt
1 oval-shaped Italian eggplant (about ½ pound), cut into ¼- to ⅓-inch-thick slices
3 to 4 yellow pattypan squash, cut into ¼- inch-thick slices
1 cup 1-inch-long, julienne red bell pepper sticks
¼ cup grated mozzarella, Cheddar, or Monterey Jack cheese (optional)

Preheat the oven to 400°F. Put the unbaked crust in the center of the oven on a pizza tray and bake until slightly golden, about 10 minutes. Remove from the oven.

In a small skillet, heat 1 tablespoon of the oil over moderately high heat, and cook the garlic, stirring, for a few seconds. Add 2 teaspoons of the dried herbs and the tomatoes and cook, stirring, until the tomatoes are mushy, 2 to 3 minutes. Mix in the fresh basil and salt continue to cook, stirring occasionally, until the tomatoes are somewhat saucy, 4 to 5 minutes. Remove from the heat and set aside.

Put the eggplant and squash slices (in 1 or 2 batches) in a ridged nonstick skillet (or a regular nonstick skillet) and grill (with no oil added) until golden on the bottom. Turn each piece over, and with a basting brush, brush each slice with a small amount of the remaining tablespoon oil. When the second side is golden, turn the pieces over again, baste with the oil, and sprinkle the remaining teaspoon of dried herbs over them.

Spread the tomato sauce over the partially baked crust. Arrange the grilled eggplants and squash over the sauce. Garnish with the red bell pepper and cheese (if using) and return to the oven. Bake until the cheese melts and the crust is crisp and golden, another 10 to 15 minutes. Cut into wedges and serve immediately.

Sourdough Pizza with Grilled Onions, Broccoli, and Asparagus

LARGE LOAVES OF SOURDOUGH or French bread are instant pizza crusts. Just cut them in half, cover them with your favorite toppings, and bake. Whenever I am in a hurry, I turn to whichever breads and vegetables are in the refrigerator to make these delicious luncheon pizzas.

2 tablespoons extra-virgin olive oil
2 small red onions, peeled, cut in half lengthwise, and thinly sliced
1 tablespoon peeled and minced fresh ginger
1 teaspoon minced garlic
1 teaspoon dried oregano
1 teaspoon ground coriander
½ teaspoon ground cumin
½ teaspoon coarsely crushed fennel seeds
1 small head broccoli, cut into 1-inch-long or smaller florets
1 bunch asparagus, bottom stems snapped off and tops cut into 1-inch pieces
4 to 6 medium-size shiitake mushrooms, stems removed and caps thinly sliced
½ teaspoon salt, or to your taste
One 1-pound long sourdough or French bread, cut in half lengthwise (or slices of sourdough bread)
1½ cups prepared pizza sauce, or more to your taste
1 cup freshly grated Parmesan or mozzarella cheese (optional), or more to your taste

In a medium skillet, heat the oil over moderately high heat and cook the onions, stirring, until they start to turn golden, 3 to 5 minutes. Add the ginger, garlic, oregano, coriander, cumin, and fennel seeds, then mix in the broccoli, asparagus, and mushrooms. Add the salt, cook for a minute or two, cover the skillet, remove from the heat, and set aside for about 5 minutes. (The steam in the skillet will make the vegetables tender-crisp.)

Preheat the oven to 400°F.

Place the 2 pieces of the bread on a cookie sheet and spread the pizza sauce on the cut sides of each. Top with the cooked vegetables and scatter the cheese over the top.

Place the pizzas on the center rack and bake until the cheese melts and the pizzas are crisp and golden, 10 to 12 minutes. Cut into pieces and serve immediately.

Makes 4 to 6 servings

SERVING IDEAS:
Perfect with a soup and a salad. This pizza can also be made on muffins, bagels, and flour tortillas.

DO AHEAD:
Assemble the pizza up to 4 hours in advance and store in the refrigerator. Bake just prior to serving.

Boboli Pizza with Spicy Meat Sauce and Potatoes

Makes 2 to 4 servings

SERVING IDEAS:
  This hearty pizza is best with Tomato, Jicama, and Scallion Salad on Endive Boats (page 51).

DO AHEAD:
  Make the meat sauce up to a week in advance. Assemble the pizza a few hours ahead of time and bake just prior to serving.

NOTE:
  Add more yogurt once the meat is tender and bring to a boil once again if you desire a thinner sauce.

MEAT SAUCE TAKES ON a brand-new identity when it is made with yogurt and Indian seasonings.

2 tablespoons extra-virgin olive oil
1 cup finely chopped onions
3 small russet potatoes, peeled and cut into wedges or dice
2 teaspoons fennel seeds
2 teaspoons minced garlic
2 tablespoons peeled and minced fresh ginger
1 pound extra lean ground meat (lamb, beef, chicken, or turkey)
1 tablespoon ground coriander
1 teaspoon dried fenugreek leaves
½ teaspoon garam masala
½ teaspoon paprika or cayenne pepper
¼ teaspoon ground turmeric
1 teaspoon salt, or to your taste
1 cup nonfat plain yogurt, whisked until smooth
One 12-inch Boboli pizza crust (or any other pizza crust)
Chopped cilantro (fresh coriander) leaves for garnish
½ cup grated part-skim mozzarella or smoked gouda cheese
Sprinkling of freshly grated Parmesan cheese to taste

In a large, nonstick saucepan, heat the oil over moderately high heat and cook the onions, stirring, until golden, 3 to 5 minutes. Add the potatoes, fennel seeds, garlic, ginger, and ground meat and cook, stirring and breaking up any lumps, until the meat turns golden, 5 to 7 minutes.

Mix in the coriander, fenugreek, garam masala, paprika, turmeric, and salt; cook for another minute. Add the yogurt in a thin stream, stirring constantly to prevent curdling. Bring to a boil over high heat. Reduce the heat to moderate, cover, and cook until the meat is tender and the sauce is thick, 10 to 15 minutes. Set aside.

Preheat the oven to 400°F. Put the crust on a pizza tray or a cookie sheet and spread the meat sauce over the pizza crust. Garnish with the cilantro leaves and cover with the mozzarella and Parmesan cheese. Transfer the pizza to the center rack of the oven and bake until crisp and golden, 15 to 18 minutes. Remove from the oven and serve hot with crushed red pepper on the side.

Leftover Thanksgiving Turkey Pizza on Boboli Crust

HERE'S AN EXCITING WAY to use leftover Thanksgiving turkey.

2 tablespoons safflower oil
1 small onion, peeled and cut into half lengthwise and thinly sliced
1 cup diced roasted turkey
6 to 8 small mushrooms, quartered
2 teaspoons ground coriander
1 teaspoon ground cumin
2 large, vine-ripened tomatoes, coarsely chopped
½ cup loosely packed finely chopped cilantro (fresh coriander) leaves, soft stems included
1 to 3 serrano peppers (optional), to your taste, finely sliced
1 tablespoon peeled and minced fresh ginger
1 teaspoon minced garlic
½ teaspoon salt, or to your taste
One 12-inch Boboli pizza crust (or any other pizza crust)
1½ cups grated part-skim mozzarella cheese
½ cup freshly grated Parmesan cheese
1 teaspoon ground dried herbs of your choice—such as basil, oregano, fenugreek, thyme

Makes 2 to 4 servings

SERVING IDEAS:
  Present this with Cranberry-Orange Chutney (page 263) and a tossed green salad.

DO AHEAD:
  Assemble the pizza up to 4 hours in advance and store in the refrigerator. Bake just prior to serving.

In a medium saucepan, heat 1½ tablespoons of the oil over moderately high heat and cook the onions, stirring, until golden, 2 to 4 minutes. Add the turkey and mushrooms and cook, stirring, until the mushrooms release their juices and the juices evaporate, 5 to 7 minutes. Set aside in a bowl.

Add the remaining ½ tablespoon oil to the same pan and cook the coriander and cumin, stirring, for about 30 seconds over moderately high heat. Add the tomatoes, cilantro, peppers, ginger, and garlic and cook, stirring lightly, until the tomatoes are soft, 3 to 4 minutes. Mix in the salt and remove from the heat.

Preheat the oven to 400°F. Put the crust on a pizza tray, spread the chutney sauce over the crust, and top with the mozzarella. Place the pizza on the center rack and bake until the cheese melts (do not let it turn golden). Remove from the oven and spread the cooked onions, turkey, and mushrooms over the melted cheese. Top with the Parmesan cheese and sprinkle your favorite dried herbs over it. Return to the oven and bake until crisp and golden, another 5 to 10 minutes. Cut into wedges and serve immediately.

Naan Pizza with Green Cilantro Chutney and Grilled Saffron Kebab Rolls

Makes 2 to 4 servings

SERVING IDEAS:

This salady pizza calls for a tall glass of iced cappucino or a fruity yogurt shake.

DO AHEAD:

The pizza dough, kebabs, and chutney can all be prepared ahead of time. Bake the naan pizza and assemble closer to serving time or the pizza will get soggy. Remember, once you bake the naan pizza crust, there is no further baking required.

DIAGONAL SLICES OF SAFFRON kebab rolls and finely diced vine-ripened tomatoes sit elegantly on a jade-green cushion of shredded lettuce, which in turn rests on crispy naan pizza breads that have been slathered with a fresh green chutney. This is decidedly one of my best inventions.

This pizza does involve turning to four different recipes, but the final product is so spectacular that, I assure you, it is worth every minute of the effort that has gone into it.

5 to 7 Grilled Saffron Seekh Kebabs, Chicken Tikka Kebabs, or Skewered Shrimp (pages 183, 181, or 189)
1 Naan Pizza Bread with Nigella Seeds (page 70)
1 cup Green Cilantro Chutney (page 257)
2 cups shredded iceberg or romaine lettuce
1 cup finely diced firm, vine-ripened tomatoes, drained
½ cup thinly sliced scallion whites (about 10)
½ to 1 teaspoon chaat masala or Roasted Peppercorn Masala (page 12), to your taste

Cut each kebab roll into 5 to 6 oval-shaped diagonal slices (cut the tikka kebabs into small pieces and the shrimp in half lengthwise). Set aside.

Put the naan pizza on a serving platter and evenly spread the cilantro chutney over it. Top with the shredded lettuce and arrange the kebab slices over the lettuce. Scatter the tomatoes, scallion whites, and cilantro over the kebabs. Garnish with the chaat masala and serve immediately.

Small Pasta Shells with Kashmiri Garam Masala, Shrimp, Asparagus, and Wild Mushrooms

KASHMIR—THE PICTURESQUE LAND of mountains, valleys, and fragrant flowers, where nature's beauty has to be seen to be believed—is the home of some of India's most prized treasures. Among these are saffron and wild mushrooms, especially the morels (*gucchiyan*) and chanterelles (*dhingriyan*). The intricately woven silk rugs and satin-smooth, hand-embroidered *satoosh* and *pashmina* wool shawls also come from Kashmir—this was where the name "cashmere" was coined.

The fragrance of Kashmir also extends to the local cuisine, as can be seen from their special garam masala, which includes black cumin seeds, mace, nutmeg, and occasionally saffron, along with the regular garam masala spices.

½ pound dried small pasta shells, cooked as directed on the package until al dente, drained, and rinsed under cold water

1 tablespoon fresh lemon juice

2 tablespoons extra-virgin olive oil

3 to 5 serrano or jalapeño peppers, to your taste, skin punctured to prevent them from bursting

3 to 5 cloves garlic, to your taste, minced

One 1-inch piece fresh ginger, peeled and minced

½ cup loosely packed finely chopped cilantro (fresh coriander) leaves, soft stems included

1 teaspoon Kashmiri Garam Masala (page 9)

¼ to ½ teaspoon cayenne pepper, to your taste

15 to 20 large shrimp

1 bunch asparagus, tough stems snapped off and tops cut into 1-inch-long pieces

1 cup chopped wild mushroom caps, fresh or reconstituted dried, or more to your taste

½ teaspoon salt, or to your taste

Kashmiri Garam Masala (page 9) for garnish

Makes 4 servings

SERVING IDEAS:
Team with Grilled Gingerbread Naan (page 72) or Grilled Ginger-Fenugreek Toast (page 82), fresh lemonade or iced tea, and a bowl of chilled seasonal fruits.

DO AHEAD:
This dish tastes best when fresh, but it may be made about 2 hours ahead of time.

continued

Transfer the pasta to a serving platter or casserole dish and mix in the lemon juice; cover and keep warm.

Prepare the vegetables while the pasta is cooking. Heat the oil in a large, nonstick skillet over moderately high heat and cook the peppers, garlic, and ginger, stirring, until just golden, 1 to 2 minutes. Mix in the cilantro, garam masala, and cayenne pepper, then add the shrimp, asparagus, mushrooms, and salt. Cook, stirring, until the shrimp firm up and turn pink, 3 to 5 minutes; cover the skillet and turn off the heat. Let everything remain in the skillet for another 5 minutes. (The steam from the vegetable juices will further cook everything.)

Transfer to the cooked pasta platter and toss gently to mix. Garnish with more garam masala and serve immediately.

Indian Pasta and Chicken Salad with Ginger Limette

ADD VINEGAR AND IT is a vinaigrette, add lime juice and we create a limette. Both are indispensable dressings.

For centuries, the Indians have been using fresh lime juice (we call them lemons—our "lemons" are more like Key limes, the smaller, softer-skinned, and tarter variety that is used to make Key lime pie—in all types of foods, from salads, pickles, and chutneys to curries and vegetable side dishes. However, the Indian use of lime juice in salads differs from the way it is used in the West, as it is never combined with oil to make a vinaigrette.

3 tablespoons extra-virgin olive oil
2 tablespoons peeled and minced fresh ginger
1½ tablespoons mixed dried Italian herbs
1 tablespoon ground coriander
1 teaspoon ground cumin
1 teaspoon chaat masala
1 teaspoon salt, or to your taste
½ teaspoon freshly ground black pepper, or to your taste
¼ cup fresh lime or lemon juice, or to your taste
1 pound dried curly pasta (rotini), cooked as directed on the package until al dente, drained, and rinsed under cold water
2 cups diced cooked chicken (boiled, roasted, or grilled)
2 cups seeded, finely diced red, yellow, and orange bell peppers
½ cup loosely packed finely chopped cilantro (fresh coriander) leaves, soft stems included
½ cup loosely packed finely chopped fresh basil leaves

In a small saucepan, heat the oil over moderate heat and cook the garlic and ginger, stirring, until they just start to turn golden, 1 to 2 minutes. Increase the heat to moderately high and add the herbs, spices, salt, and pepper. Cook, stirring, for 30 to 45 seconds, add the lime juice, and remove from the heat.

Put the pasta, chicken, and bell peppers in a large serving bowl and add the dressing, cilantro, and basil. Toss to mix well. Chill in the refrigerator for 4 to 6 hours before serving to let the flavors develop.

Makes 8 servings

SERVING IDEAS:
This makes a lovely, light lunch with a soup and focaccia bread. The dressing can also be used as a marinade for chicken and seafood.

DO AHEAD:
This salad stays fresh for about 1 week in the refrigerator. Toss once more before serving. The dressing keeps 7 to 10 days refrigerated.

VARIATION:
Make twice the dressing recipe. Lightly cook some zucchini, cauliflower, broccoli, green beans, etc., in the microwave oven (or steam them), toss them with the dressing, and mix them into the pasta salad.

Carol Berger's Oriental Salad with Twisty Noodles

Makes 8 servings

SERVING IDEAS:

For a light lunch, serve these noodles with Cream-Style Chicken Corn Soup with Pickled Jalapeño Peppers (page 20) and a tall glass of fruity iced tea.

DO AHEAD:

This salad stays fresh, refrigerated, for a week. The dressing can be refrigerated for 15 to 20 days.

CAROL, THE OWNER-CHEF of The Trail's End, a lovely restaurant in Portland, Oregon, makes this salad with the long Chinese egg noodles, but as a variation I am using short, flat egg noodles that have been lightly twisted. Carol's use of balsamic vinegar (instead of the more traditional rice vinegar) adds an exotic appeal to this salad, as does a sprinkling of Indian chaat masala.

One 12-ounce package egg noodles (or any other noodles), cooked as directed on the package until al dente, rinsed in cold water, and drained
2 cups shredded green cabbage
1 cup peeled and finely diced Japanese, English, or pickling cucumber
1 cup 1-inch-long julienne carrot sticks
2/3 cup thinly sliced scallions (white and light green parts)
2/3 cup coarsely chopped roasted peanuts with their skins
One 1-inch piece fresh ginger, peeled and cut into 3 to 4 nickel-size slices
1 large clove garlic, peeled
3 tablespoons soy sauce
2 tablespoons balsamic vinegar
1 tablespoon sesame oil
1 to 2 teaspoons hot chili oil, to your taste
1 tablespoon sugar
1 tablespoon kosher salt, or to your taste
2 tablespoons sesame seeds, lightly toasted (page 34), and 1 teaspoon chaat masala for garnish

In a large bowl, mix together the cooked noodles, cabbage, cucumber, carrots, scallions, and peanuts.

Put the ginger, garlic, soy sauce, vinegar, sesame oil, chili oil, sugar, and salt in a blender and process until the ginger and garlic are completely mixed into the sauce.

Add the sauce to the noodles and mix well. Transfer to a platter, garnish with the sesame seeds and chaat masala, and serve.

Pasta with Roasted Tomato-Balsamic Curry Sauce and Mushrooms

THIS PASTA DISH IS specially for my daughters, Sumita and Supriya, who are always asking for new pasta recipes.

2½ pounds vine-ripened tomatoes, halved or quartered lengthwise, depending on the size
1½ tablespoons balsamic vinegar
2½ tablespoons extra-virgin olive oil
1½ tablespoons minced garlic
1 tablespoon ground dried basil
2 teaspoons ground cumin
2 teaspoons ground coriander
1 teaspoon salt, or to your taste
½ teaspoon freshly ground black pepper, or to your taste
1 pound dried pasta of your choice, cooked as directed on the package until al dente, rinsed in cold water, and drained
½ pound mushrooms, trimmed and halved or quartered
1 cup thinly sliced morel mushroom caps, fresh or reconstituted dried
¼ cup firmly packed finely chopped cilantro (fresh coriander) leaves, soft stems included
Garam masala for garnish
Freshly grated Parmesan cheese

Preheat the oven to 450°F.

In a small bowl, combine the balsamic vinegar, 1½ tablespoons of the oil, garlic, basil, cumin, coriander, salt, and pepper. Brush the cut sides of each tomato with this mixture and place cut side down in a nonreactive pie dish or a casserole. Roast, uncovered, until the tomatoes are very soft, 15 to 20 minutes.

Remove the tomatoes from the oven; set aside. When cool enough to handle, pull off the skins. Return to the oven and broil 6 to 8 inches from the source of heat until the tomatoes are charred in some spots, 2 to 3 minutes. Transfer to a blender and blend until smooth. Set aside.

In a medium saucepan, heat the remaining tablespoon oil over moderate heat and cook the mushrooms, stirring, until they release all their juices, 2 to 4 minutes. Raise the heat to high and continue to cook, stirring, until all the juices dry up and the mushrooms are golden, 2 to 3 minutes. Mix in the roasted tomato sauce and cilantro; simmer moderately low heat for 2 to 4 minutes. Place the pasta in a large bowl. Mix in the sauce, garnish with garam masala, and serve with Parmesan cheese on the side.

Makes 4 to 6 servings

SERVING IDEAS:
  This novel sauce is charming with an array of pasta shapes—spaghetti, rigatoni, farfalle, and stuffed pasta—and also teams well with barbecued or pan-cooked dry meat preparations.

DO AHEAD:
  The sauce can be made 3 to 5 days in advance and refrigerated.

Penne in Tomato-Basil-Coriander Sauce

SERVING IDEAS:

Delicious with Garlic and Roasted Peppercorn Chicken (page 128) or Garlicky Karahi Shrimp with Thyme (page 150) and a salad of bitter greens.

DO AHEAD:

Make the sauce up to 2 days in advance and refrigerate or freeze for 2 to 3 months. Leftovers stay fresh 3 to 4 days.

MY HUSBAND, PRADEEP, LOVED the way his favorite Italian restaurant prepared penne. So one day I went up to the chef to ask him the recipe. His answer was very vague—add this and this and then that. I politely thanked him and came home, determined to make something Pradeep would like.

In my kitchen, I added a bit of this and a bit of that and this is what I made—something that not only Pradeep, but my daughters also loved.

½ pound dried penne pasta cooked as directed on the package until al dente, rinsed in cold water, and drained

2 tablespoons extra-virgin olive oil

3 to 5 serrano or jalapeño peppers, to your taste, skins punctured to prevent them from bursting

4 to 7 cloves garlic, to your taste, minced

¼ cup minced fresh Italian parsley leaves

¼ cup minced fresh basil leaves

1 tablespoon ground coriander

1 teaspoon ground cumin

¼ to ½ teaspoon crushed red pepper flakes, to your taste

Three 15-ounce cans tomato sauce

¼ to ½ cup half-and-half or whipping cream

Coarsely chopped fresh basil leaves, freshly grated Parmesan cheese, and garam masala for garnish

Transfer the cooked pasta to a serving casserole, cover, and keep warm.

Prepare the sauce while the pasta is cooking. Heat the oil in a medium, non-stick saucepan over moderate heat and cook the peppers and garlic, stirring, until the garlic just turns golden, 1 to 2 minutes. Mix in the parsley, basil, coriander, cumin, and red pepper flakes and add the tomato sauce.

Cook, stirring, over high heat for 4 to 6 minutes (if the sauce splatters, reduce the heat or cover the pan), reduce the heat to moderate, and simmer until the sauce thickens, 15 to 20 minutes. Add the cream and cook for another 5 to 7 minutes to blend the flavors.

Pour the sauce over the warm penne and stir gently to mix. Garnish with more chopped basil, Parmesan cheese, and a touch of garam masala; serve hot.

Stir-fried Pasta with Garlic and Assorted Herbs

LOTS OF FRESHLY COOKED pasta with a little bit of olive oil, golden slivers of garlic, and a scattering of aromatic herbs and spices all come together to make this modest, unsaucy pasta dish, an ideal addition to any type of a banquet.

1 pound dried pasta (spaghetti, linguine, fettuccine), cooked as directed on the package until al dente, rinsed in cold water, and drained
2 tablespoons extra-virgin olive oil
4 to 6 large cloves garlic, to your taste, peeled and cut into thin slivers
¼ cup firmly packed finely chopped fresh basil leaves or 2 teaspoons dried
¼ cup firmly packed finely chopped cilantro (fresh coriander) leaves, soft stems included
2 tablespoons finely chopped fresh oregano leaves or 1 teaspoon dried
2 tablespoons finely chopped fresh Italian parsley leaves or 1 teaspoon dried
1 tablespoon finely chopped fresh mint leaves
1 tablespoon ground coriander
1 tablespoon freshly ground cracked black peppercorns, or to your taste
½ teaspoon salt, or to your taste
1 large red bell pepper, seeded and finely diced
¼ cup minced fresh chives or scallion greens for garnish

In a large, nonstick skillet, heat the oil over moderately high heat and cook the garlic slivers stirring, until golden, about 1 minute. Add all the herbs and cook, stirring, until they wilt and turn brown, 2 to 4 minutes. Mix in the coriander, black pepper, and salt, then add the red bell pepper and cooked pasta. Cook, turning the pasta gently with a spatula, until it becomes completely coated with the herbs. (Taste and adjust the seasonings and add some red pepper flakes, if desired.) Transfer to a serving bowl, garnish with the chives, and serve hot.

Makes 6 to 8 servings

SERVING IDEAS:
Great by itself, you can also smother it in Creamy Tomato Sauce (page 252) or crown with your favorite grilled or sautéed vegetables, shrimp, or chicken. Or serve it with Wilted Red Swiss Chard with Sautéed Goat Cheese (page 46).

DO AHEAD:
Make up to 2 days ahead and refrigerate. Cover and reheat with a scant sprinkling of water and your dish will be as good as new. Just garnish and serve.

Ravioli with Dandelion Greens and Garam Masala

I WAS ASKED TO make saag paneer (a popular Indian dish made with spinach and paneer cheese) for an Indian banquet. Upon opening my refrigerator, I noticed that I had very little spinach and no paneer at all. But I did have dandelion greens and I had cheese ravioli. Suddenly, I had a flash—who would know the difference between spinach and dandelion greens? And ravioli does look like pieces of paneer and it does contain cheese, and cheese translates to *paneer* in Hindi. This dish, though quite different from the traditional recipe, is still a real treat.

Loaded with calcium and vitamins, dandelion greens—a member of the sunflower family—tend to be slightly bitter by themselves, so it is a good idea to combine them with spinach.

1 large bunch fresh dandelion greens (about ½ pound), trimmed of tough stems, thoroughly washed, and coarsely chopped

1 medium-size bunch fresh spinach (about ½ pound), trimmed of tough stems, thoroughly washed, and coarsely chopped

3 tablespoons extra-virgin olive oil

1 cup finely chopped onions

1 teaspoon minced garlic

1 teaspoon garam masala

1 cup loosely packed finely chopped cilantro (fresh coriander) leaves, soft stems included

½ teaspoon salt, or to your taste

One 1-pound package fresh cheese ravioli, cooked as directed on the package until al dente, rinsed in cold water, and drained

2 large cloves garlic, cut into thin slivers

1 tablespoon ground coriander

1 teaspoon fresh thyme leaves or ½ teaspoon dried

1 large red bell pepper, seeded and finely diced

Garam masala for garnish

In a large, nonstick skillet, heat 2 tablespoons of the oil over moderately high heat and cook the onions, stirring, until golden, 3 to 5 minutes. Add the minced garlic, garam masala, and cilantro, and mix in the dandelion greens and spinach a little at a time, adding more as each batch wilts until all of it is used up. Add the salt, cover the skillet, and cook for about 5 minutes, stirring occasionally. Remove to a bowl and set aside.

To the same skillet, add the remaining tablespoon oil and the ravioli and garlic slivers and cook, turning the ravioli carefully, until golden. Add the coriander, thyme, and red bell peppers. Cover the skillet and let sit for 3 to 5 minutes to blend flavors. (This allows the peppers to become slightly tender and the ravioli to stay moist.)

Mix in the reserved greens and stir over moderate heat for 2 to 4 minutes. Transfer to a serving dish and serve hot.

VARIATION: Cook the ravioli with the garlic and spices and serve it with Pasta Sauce with Roasted Japanese Eggplants and Peppers (page 251).

Potato and Tortellini Curry

Makes 6 to 8 servings

SERVING IDEAS:

Great as is, or present it as they would in India—with a side of vegetables, yogurt, rice, and breads.

DO AHEAD:

Can be made up to 2 days ahead and refrigerated. As the dish cools down, the potatoes and tortellini will absorb most of the water. Reheat with an additional ½ cup water just before serving. It should have a thickish gravy.

THIS INSPIRED RECIPE IS a true Indian-style curry (a dish with a sauce) made with Indian seasonings and flavors.

3 tablespoons extra-virgin olive oil
1 tablespoon peeled and minced fresh ginger
1 teaspoon minced garlic
3 to 5 serrano peppers, to your taste, skins punctured to prevent them from bursting
1 teaspoon cumin seeds
1 tablespoon ground coriander
1 teaspoon ground cumin
½ teaspoon ground turmeric
½ teaspoon paprika
1 teaspoon salt, or to your taste
3½ cups finely chopped vine-ripened tomatoes (about 6 medium-size tomatoes)
1 cup firmly packed finely chopped cilantro (fresh coriander) leaves, soft stems included
2 large russet potatoes, peeled and cut into ¾-inch cubes
3½ cups water, or more as needed
12 to 16 ounces cheese tortellini or ravioli (choose the smaller ones stuffed with mild cheese), cooked as directed on the package until al dente rinsed in cold water and drained
Garam masala and chopped cilantro leaves for garnish

In a large, nonstick saucepan, heat the oil over moderately high heat and cook the ginger and garlic, stirring, until golden, 30 to 60 seconds. Add the peppers and cumin seeds; they will sizzle upon contact with the hot oil. Stir in the coriander, ground cumin, turmeric, paprika, and salt. Add the tomatoes and cilantro and cook, stirring as necessary, until most of the liquid from the tomatoes evaporates, 7 to 10 minutes. Add the potatoes, and cook, stirring over moderate heat for 5 to 7 minutes, then add the water. Raise the heat to high and bring to a boil. Reduce the heat to moderate, cover the pan, and cook, stirring occasionally, until the potatoes are soft, 7 to 10 minutes. Add the tortellini and simmer for 3 to 4 minutes.

Transfer to a serving casserole, garnish with garam masala and cilantro, and serve hot.

The Skillful Skillet

HAVE YOU EVER TRIED to make stew in a skillet or an omelette in a pot? Why is it that we intuitively reach for a wok when we stir-fry or a griddle when pancakes are in order? Because there are some untaught, unspoken, and unwritten "laws" guiding our selection of pots and pans and, like law-abiding citizens in the world of cuisine, we follow those to the letter.

Preparation of memorable and captivating dishes may be an art that comes from the heart, but the proper cooking of the foods lies in the shape of the pan—flat, deep, oval, or round—each serving a specific purpose. Cook your vegetables and meats in deep pots or saucepans and you'll end up with a stew or a mush of steamed vegetables. (In the constrained space in a pot or a saucepan, the foods end up one on top of the other. The foods at the bottom brown nicely, but they are prone to being crushed by the weight of what's on top. On the other hand, the food on top cooks from the steam generated by the heat below. Stirring causes havoc—everything disintegrates into a big heap. Cook them in an open skillet and they get a chance to breathe and cook at their own pace, with each morsel in direct contact with the heated metal.

A skillet is a pan with a multitude of names—frying pan, omelette pan, sauté pan. This humble, old-fashioned pan with a flat bottom and raised (straight or slanting) sides has the power to transform each of us into a gourmet chef. Just add the foods and the seasonings and the skillet does the rest—braising, grilling, roasting, sautéing, pan- or stir-frying. The cooked foods look so pretty and colorful that they can go from the stove top to the table, all in the same versatile pan.

If today's pace of life has put a damper on your yearnings to become an exceptional home cook, don't panic. Just go out and purchase a large, heavy (preferably nonstick, if oil is an issue) skillet, read these recipes, and then create your own favorite foods with flair and spontaneity.

Garlic and Roasted Peppercorn Chicken

Makes 4 servings

SERVING IDEAS:

Present with a side of pan-cooked or grilled vegetables, a yogurt raita, and any type of bread. Make more than you need; leftovers are wonderful in green salads and in sandwiches, pita pockets, tacos, burritos, and other Mexican fare.

DO AHEAD:

Best when served fresh, though it can be made a few hours ahead of time.

WHETHER USED FOR A simple family dinner or elaborate entertaining, this priceless recipe is a definite crowd pleaser. For a grilled look, cook in a skillet with a ridged bottom.

1½ pounds boneless, skinless chicken tenders, tendons removed
1 tablespoon minced garlic
1 tablespoon peeled and minced fresh ginger
1 teaspoon roasted (page 12) and coarsely ground black peppercorns, or to your taste
¾ teaspoon coarsely ground carom seeds
¼ cup fresh lemon or lime juice
1 cup firmly packed finely chopped cilantro (fresh coriander) leaves, soft stems included
1 teaspoon salt, or to your taste
2 to 3 tablespoons peanut oil
¾ cup seeded and finely diced red bell peppers
Garam masala for garnish

Put the chicken tenders in a medium-size bowl. Combine the garlic, ginger, peppercorns, carom seeds, lemon juice, ½ cup of the cilantro, and the salt in another bowl. Mix with the chicken until it is fully coated. Cover with plastic wrap and marinate for at least 12 and up to 48 hours in the refrigerator.

In a large, nonstick skillet, heat the oil over moderately high heat and add the marinated chicken tenders one at a time, so that all the pieces lie straight in the skillet. (Do it in two batches if the skillet is not large enough.) Cook, turning the pieces once or twice, until they are golden and tender, 5 to 7 minutes. Sprinkle the diced peppers and the remaining ½ cup cilantro on top, stir to combine, and cook for another 2 to 3 minutes.

Transfer the chicken to a platter, garnish with garam masala and serve.

Chicken Thighs with Basil, Cilantro, and Macadamia Nuts

HERE WE MARINATE CHICKEN thighs in a pesto-style blend of basil, cilantro, and macadamia nuts and then cook them until they are tender and fragrant. If you wish, add some pineapple juice to give a Hawaiian touch to this dish.

One 1-inch piece fresh ginger, peeled and cut into thin slices
5 large cloves garlic, peeled
1 to 4 jalapeño peppers, to your taste, stems removed
⅓ cup coarsely chopped macadamia nuts
2 tablespoons extra-virgin olive oil
2 tablespoons fresh lemon or lime juice
½ cup nonfat plain yogurt
¾ cup firmly packed fresh basil leaves
½ cup firmly packed cilantro (fresh coriander) leaves, soft stems included
1 tablespoon ground coriander
1¼ teaspoons garam masala
½ teaspoon ground cumin
1 teaspoon salt, or to your taste
1½ pounds boneless chicken thighs, all fat and skin removed and cut into 1½- to
  2-inch pieces
Chopped fresh basil or cilantro leaves for garnish

In the work bowl of food processor fitted with the metal S-blade and with the motor running, process the ginger, garlic, and peppers until minced by adding them through the feed tube. Add the macadamia nuts and process until minced. Add the oil, lemon juice, yogurt, basil, and cilantro and process until everything is smooth. (Stop the machine and scrape down the sides of the work bowl once or twice.) Add the spices and salt and process again to incorporate.

Put the chicken thighs in a medium bowl. Add the processed mixture and mix until the pieces are fully coated with it. Cover with plastic wrap and marinate the chicken thighs for at least 12 and up to 48 hours in the refrigerator.

Transfer the chicken and its marinade to a large skillet and cook, stirring occasionally, over moderately high heat until the thighs are golden and tender and the marinade sticks to the pieces, 20 to 25 minutes.

Transfer to a serving platter or dish, garnish with basil or cilantro, and serve.

Makes 4 servings

SERVING IDEAS:
This dry-style chicken dish is remarkable when presented with a saucy lentil or bean dish along with naan or parantha and a side of vegetables or a salad.

DO AHEAD:
Can be made 1 to 2 days in advance and refrigerated. Reheat with additional yogurt if required. Leftovers stay fresh for about 5 days in the refrigerator.

Yogurt-Glazed Lamb Chops

Makes 8 servings

SERVING IDEAS:

For meat and potato lovers, present this with Peppery Mashed Potatoes (page 137); for everyone else, choose any dry-cooked vegetable side dish. And don't forget to chill a bottle of your favorite Gewürztraminer.

DO AHEAD:

Can be made 2 to 3 days ahead of time and refrigerated. Reheat with additional yogurt, if required.

SUCCULENT AND TENDER, THE lamb is glazed with a spicy yogurt sauce that can be made hot or mild to suit your taste.

Notice that this recipe contains no oil. The lamb chops render enough fat as they cook, so extra oil is not necessary.

4 to 6 lamb chops (5 to 6 ounces each), all fat removed and washed
¾ to 1 cup nonfat plain yogurt, whisked until smooth
2 tablespoons fresh lime or lemon juice
2 teaspoons minced garlic
1 tablespoon peeled and minced fresh ginger
¼ cup ground raw almonds
1 tablespoon ground coriander
2 teaspoons garam masala
2 teaspoons ground dried fenugreek leaves
1 teaspoon white poppy seeds
¼ to ½ teaspoon ground red chili peppers (optional), to your taste
1 teaspoon salt, or to your taste
One 1-inch piece fresh ginger, peeled and cut into 1-inch-long julienne sticks
¼ cup minced scallion greens and garam masala for garnish

Put the lamb chops in a medium-bowl. Combine the yogurt, lime juice, garlic, ginger, almonds, coriander, garam masala, fenugreek leaves, poppy seeds, peppers, and salt in another bowl. Mix with the chops until they are fully coated with the mixture. Cover with plastic wrap and marinate for at least 12 and up to 48 hours in the refrigerator.

Put the lamb chops and their marinade and the ginger julienne in a large, nonstick skillet. Cover and cook over moderately high heat for about 5 minutes, reduce the heat to moderate and continue to cook until the lamb chops are fork-tender and the gravy appears like a glaze over the chops, 25 to 35 minutes. (Add some more yogurt or water if the juices dry up too fast, or uncover and finish cooking if there is too much sauce.) Turn the chops over occasionally.

Transfer to a serving casserole, garnish with the scallion greens and some more garam masala, and serve.

Minty Meatballs in Citrus Juices

MEATBALLS SIMMERED IN SWEET and tart citrus juices with dried red peppers, ginger, and garlic lend themselves to all types of cuisines. This dish works well hot or cold, so it is also ideal for picnics and packed lunches.

2 pounds extra-lean ground beef or lamb
½ cup minced scallion whites
2 tablespoons minced fresh mint leaves
1 teaspoon salt, or to your taste
1 teaspoon freshly ground black pepper, or to your taste
3 to 4 tablespoons peanut oil
2 to 4 dried red chili peppers, to your taste
2½ cups finely chopped onions
2 tablespoons peeled and minced fresh ginger
2 teaspoons minced garlic
1 cup loosely packed finely chopped cilantro (fresh coriander) leaves, soft stems
    included
½ cup pineapple juice
½ cup orange juice
½ cup fresh lemon or lime juice
Chopped cilantro leaves and finely diced red bell pepper for garnish

In a large bowl, mix together the beef, scallions, mint, ½ teaspoon of the salt, and ½ teaspoon of the pepper. Divide and shape the mixture into twenty-five to thirty 1-inch balls. Set aside.

In a large, nonstick skillet, heat the oil over moderately high heat and cook the hot red peppers, stirring, for 45 seconds. (Stand as far away from the skillet as you can, in case the peppers burst.) Add the onions and cook, stirring occasionally, until they turn dark brown, 10 to 12 minutes. Stir in the ginger, garlic, cilantro, and the remaining ½ teaspoon salt and ½ teaspoon pepper. Add the meatballs and the pineapple, orange, and lemon juices.

Cover the skillet and cook over high heat for the first 3 to 5 minutes, then reduce the heat to moderate and continue to cook, stirring occasionally, until the meatballs are fork-tender, all the liquid is absorbed, and the oil separates to the sides of the skillet, 20 to 25 minutes. If the sauce is too thin, uncover the skillet during the last 5 to 7 minutes of cooking. Transfer to a serving dish, garnish, and serve hot.

Makes 4 to 6 servings

SERVING IDEAS:

Even though these meatballs are great by themselves, I usually serve Green Cilantro Chutney (page 257) to further perk up their flavor. As an entrée, I pair them with a soup, salad, and a side of slightly saucy vegetables, rice, and bread.

DO AHEAD:

Uncooked meatballs can be frozen in a single layer on a cookie sheet and then stored in zipper-top plastic bags for 2 to 3 months. They can go straight from the freezer to the pan. Prepared meatballs stay fresh for 3 to 5 days in the refrigerator.

Pacific Sea Bass with Garlic and Cayenne Pepper

Makes 4 to 6 servings

SERVING IDEAS:

Ideal paired with grilled vegetables and pasta or served on a bed of sautéed root vegetables (A Medley of Roots, page 140) and garlic bread. Don't forget to offer your favorite red wine.

DO AHEAD:

The fish can be marinated up to a day in advance, but it is best when cooked and served fresh.

DIFFERENT TYPES OF SPECIALTY mustards and assorted herbs add subtle flavor changes to this recipe. So go ahead, use whatever happens to be in your refrigerator and create a new recipe every time.

2 pounds fillets of Pacific or Chilean sea bass, halibut, cod, swordfish, or any other firm fish, cut into 1- to 1½-inch pieces
¼ cup fresh lime or lemon juice
1 tablespoon peppercorn mustard or any other specialty mustard
1½ tablespoons minced garlic
1 tablespoon peeled and minced fresh ginger
½ cup loosely packed minced fresh basil leaves or 1 tablespoon dried
3 tablespoons minced fresh oregano leaves or 1 teaspoon dried
½ teaspoon salt, or to your taste
½ teaspoon freshly ground black pepper, or to your taste
¼ to ½ teaspoon cayenne pepper, to your taste
2 tablespoons olive oil
Shredded lettuce, paprika, garam masala, and lemon wedges for garnish

Put the fish pieces in a large bowl. Combine the lime juice, mustard, garlic, ginger, basil, oregano leaves, salt, and black and cayenne pepper in another bowl and add to the fish, mixing gently with your fingers to make sure that all the pieces are well coated. Cover with plastic wrap and place in the refrigerator for at least 1 and up to 24 hours.

In a large, nonstick skillet, heat the oil over moderately high heat and add the fish and its marinade in a single layer. Cook until all the marinade evaporates and the pieces are golden on the bottom, 5 to 7 minutes. Turn the pieces over and cook until they are golden and the fish is flaky, another 5 to 7 minutes, depending on the thickness of the fillets.

Transfer to a platter lined with shredded lettuce, garnish with a light sprinkling of paprika, garam masala and lemon wedges, and serve.

Orange Roughy with Soy Sauce and Garam Masala

THIS COMBINATION OF INDIAN and oriental flavorings produces one of the best seafood preparations that I have tasted. It also gets a very high rating from my husband, Pradeep.

Watch the salt, there is already some in the soy sauce.

2 pounds fillets of orange roughy or any other firm fish, cut into
    3-inch cubes
¼ cup soy sauce
1 tablespoon rice vinegar
2 teaspoons sesame oil
½ cup minced fresh green garlic or 1 tablespoon minced garlic and ¼ cup minced
    scallion greens
1 tablespoon peeled and minced fresh ginger
1 tablespoon ground coriander
½ teaspoon garam masala
¼ teaspoon salt, or to your taste
2 to 3 tablespoons peanut oil
¼ teaspoon cayenne pepper (optional), garam masala, or chopped cilantro (fresh
    coriander) leaves for garnish

Place the fish pieces in a large bowl. Combine the soy sauce, vinegar, sesame oil, garlic, ginger, coriander, garam masala, and salt in another bowl and add to the fish, mixing gently with your fingers to make sure all the pieces are well coated. Cover with plastic wrap and place in the refrigerator for at least 1 and up to 24 hours.

In a large, nonstick skillet, heat the oil over moderately high heat and add the fish and its marinade in a single layer. Cover and cook until the bottom of the fish is golden brown, 5 to 7 minutes. Uncover the skillet and carefully turn each piece over with a spatula. Cover the skillet again and cook until the second side is golden brown and the fish is flaky, another 5 to 7 minutes, depending on the thickness of the fillets.

Transfer the fish to a platter, sprinkle some cayenne pepper and garam masala on each piece, garnish with chopped cilantro, and serve.

Makes 4 to 6 servings

SERVING IDEAS:
Present with steamed basmati or jasmine rice or with couscous and a side of Stir-fried Vegetables with Fresh Green Garlic (see page 153), or your favorite fiery hot stir-fried vegetable dish.

DO AHEAD:
The fish can be marinated up to a day in advance, but it is best when cooked and served fresh.

Scrambled Eggs with Potatoes and Mushrooms

Makes 8 servings

SERVING IDEAS:

A perfect addition to a Sunday brunch with Indian paranthas or warm, buttered rolls, lots of fresh fruits, and a fruity yogurt shake.

DO AHEAD:

Best when served fresh. To save time, cook the mushrooms, onions, potatoes, bell pepper, and ginger and set aside for up to 3 hours. Just prior to serving, add the eggs and the remaining ingredients and proceed with the recipe.

MY CHILDHOOD FAVORITE WITH a difference—the earlier one did not contain mushrooms. Somehow, good-quality domesticated mushrooms were not readily available in the markets and even when my mother saw them, she always hesitated to purchase them, because they were not too fresh looking and she worried about their nonhygienic packing.

6 to 8 large mushrooms (about ½ pound), rinsed and diced
2 tablespoons vegetable oil
¾ cup finely chopped onions
2 medium-size russet potatoes, boiled in lightly salted water to cover until tender, drained, peeled, and cut into ½-inch dice
1 small red bell pepper, seeded and cut into ¼-inch dice
2 teaspoons peeled and minced fresh ginger
6 to 8 extra-large eggs, lightly beaten
½ cup lightly packed, finely chopped cilantro (fresh coriander) leaves, soft stems included
2 teaspoons fresh thyme leaves
½ teaspoon freshly ground black pepper, or to your taste
½ teaspoon salt, or to your taste
¼ cup finely chopped scallion greens and pinch of paprika for garnish

Put the mushrooms in a medium, nonstick skillet and cook, stirring, over moderately high heat until they release their juices, 2 to 3 minutes. Continue to cook until all the juices evaporate and the mushrooms turn golden, 3 to 4 minutes. Set aside.

In a large, nonstick skillet, heat the oil over moderately high heat and cook the onions, stirring occasionally, until they just start to turn golden, 3 to 5 minutes. Mix in the potatoes and continue to cook, turning occasionally, until the potatoes are golden, 3 to 5 minutes. Stir in the bell pepper and ginger and cook for another minute or two, until slightly softened. Reduce the heat to moderate and add the beaten eggs, cilantro, black pepper, and salt. Stir gently until the eggs are firm and start to turn golden, 3 to 5 minutes.

Transfer to a serving casserole, garnish with the scallion greens and paprika, and serve at once.

Medley of Colorful Potatoes with Garlicky Balsamic Vinegar

THERE WAS A TIME when my daughters, Sumita and Supriya, eyed my purple potatoes rather suspiciously. Today, they look strangely at people who are reluctant to try them.

If you haven't seen these wonderful treasures, ask your grocer to get them for you. Then make this unusual recipe that my daughters heartily recommend.

2 pounds mixed small purple, red, russet, and Yukon Gold potatoes, boiled in lightly
    salted water to cover until tender, drained, and cut into ¼-inch-thick slices
1 to 1½ cups water
¼ cup balsamic vinegar
3 tablespoons extra-virgin olive oil
4 teaspoons minced garlic
½ cup firmly packed finely chopped fresh basil leaves
1 teaspoon salt, or to your taste
1½ cups coarsely chopped vine-ripened tomatoes (about 3 medium-size tomatoes)
Freshly ground black pepper for garnish

In a small bowl, combine the vinegar, 1 tablespoon of the olive oil, 2 teaspoons of the garlic, the basil, and salt.

In a large, nonstick skillet, heat the remaining 2 tablespoons of oil over moderately high heat and cook the remaining 2 teaspoons garlic, stirring, until barely golden, about 1 minute. Add the tomatoes and cook until saucy, about 2 minutes, then mix in the potatoes and vinegar mixture. Cook the potatoes, turning carefully as necessary with a spatula, until all the juices evaporate and the potato slices are crisp on both sides, 10 to 15 minutes.

Transfer to a serving dish, top with freshly ground black pepper, and serve as a side dish.

Makes 6 to 8 servings

SERVING IDEAS:
Superb with any pasta, curried lentil, bean, or meat preparation, or as a snack by itself. The garlicky balsamic mixture doubles as a lovely salad dressing for mixed greens.

DO AHEAD:
Stays fresh for 3 to 5 days in the refrigerator; however, the potatoes will not remain crisp. To restore their crispy texture, reheat them in a skillet.

Multicolored Potatoes with Glazed Cherry Tomatoes

Makes 6 to 8 servings

SERVING IDEAS:

Present as a side dish with any meat, curry, or lentil dish, as an appetizer with a green chutney, or as a salad over a bed of wilted spinach or chopped lettuce.

DO AHEAD:

The potatoes can be boiled a day in advance. The dish can be made a few hours ahead of time and reheated, preferably in the skillet in which it was cooked.

WHY STOP AT ONE potato dish only when we can make so many with this popular root vegetable? Here is another spectacular potato recipe, infused with ginger, coriander, and lemon juice and decorated with spice-glazed cherry tomatoes.

5 to 6 medium-size purple potatoes (about 1¼ pounds)
18 to 20 baby (1-inch) new white potatoes (about ¾ pound)
3 tablespoons olive oil
One 1½-inch piece fresh ginger, peeled and cut into julienne sticks
1 tablespoon peeled and minced fresh ginger
2 tablespoons ground coriander
1 teaspoon salt, or to your taste
1 cup loosely packed finely chopped cilantro (fresh coriander) leaves, soft stems included
¼ cup fresh lemon juice, or to your taste
20 to 25 small cherry or pear-shaped red or yellow tomatoes

Put the two types of potatoes into separate pans in lightly salted water to cover until they are tender but not broken. Let cool, then cut the purple potatoes in ½-inch rounds and the baby potatoes in half. (Do not peel either type.) Cover and set aside.

In a large, nonstick skillet, heat 2 tablespoons of the oil over moderate heat and cook the ginger julienne, stirring, until golden, 2 to 3 minutes. Remove to paper towels to drain. Reserve for garnish.

Add the remaining 1 tablespoon oil to the skillet and stir in the minced ginger, ground coriander, and salt over moderate heat. Then add the potatoes, one at a time, so that each piece lies flat in the skillet. (Use two skillets if one is not large enough, or cook in two batches). Add the cilantro, increase the heat to moderately high, and cook, turning the potatoes gently as necessary, until golden on both sides, 8 to 10 minutes. Top with the lemon juice and cook for another minute. Transfer to a serving platter and keep warm.

Add the cherry tomatoes to the same skillet and cook, shaking the skillet, until the tomatoes are glazed with the spices remaining in the skillet, 2 to 3 minutes. Transfer to the potato platter. Garnish with the reserved stir-fried ginger and serve.

Peppery Mashed Potatoes

WHO SAYS THAT MASHED potatoes are boring? That person obviously hasn't tasted this gutsy version with jalapeño peppers.

3 tablespoons safflower oil
1 tablespoon peeled and minced fresh ginger
1 to 3 teaspoons minced jalapeño or serrano peppers, to your taste
2 tablespoons ground coriander
5 to 6 large russet potatoes (about 2 pounds), boiled in lightly salted water to cover
    until tender, peeled, drained, and coarsely mashed
1 teaspoon salt, or to your taste
½ teaspoon freshly ground black pepper, or to your taste
1 cup loosely packed finely chopped cilantro (fresh coriander) leaves, soft stems
    included
¼ cup fresh lemon juice
1 teaspoon paprika
Finely chopped cilantro (fresh coriander) leaves and freshly ground black pepper
    for garnish

In a large, nonstick skillet, heat the oil over moderately high heat and cook the ginger, stirring, until it turns golden, about 1 minute. Stir in the peppers and coriander, add the potatoes, and stir until well mixed. Add the salt, pepper, cilantro, and lemon juice. Reduce the heat to moderately low and cook, stirring and turning occasionally, until the potatoes are slightly crusty and golden, 5 to 7 minutes. Sprinkle the paprika on top and continue to cook, stirring occasionally, for another 5 to 7 minutes to allow flavors to develop.

Transfer to a serving dish, garnish with cilantro and black pepper, and serve.

Makes 6 to 8 servings

SERVING IDEAS:
  Perfect with a summer barbecue or as a breakfast accompaniment in place of hash browns, these mildly (or fiery) hot potatoes never fail to please our seasoned palates.

DO AHEAD:
  Best when served fresh, but it can be made a few hours ahead of time and reheated, preferably in the skillet it was made in or in the microwave oven.

Okra Bits with Potatoes and Tomatoes

Makes 8 servings

SERVING IDEAS:
Present this dry-cooked side dish with any meat or vegetable curry or roll it burrito-style in warm chapatis or paranthas or in flour or whole-wheat tortillas.

DO AHEAD:
Stays fresh for 3 to 5 days in the refrigerator.

IF POSSIBLE, MAKE THIS recipe with fresh okra. If that is not available, use frozen, provided you understand the proper handling of this vegetable. Okra is a very gooey and starchy vegetable. To make it into a crispy and appetizing dish, you must make sure that that each piece is completely dry. (That is the reason each individual okra pod must be wiped dry before cooking it.)

Since frozen okra is full of moisture, the first step of the recipe is to get rid of the moisture before starting. To do this, place thawed frozen okra in a non-stick skillet (without oil) and cook it for 10 to 15 minutes over moderate heat, turning it very carefully, until all the water evaporates and the okra pieces start to turn golden. Then add the oil and proceed with the recipe.

2½ to 3 pounds young okra
3 tablespoons peanut oil
2 large potatoes, boiled in lightly salted water to cover until tender, peeled, drained, and cut into ¾-inch dice
3 medium-size, vine-ripened tomatoes, cut into ½- to ¾-inch cubes
2 tablespoons ground coriander
2 teaspoons ground cumin
1½ teaspoons mango powder
¾ teaspoon ground turmeric
1 teaspoon salt, or to your taste
¼ cup loosely packed finely chopped cilantro (fresh coriander) leaves for garnish

Wash and wipe each okra dry. Cut off the stem and slice each okra into ½-inch-long pieces. Discard the tips only if they look too brown.

In a large, nonstick skillet, heat 2 tablespoons of the oil over moderately high heat and cook the okra, stirring occasionally, until it turns golden brown, 5 to 7 minutes. Remove to a bowl.

Add the remaining 1 tablespoon oil and the potatoes and cook, stirring occasionally, until they turn golden, 5 to 7 minutes. Remove to the bowl with the okra.

Add the tomatoes to the skillet and cook, stirring, until they are soft, 3 to 5 minutes. Return the okra and potatoes to the skillet and add the coriander, cumin, mango powder, turmeric, and salt. Cook for another 5 to 7 minutes to blend the flavors.

Transfer to a serving dish, garnish with the chopped cilantro, and serve.

Sautéed Taro Root

TARO ROOT IS CALLED *arbi* or *ghuiyan* in India. When they see my hands in the taro root bin, people often ask me what I do with this vegetable—why, I cook it, of course. When cooked in this recipe, this starchy root becomes slightly crisp on the outside while remaining moist and tender inside. It looks deceiving and unless people know it, you can pass it off as fried fish.

1½ pounds small taro roots (20 to 25)
2 to 3 tablespoons peanut oil
2 tablespoons peeled and minced fresh ginger
2 tablespoons ground coriander
1 tablespoon fresh thyme leaves or 1 teaspoon dried
½ teaspoon coarsely crushed carom seeds
¾ teaspoon salt, or to your taste
Freshly ground black pepper to taste
½ cup lightly packed finely chopped cilantro (fresh coriander) leaves, soft stems
  included
¼ cup fresh lime or lemon juice
2 cups shredded curly leaf lettuce
Garam masala for garnish

In a large saucepan, boil the taro roots in lightly salted water to cover until they are very tender, 10 to 12 minutes. Drain, remove from the pan, and let cool. Peel and cut each taro root lengthwise into halves or quarters, depending on the size. Set aside.

In a large, nonstick skillet, heat 1 tablespoon of the oil over moderately high heat and cook (in one or two batches, adding more oil as needed), the taro root pieces, turning them once or twice, until they are golden, 3 to 5 minutes. Set aside in a bowl. When cool enough to handle, press each root gently between the palms of your hands to flatten them to an even thickness so the flavors penetrate better. Set aside. (Use paper towels to protect your hands if the pieces are hot.)

Add the remaining 1 tablespoon oil to the skillet and cook the ginger, stirring, over moderate heat until golden, 30 to 60 seconds. Mix in the coriander, thyme, carom seeds, salt, pepper, and cilantro. Add the taro pieces and cook, turning gently, until well coated with the spices in the skillet, 2 to 3 minutes. Mix in the lime juice. Transfer to a serving platter lined with the lettuce, garnish, and serve.

Makes 6 to 8 servings

SERVING IDEAS:
  This dry-cooked side dish teams perfectly with lentils, vegetable curries, and saucy meat or chicken dishes and doubles as a substantial snack when served by itself or with Yogurt-Cilantro Chutney (page 258).

DO AHEAD:
  Even though this dish keeps in the refrigerator for 3 to 5 days, I prefer to serve it as fresh as possible. Kept for a long time, it loses its crispy texture, but still tastes good. Reheat it preferably in a skillet (or a preheated 400°F oven) in a single layer.

A Medley of Roots

For formal dinners, place some shredded red romaine or bronze leaf lettuce on separate plates, cover somewhat with individual helpings of this dish, and then position some sautéed or grilled firm fish, shrimp, or chicken over the top. Drizzle some Yogurt Raita Sauce with Crispy Minced Ginger (page 245) over that and serve with more sauce on the side.

DO AHEAD:

For a very fresh taste, make no more than 3 to 4 hours in advance. Or, cook the root pieces until golden and keep in the refrigerator for up to 3 days. Reheat in a skillet, add the spices, cilantro, and lime juice, and finish cooking closer to serving time.

HERE'S A RECIPE THAT transforms everyday root vegetables into an exciting and colorful dish. To make it even livelier, use a griddle with a ridged bottom for more of a grilled taste and look.

Choose small and even-sized yams and sweet potatoes.

2 pounds mixed yams, sweet potatoes, colorful potatoes, taro roots, turnips, etc.
3 tablespoons peanut oil
2 tablespoons peeled and minced fresh ginger
1 tablespoon ground coriander
1 teaspoon ground cumin
½ teaspoon salt, or to your taste
½ cup firmly packed finely chopped cilantro (fresh coriander) leaves, soft stems included
¼ cup fresh lime or lemon juice, or more to your taste
½ teaspoon freshly ground black pepper, or to your taste

In a large saucepan, boil the root vegetables in lightly salted water to cover until soft. (Watch carefully, because some root vegetables cook faster than others.) Let cool, then peel and cut into ¾-inch cubes or ¼-inch-thick rounds.

In a large, nonstick skillet, heat the oil over moderately high heat and cook the ginger, stirring, for a few seconds until golden. Add the root vegetables (in 1 or 2 batches) and cook them without stirring until they are golden on the bottom, 7 to 10 minutes. Turn them over carefully and cook the second side till golden, another 4 to 6 minutes. Sprinkle the coriander, cumin, and salt over the top and cook for 2 to 4 minutes, turning once or twice to coat with spices and pan roast lightly. Add the cilantro and lime juice and cook for another 3 to 5 minutes, turning occasionally to blend flavors.

Transfer to a serving platter, garnish with black pepper, and serve.

Mixed Vegetables with Fresh Curry Leaves

THE AROMA OF CURRY leaves is intensified when the leaves are combined with asafetida and mustard seeds. This herb and spice combination is most popular in southern and western India where it is used to prepare a vast selection of spectacular dishes.

3 tablespoons peanut oil
3 stalks fresh curry leaves (25 to 30 leaves)
1 teaspoon brown mustard seeds
½ teaspoon coarsely ground fenugreek seeds
¼ teaspoon ground asafetida
1 tablespoon ground coriander
15 to 20 unpeeled baby russet potatoes, halved, or 2 to 3 large potatoes,
    cut into 1-inch cubes
2 cups finely chopped vine-ripened tomatoes (about 2 large tomatoes)
¾ teaspoon salt, or to your taste
1 cup green beans, strings discarded and cut into 1-inch pieces
2 to 4 small zucchini, cut into thin, diagonal slices
1 large red bell pepper, seeded and cut into 1-inch cubes
1 large yellow bell pepper, seeded and cut into 1-inch cubes
Chopped cilantro (fresh coriander) leaves and freshly ground black pepper
    for garnish

In a large, nonstick skillet, heat the oil over moderately high heat and cook the curry leaves, stirring, until they turn golden, 1 to 2 minutes. With the lid of the skillet in your hand, add the mustard seeds and immediately cover the skillet; the seeds start popping upon contact with the hot oil. Stir by shaking the skillet. When the popping subsides, remove the lid and add the fenugreek seeds, asafetida, and coriander. Cook, stirring, for about 1 minute, and add the potatoes, tomatoes, and salt. Cover the skillet and cook over moderately low heat until the potatoes are almost tender, 15 to 20 minutes.

Add the beans and zucchini, cover the skillet, and continue to cook, stirring occasionally, for 3 to 4 minutes. Add the bell peppers and cook for another 3 to 4 minutes.

Transfer to a platter, garnish with cilantro and black pepper, and serve.

Makes 6 to 8 servings

SERVING IDEAS:
These "curry"-flavored vegetables are perfect partners to steamed basmati rice or can be served on the side with any curried or grilled meat preparation.

DO AHEAD:
Cook the dish until the potatoes are soft and set aside for up to 1 day in the refrigerator. Reheat and finish making the recipe closer to serving time. If the vegetables are cooked too far in advance, they will become soggy.

Grilled Fillet of Cod

Makes 4 to 6 servings

SERVING IDEAS:

Chopped Tomato and Zucchini Julienne in Balsamic-Basil Dressing (page 50), Saffron Rice with Spinach, Red Bell Peppers, and Wild Mushrooms (page 273), or any other rice with lots of vegetables.

DO AHEAD:

Marinate the fish up to a day in advance. Leftovers can be reheated in the microwave oven or in a skillet.

THE DELICATE AND THIN fillets of cod crumble very easily if they are handled too much. For this reason, I cook the bottom sides in a skillet, then broil the tops in the oven until they become golden. This way the fillets do not have to be turned and both sides of the fish cook beautifully.

2 tablespoons plain nonfat yogurt, whisked until smooth
2 tablespoons fresh lime or lemon juice
2 teaspoons minced garlic
2 to 3 teaspoons mixed dried Italian herbs, to your taste, crumbled or ground
1 tablespoon garbanzo bean flour or all-purpose flour
1 tablespoon ground coriander
1 teaspoon coarsely crushed carom seeds
1 teaspoon ground ginger
1 teaspoon salt, or to your taste
½ teaspoon freshly ground black pepper, or to your taste
2 to 4 tablespoons olive or peanut oil
1½ to 2 pounds thin fillets of cod, dover sole, snapper or any other firm fish
  (10 to 12 per pound)
Paprika, garam masala, minced fresh chives and lemon wedges for garnish

Mix the yogurt, lime juice, garlic, Italian herbs, flour, coriander, carom seeds, ginger, salt, and pepper together in a small bowl. Place the fish in a large, flat baking dish and rub both sides of each fillet with the yogurt mixture. Cover with plastic wrap and refrigerate for at least 4 or up to 24 hours.

In a large, nonstick, ovenproof skillet (or cover the handle of any skillet with 4 layers of aluminum foil) heat 1 tablespoon of the oil. Transfer the fillets to the skillet in a single layer (you may have to do this in 2 or 3 batches), drizzle some of the remaining oil over them and cook on moderately high heat until all the marinade dries up and the fillets become golden on the bottom, 3 to 5 minutes per batch.

Preheat the broiler in the oven and and place the skillet about 6 inches from the heat source. Broil the fish until the tops are golden and the fillets become flaky, 4 to 7 minutes depending on the thickness of the fillets.

Transfer to a warm platter, garnish with a light sprinkling of paprika, garam masala, and chives, and serve.

Wok on Fire

THE CHINESE STIR-FRY IN a wok, Americans use a skillet, and in India, we depend upon the *karahi-wok*. Whatever the pan this quick cooking procedure allows us to turn out delicious recipe after recipe with our favorite meats, vegetables, and grains. Indian karahi-woks are concave pans with round bottoms. The biggest advantage of cooking in a karahi-wok is the fact that the use of oil can be minimized—all the oil collects in the center of the rounded bottom, instead of spreading out as it does in the flat-bottomed pans. This allows perfect browning of the basic masala ingredients—ginger, garlic, onion, and spices—as they fry in the smallest amounts of oil possible. And because of its size and shape, more of the food comes in direct contact with the heated metal.

Karahi-woks are available in a variety of metals, ranging from cast-iron and tin-coated brass to aluminum and stainless steel. They can be purchased in Indian stores all over the country.

In Indian homes, karahi-woks are considered the most utilitarian and multipurpose of cooking utensils. They are used in preparing a large array of dishes—from deep-fried appetizers and main courses to side dishes and desserts. (Along with numerous puddings and halvahs, my mother often made her caramel custard in a karahi. The custard container was sealed properly and placed in a water bath in the karahi-wok. The karahi was then set on a portable coal-burning stove and the custard cooked as it simmered in the karahi. Remember, we had no ovens when I was growing up.)

About Karahi Dishes

INDIAN KARAHI DISHES DIFFER significantly from traditional Chinese wok-cooked dishes. In Chinese cuisine, the meats and vegetables are stir-fried separately, then combined with a sauce or a glaze. In authentic karahi cooking, most of the meats and vegetables are quickly cooked in a thick tomato-based sauce, with absolutely no water or juices added. Over the years, a distinctive savory garlic-ginger-fenugreek flavor has become synonymous with these unique dishes.

If you don't have a karahi-wok, by all means use a Chinese wok, skillet, or a saucepan, but do give these dishes a try. (You may need more oil than the recipes call for. Skillets and saucepans have a wider base and the oil spreads over a larger surface.)

Karahi Chicken

AS KIDS, WE LOVED to sop up leftover masala (spicy sauce) in the *karahi-wok* with bite-size pieces of freshly made chapati breads. In the back of our minds was the haunting thought that this act may upset Inder Devta—the god of rain—and he would put a damper on our wedding day by sending showers of rain. Our elders always said that if we licked clean any plates or utensils, the gods would drop rain on the most auspicious day of our lives. Maybe this was their way of teaching us proper etiquette. But I'm proud to say that my wedding day was completely rain free, despite repeatedly committing this crime. Maybe, in the eyes of God, sopping up masalas with chapati bites was not a sin after all.

2 tablespoons peanut oil

One 1-inch piece fresh ginger, peeled and cut into julienne strips

1 medium onion, cut in half lengthwise and thinly sliced

2 teaspoons minced garlic

3 cups coarsely chopped vine-ripened tomatoes (about 3 large tomatoes)

1 cup loosely packed, finely chopped cilantro (fresh coriander) leaves, soft stems included

1 tablespoon ground coriander

1 teaspoon ground cumin

1 teaspoon salt, or to your taste

Freshly ground black pepper to taste

1½ pounds boneless, skinless chicken tenders, tendons removed and each cut into 3 pieces

8 to 10 medium-size mushrooms, quartered

2 cups 2-inch-long julienne strips mixed red, yellow, and green bell peppers

1 teaspoon dried fenugreek leaves

Garam masala and a few cilantro leaves for garnish

In a large wok or karahi, heat the oil over moderately high heat and stir-fry the ginger and onion until golden, 5 to 7 minutes. Mix in the garlic, add the tomatoes, and cook, stirring, until a thick sauce forms, 5 to 7 minutes. Mix in the cilantro, coriander, cumin, salt, and pepper, add the chicken and mushrooms, and cook, stirring gently, until the chicken is tender, 7 to 10 minutes. Add the bell peppers and fenugreek leaves and cook, stirring occasionally, 4 to 5 minutes to blend the flavors.

Garnish with the garam masala and cilantro and serve as a main dish.

Makes 6 to 8 servings

SERVING IDEAS:

Present with steamed basmati rice or Indian bread, a side of vegetables, and yogurt raita.

DO AHEAD:

Stays fresh in the refrigerator for 4 to 5 days.

Ginger, Garlic, and Sesame Chicken

Makes 4 to 6 servings

SERVING IDEAS:

Served with tooth-picks on a bed of shred-ded greens, this doubles as a starter course. Place over prebaked cheese pizza and it is probably one of the best toppings you'll ever taste. (Go light on the cheese.)

DO AHEAD:

Marinate the chicken up to a day ahead, then cook just prior to serv-ing. Or cook it a few hours in advance and reheat before serving. Leftovers stay fresh for 3 to 5 days in the refriger-ator.

GET DARING. MARINATE YOUR chicken pieces in citrus juices, ginger, garlic, honey, garam masala, and sesame seeds, then cook them in a karahi until they are juicy and tender.

4 to 6 boneless, skinless chicken breast halves (about 2 pounds), skin removed and cut into 1-inch pieces
½ cup orange juice
¼ cup fresh lemon juice
2 tablespoons soy sauce
3 tablespoons honey
2 tablespoons peeled and minced fresh ginger
2 teaspoons minced garlic
1 teaspoon garam masala
1 teaspoon salt, or to your taste
½ teaspoon freshly ground black pepper, or to your taste
3 tablespoons peanut oil
1 teaspoon sesame oil
1 cup loosely packed finely chopped cilantro (fresh coriander), soft stems included
1 tablespoon sesame seeds, toasted (page 34), and chopped cilantro leaves for garnish

Put the chicken in a large bowl. Combine the orange and lemon juices, soy sauce, honey, ginger, garlic, garam masala, salt, and pepper, pour over the chicken, and mix until the chicken is fully coated. Cover with plastic wrap and marinate the chicken for at least 12 and up to 24 hours in the refrigerator.

In a large wok or karahi, heat the oils together over moderately high heat, and add the chicken and its marinade. Cover and cook for about 5 minutes to soften slightly. Uncover the wok, reduce the heat to moderate, add the cilantro, and continue to cook the chicken, turning occasionally, until it is tender and the gravy is thick and clings to the pieces almost like a glaze, 10 to 12 minutes.

Transfer to a serving dish, garnish with the toasted sesame seeds and cilantro, and serve.

Chili Chicken Thighs in a Wok

BRAISE THE CHICKEN IN a wok with stir-fried dried red chilies and ginger until all the liquids dry up and a shimmering glaze coats the chicken pieces. To avoid accidentally breaking the chilies during cooking, stir very carefully.

2 tablespoons peanut oil

1 teaspoon sesame oil

5 to 10 dried red chili peppers, to your taste (choose only unbroken whole chilies)

Two 1-inch pieces fresh ginger, peeled and cut into julienne strips

1 large onion, cut in half and thinly sliced

1 cup loosely packed finely chopped cilantro (fresh coriander) leaves, soft stems included

16 to 20 bone-in chicken thighs, skin removed (if desired, cut each piece in half widthwise)

¾ cup water

½ cup white vinegar

2 tablespoons soy sauce

½ teaspoon freshly ground black pepper, or to your taste

1 teaspoon salt, or to your taste

Toasted (page 34) almond slivers and sesame seeds and chopped cilantro leaves for garnish

Makes 8 servings

SERVING IDEAS:
Here is an entrée that can double as an appetizer. Serve over a cushion of shredded lettuce, with or without chutneys or sauces.

DO AHEAD:
Stays fresh in the refrigerator for 4 to 5 days.

In a large wok or karahi, heat the oils together over moderately high heat and stir-fry the chilies and ginger until the ginger turns golden, 2 to 4 minutes. (Stand away from the wok while you are doing this in case the chilies burst and accidentally fly toward your face.) Add the onion and continue to cook, stirring as necessary, until it turns medium to dark brown, 10 to 12 minutes. Mix in the cilantro, and add the chicken, water, vinegar, soy sauce, pepper, and salt. Bring to a boil over high heat, cover the wok, reduce the heat to moderate, and cook until the chicken is tender and all the liquid has evaporated, 20 to 25 minutes. (If the chicken is tender but there is still extra liquid in the wok, uncover the wok and cook over high heat until it dries up completely.)

Remove to a serving platter, garnish with toasted almond slivers and sesame seeds and chopped cilantro, and serve.

Garlic and Fenugreek-Scented Beef Curry

Makes 4 to 6 servings

SERVING IDEAS:
Great hot with paranthas or naans and a dry-cooked vegetable side dish. Or place atop Simply Cumin Basmati (page 270) and serve with a yogurt raita.

DO AHEAD:
Can be made 2 to 3 days in advance and stored in the refrigerator. Reheat with additional water.

VARIATION:
Swap the fenugreek leaves with 1 or 2 tablespoons of mixed Italian herbs and serve it over cooked pasta.

THIS BEEF CURRY HAS been spiced up with ginger, garlic, and fenugreek leaves.

3 tablespoons safflower or peanut oil
1 tablespoon minced garlic
1 tablespoon peeled and minced fresh ginger
3 bay leaves, crumbled
2 pounds boneless beef (top sirloin or any other tender cut), fat removed and cut into 1-inch cubes
1 teaspoon chopped fresh rosemary leaves or ½ teaspoon dried
½ teaspoon ground turmeric
1 teaspoon salt, or to your taste
½ teaspoon freshly ground black pepper, or to your taste
1 tablespoon ground coriander
1 teaspoon ground cumin
¼ cup ground dried fenugreek leaves
2 cups coarsely chopped vine-ripened tomatoes (about 2 large tomatoes)
½ cup nonfat plain yogurt, whisked until smooth
½ cup firmly packed finely chopped cilantro (fresh coriander) leaves, soft stems included
½ cup water
1 cup finely sliced scallion greens and garam masala for garnish

In a large, nonstick wok, heat 2 tablespoons of the oil over moderately high heat and stir-fry the garlic, ginger, and bay leaves for a few seconds to release flavors. Add the beef cubes, rosemary, turmeric, salt, and pepper and cook, stirring, until the beef is golden on all sides, 8 to 10 minutes. Remove to a bowl.

Heat the remaining tablespoon oil in the same wok over moderately high heat and cook the coriander, cumin and fenugreek, stirring for about 1 minute. Add the tomatoes, yogurt, and cilantro and cook, stirring, for 2 to 3 minutes. Mix in the beef and water, cover, and bring to a boil over high heat. Reduce the heat to moderately low and simmer until the beef is fork-tender and the gravy is thick, 15 to 30 minutes. (Add additional ¼ to ½ cup water if you prefer a thinner sauce.) Transfer to a serving dish, garnish, and serve hot.

Beef and Garbanzo Bean Chili

ALTHOUGH THIS DISH IS not stir-fried, it is prepared in a wok, so I have included it here. In India, this dish is made with ground mutton (goat meat) and fresh peas. I make it here with extra-lean ground beef and canned garbanzo beans.

1 tablespoon extra-virgin olive oil
1 tablespoon peeled and minced fresh ginger
2 teaspoons minced garlic
1 to 3 serrano peppers, to your taste, finely chopped
1 tablespoon ground coriander
1 teaspoon ground cumin
1 teaspoon dried fenugreek leaves
1 teaspoon dried rosemary
½ teaspoon salt, or to your taste
1 pound extra-lean ground beef
1 cup finely chopped vine-ripened tomatoes (about 1 large tomato)
One 15-ounce can garbanzo beans, drained and rinsed
1 cup nonfat plain yogurt, whisked until smooth
1 cup loosely packed finely chopped cilantro (fresh coriander) leaves, soft stems included
½ teaspoon garam masala
Garam masala and chopped cilantro leaves for garnish

Makes 4 to 6 servings

SERVING IDEAS:
Great as an entrée with steamed rice or chapatis. Or serve atop cooked pasta or pizza instead of meat sauce.

DO AHEAD:
Can be made a couple of days in advance and refrigerated.

In a large wok or karahi, heat the oil over moderately high heat and stir-fry the ginger and garlic until golden, 1 to 2 minutes. Add the peppers, coriander, cumin, fenugreek leaves, rosemary, and salt, and mix in the ground beef. Cook, stirring and breaking any lumps that might form, until the meat is golden and completely dry, 5 to 7 minutes. (Lower the heat somewhat if the meat sticks to the wok.)

Add the tomatoes and cook until the tomatoes become saucy, 2 to 4 minutes, then mix in the garbanzo beans. Cook, stirring, until the garbanzo beans are slightly softened, another 2 to 4 minutes, then mix in the yogurt, cilantro, and garam masala. Cook, stirring occasionally, until the yogurt is completely absorbed into the dish and the garbanzo beans become very soft, 8 to 10 minutes.

Transfer to a serving bowl, garnish with garam masala and cilantro, and serve hot.

Garlicky Karahi Shrimp with Thyme

Makes 6 to 8 servings

SERVING IDEAS:

Pile the shrimp on a fluffy pillow of Steamed Basmati Rice (page 269), cooked penne, or pizza. Or partner it with freshly made Indian flat breads or warmed sourdough rolls or baguettes.

DO AHEAD:

Marinate the shrimp and cook the sauce up to 4 hours ahead. Finish cooking closer to serving because the shrimp will toughen if reheated.

IN THIS RECIPE, AUTHENTIC karahi cooking is given a slight twist. Here we marinate and stir-fry the shrimp separately, and then combine it with the familiar tomato-based karahi sauce. Also, the familiar carom seeds are substituted with fresh thyme leaves. (Carom seeds and thyme leaves both contain thymol oil and add a somewhat similar flavor to the dish.)

1 pound extra-large shrimp (35 to 40 shrimp), peeled and deveined
3 tablespoons peanut oil
2 tablespoons fresh lemon or lime juice
2 teaspoons minced garlic
1½ teaspoons fresh thyme leaves or ½ teaspoon dried
1 teaspoon paprika
1 teaspoon salt, or to your taste
1 medium-size onion, cut in half lengthwise and thinly sliced
One 1-inch piece fresh ginger, peeled and cut into 1-inch-long julienne strips
1 tablespoon ground coriander
1 teaspoon dried fenugreek leaves
Freshly ground black pepper to taste
3 cups coarsely chopped vine-ripened tomatoes (about 3 large tomatoes)
1 cup loosely packed finely chopped cilantro (fresh coriander) leaves, soft stems included
2 Anaheim peppers, cut into ¼-inch rounds and garam masala for garnish
A few cilantro leaves for garnish

Put the shrimp in a large bowl. Combine 1 tablespoon of the oil, the lemon juice, garlic, thyme, paprika, and ½ teaspoon of the salt. Add to the bowl and toss together until the shrimp are fully coated with the mixture. Cover with plastic wrap and let marinate in the refrigerator for at least 1 and up to 4 hours.

In a large wok or karahi, heat the remaining 2 tablespoons oil over moderately high heat and cook the onion and ginger, stirring, until golden, 4 to 5 minutes. Mix in the coriander, fenugreek leaves, the remaining ½ teaspoon salt, and the pepper. Add the tomatoes and cilantro and cook, stirring, until a thick sauce forms, 7 to 10 minutes. Remove to a bowl.

To the same wok (do not clean it), add the shrimp and their marinade and cook over moderately high heat, stirring occasionally, until all the liquid evaporates and the shrimp are cooked through, 3 to 5 minutes. Remove to the bowl with the sauce.

Add the pepper rounds to the same wok and cook over moderate heat, stirring occasionally, until crisp-tender, 2 to 3 minutes. Remove to a separate bowl and reserve for garnish.

Return the shrimp and tomato sauce to the wok. Cook, stirring gently, over moderate heat, for another 3 to 4 minutes to blend the flavors. Transfer to a serving dish, garnish with the reserved pepper rounds, garam masala, and cilantro, and serve.

Scrambled Tofu with Shiitake Mushrooms and Peas

THIS JUMBLE OF TOFU, tomatoes, and peas is based on a popular Indian dish called *paneer bhurji* (scrambled paneer cheese).

SERVING IDEAS:

Present as a side dish with a curry or lentil preparation or atop pizza, pasta, or toasted bread with a mango or peach yogurt shake.

DO AHEAD:

Stays fresh for 3 to 5 days in the refrigerator.

3 tablespoons canola oil

2 ounces dried shiitake mushrooms, soaked in hot water to cover for 30 minutes, drained, stemmed, and sliced

2 cups finely diced onions

1 tablespoon minced garlic

1 to 3 serrano peppers (optional), to your taste, minced

1 tablespoon ground coriander

1 teaspoon ground cumin

¼ teaspoon ground turmeric

1 teaspoon salt, or to your taste

3 cups finely diced vine-ripened tomatoes (about 3 large tomatoes)

1 cup loosely packed finely chopped cilantro (fresh coriander) leaves, soft stems included

1 pound firm or extra-firm tofu, pressed dry between paper towels and coarsely crumbled

1½ cups frozen peas, thawed and drained

1 tablespoon fresh lime or lemon juice

Chopped cilantro leaves and garam masala for garnish

In a large wok or karahi, over moderately high heat and stir-fry the shiitake mushrooms for 1 to 2 minutes to dry out the moisture. Remove to a bowl and set aside.

Add the remaining 2½ tablespoons oil to the same karahi and cook the onions, stirring, over moderate heat until golden, 7 to 10 minutes. Add the garlic and peppers and stir until the garlic is golden, about 1 minute. Mix in the coriander, cumin, turmeric, and salt. Add the tomatoes and cilantro, raise the heat to high, and cook, stirring, until most of the liquid evaporates, 5 to 7 minutes.

Mix in the tofu and cook, stirring very gently, until most of the liquid dries up. Add the peas and lime juice and cook until the dish is completely dry, 3 to 5 minutes.

Transfer to a serving dish, mix in the reserved shiitake mushrooms, garnish with cilantro and garam masala, and serve.

Stir-fried Vegetables with Fresh Green Garlic

THIS CHINESE-STYLE STIR-FRIED vegetable dish is enhanced with the delicate flavor of fresh green garlic (young garlic, which looks like green onion and available in Asian, Middle Eastern, and farmers' markets) and a sprinkling of garam masala. (If necessary, substitute the green garlic with 1 clove garlic and 2 to 4 scallion whites or 1 leek white.) For the snow peas, select tender baby pods not more than 2 inches long.

Makes 6 to 8 servings

SERVING IDEAS:
This pairs equally well with steamed or stir-fried sticky rice and basmati rice.

DO AHEAD:
Cut the vegetables and make the cornstarch mixture up to 4 hours in advance. Prepare the dish closer to serving time.

1 teaspoon cornstarch
¼ cup water
2 tablespoons soy sauce
1 tablespoon rice vinegar
2 tablespoons peanut oil
2 teaspoons sesame oil
2 to 4 green garlic stalks, to your taste, minced
1 tablespoon peeled and minced fresh ginger
1 medium head broccoli, cut into 1-inch florets
8 to 10 baby zucchini (green, yellow, and light green), sliced diagonally
1 large red bell pepper, seeded and cut into 1-inch squares
20 to 25 Chinese snow peas
1 cup loosely packed finely chopped cilantro (fresh coriander) leaves, soft stems included
½ teaspoon cayenne pepper or paprika and garam masala for garnish

Mix together the cornstarch, water, soy sauce, and rice vinegar. Set aside. (Mix again with a spoon prior to using, because the cornstarch will settle to the bottom.)

In a large wok or karahi, heat the oils together over moderately high heat and stir-fry the garlic and ginger until golden, 2 to 3 minutes. Add the broccoli and zucchini and stir-fry until they soften slightly, 3 to 4 minutes. Then mix in the bell pepper, pea pods, and cilantro and cook until all the vegetables are crisp-tender, 2 to 4 minutes. Add the cornstarch mixture and stir for about 30 seconds. This will give the vegetables a lovely glaze. There should be no sauce in this dish.

Transfer to a platter, garnish with the cayenne pepper and garam masala, and serve.

Baby Squash Medley

SERVING IDEAS:
  Incredible with grilled and barbecued meats, poultry, and seafood, and Indian curries and breads.

DO AHEAD:
  This dish is best when served fresh.

MADE WITH AN ARRAY of different squash, this side dish is flavored with an innovative blending of Indian and Italian seasonings and finely diced turnips.

2 tablespoons vegetable oil
1 large onion, cut in half lengthwise and thinly sliced
1 teaspoon minced garlic
1 tablespoon mixed dried Italian herbs
2 teaspoons ground coriander
¾ teaspoon salt, or to your taste
½ teaspoon freshly ground black pepper to taste
1 small turnip, peeled and finely diced
2 pounds mixed baby squash: zucchini (yellow, white, and green) and pattypan
    squash (pale green, dark green, and yellow), cut into ¾-inch-thick rounds or cubes
1 to 2 tablespoons fresh lemon or lime juice, to your taste
Chopped cilantro (fresh coriander) leaves for garnish

In a large wok or karahi, heat the oil over moderately high heat and cook the onion, stirring, until golden in color, 5 to 7 minutes. Add the garlic, herbs, coriander, salt, pepper, turnip, and squash. Reduce the heat to moderate, cover the wok, and cook, stirring occasionally and very carefully, until the vegetables are crisp-tender, 10 to 15 minutes. Add the lemon juice.

Transfer to a serving dish, garnish with cilantro, and serve.

Karahi Mushrooms and Peas

IN THIS RECIPE, I have deviated from the popular Indian herbs and spices and added Western herbs to give a traditional dish a new identity.

This dish calls for pasilla chilies, a Mexican specialty that can be quite hot; you can use green bell peppers instead, if you wish.

I like to cook the mushrooms separately, in a different pan, before combining them with the other ingredients for two reasons: They make the dish very watery as they release their juices and, as they dry, a thin, brown film coats the bottom of the pan. This film burns as soon as the oil is heated to cook the onions.

2 pounds small mushrooms, rinsed, trimmed, and left whole
2 tablespoons extra-virgin olive oil
1 medium-size onion, cut in half lengthwise and thinly sliced
1 tablespoon peeled and minced fresh ginger
1 teaspoon minced garlic
3 cups coarsely chopped vine-ripened tomatoes (about 3 large tomatoes)
1 tablespoon ground coriander
½ cup firmly packed finely chopped fresh basil leaves
1 teaspoon fresh thyme leaves
1 teaspoon chopped fresh marjoram leaves
1 to 2 pasilla peppers, to your taste, cut into 1-inch pieces
One 1-pound package frozen peas, thawed and drained

Put the mushrooms in a large, nonstick skillet (with no oil) and cook, stirring occasionally, over moderate heat until they release all their juices, 3 to 5 minutes. Increase the heat to high and cook until all the juices evaporate and the mushrooms turn golden, 5 to 7 minutes. Set aside.

In a large wok or karahi, heat the oil over moderately high heat and cook the onion, stirring, until golden, 5 to 7 minutes. Add the ginger and garlic and cook, stirring, for another minute. Mix in the tomatoes and cook, stirring occasionally, until a thick sauce forms, 7 to 10 minutes.

Add the coriander, basil, thyme, and marjoram, and mix in the peppers and peas. Cook, stirring, for 2 to 4 minutes, then add the reserved mushrooms. Cook for another 3 to 5 minutes to blend the flavors. Transfer to a serving dish and serve.

Makes 6 to 8 servings

SERVING IDEAS:
Superb as a side dish and great over cooked pasta, as a pizza topping, and in hot and cold sandwiches with some of the perky Green Cilantro Chutney (page 257).

DO AHEAD:
Best when served fresh, but may be made up to 2 hours ahead of time—it will get watery with the passage of time.

Blue Lake Green Beans in a Wok

Perfect dry-cooked vegetable side dish to pair with curries.

Best served fresh, though it can be made a few hours ahead of time and reheated.

THESE 4-TO 5-inch-long and round, deep-green stringless beans are a treat eaten raw or when lightly cooked. This authentic Punjabi version is made by my mother-in-law. She uses the regular green beans instead of this special variety, which is not available in India.

2 tablespoons peanut oil
1 tablespoon peeled and minced fresh ginger
1 teaspoon cumin seeds
1 tablespoon ground coriander
½ teaspoon ground turmeric
¼ teaspoon ground red or cayenne pepper
1 large vine-ripened tomato, finely chopped
1 large red potato, unpeeled and cut into ½-inch cubes
1½ pounds Blue Lake beans, trimmed and cut diagonally into ¼-inch dice
½ teaspoon mango powder
½ teaspoon garam masala

In a large wok or karahi, heat the oil over moderate heat and cook the ginger, stirring, until golden, about 1 minute. Stir in the cumin seeds (they will sizzle upon contact with the hot oil), coriander, turmeric, and ground red pepper, and add the tomato. Cook, stirring, for 1 minute, then add the potato. Cover the pan and cook, stirring occasionally, until the potatoes are slightly soft, 6 to 8 minutes. Add the beans, reduce the heat to low, cover the wok, and cook, stirring as necessary, until the potatoes are soft, 12 to 15 minutes. Stir in the mango powder and garam masala, transfer to a serving platter, and serve.

Japanese Eggplants with Baby Russet Potatoes

IF BABY RUSSET POTATOES are not available, cut larger ones into ¾-inch cubes. To add a "meaty" character to this dish, do not discard the eggplant caps; instead, cook them with the rest of the eggplant and the potatoes.

For an authentic Indian flavor, make this dish in a cast-iron karahi with ghee (page 19) or mustard oil. (To use mustard oil, first heat it until smoking, remove from the heat and let it cool a bit, then proceed with the recipe.)

2 tablespoons extra-virgin olive oil
4 large cloves garlic, cut into thin slivers
1 tablespoon ground coriander
1 teaspoon ground cumin
½ teaspoon ground turmeric
1 teaspoon salt, or to your taste
1½ pounds Japanese eggplants, cut into ½-inch-thick rounds or cubed (do not peel)
1 pound baby russet potatoes, unpeeled and halved or quartered lengthwise
1 cup coarsely chopped vine-ripened tomatoes (about 1 large tomato)
1 cup loosely packed, finely chopped cilantro (fresh coriander) leaves, soft stems included
Garam masala and ½ teaspoon mango powder for garnish

In a large wok or karahi, heat the oil over moderately high heat and stir-fry the garlic until golden, 30 to 60 seconds. Stir in the coriander, cumin, turmeric, and salt, and add the eggplants and potatoes. Cook, stirring gently, until the vegetables are well covered with the spices, 3 to 4 minutes.

Add the tomatoes, cover the wok, reduce the heat to low and cook until the potatoes are soft, 25 to 30 minutes. Stir occasionally, taking care to not break the potatoes. Add the cilantro and cook until it is wilted but still green, another 1 to 2 minutes.

Transfer to a serving dish, garnish with the garam masala and mango powder, and serve.

Makes 6 to 8 servings

SERVING IDEAS:

I love this dish rolled in fresh-off-the-stove chapatis brushed generously with sweet butter. It is a great side dish to serve with curries and stews.

DO AHEAD:

Can be made a few hours ahead of time and reheated just prior to serving. Leftovers stay fresh 3 to 5 days in the refrigerator.

Savory Stir-fried Cumin Potatoes

Makes 6 to 8 servings

SERVING IDEAS:

Present rolled in freshly made parantha breads with a yogurt raita and a glass of fresh orange juice or lemonade. Or pair with grilled hamburgers, chicken, or steak.

DO AHEAD:

Best when served fresh. Leftovers will keep, refrigerated, for 3 to 5 days.

BREAKFAST, LUNCH, OR DINNER, this home-style cooking technique produces one of the best potato dishes I've ever eaten. My mother turned to this quick and easy dish whenever she was in a hurry. And to further speed up matters, she boiled her potatoes in a pressure cooker.

To make it look more elaborate, Mama often added diced bell peppers, fresh peas, or soft-cooked diced tomatoes and showcased it alongside an array curries.

3 tablespoons canola oil or clarified butter (page 19)

2 teaspoons cumin seeds

1 to 3 serrano peppers (optional), to your taste, minced

1 tablespoon ground coriander

1 teaspoon ground cumin

½ teaspoon paprika

½ teaspoon mango powder

1 teaspoon salt, or to your taste

7 to 8 large russet potatoes (about 3 pounds), boiled in lightly salted water to cover until tender, peeled, drained, and cut into ½- or ¾-inch cubes

1 cup loosely packed, finely chopped cilantro (fresh coriander) leaves, soft stems included

Freshly ground black pepper, garam masala, or seeded and finely diced red or purple bell peppers for garnish

In a large wok or karahi heat the oil over moderately high heat and add the cumin seeds (they should sizzle upon contact with the hot oil) and peppers. Add the coriander, cumin, paprika, mango powder, and salt. Mix in the potatoes and cilantro, reduce the heat to moderately low, and cook, turning occasionally with a spatula, until the potatoes are slightly crusty, 5 to 7 minutes. (If the masala (spices) sticks to the bottom, cover the pan and set it aside for a short while. The steam from the hot potatoes will soften the masala, which, in my opinion, is really the best part of the dish.) Transfer to a serving dish, garnish with black pepper and diced red bell pepper, and serve.

Cooking Under Pressure

A SUDDEN LOUD WHISTLING sound and the rocking of the pressure regulator sends my mother rushing to the kitchen. She summons the family to the table. *"Sab Aa Jao, khaana tayyar hai,"* she says (Come everybody, the food is ready), and while the family leisurely finds its way to the table, the food is already there, spreading a mesmerizing aroma throughout the house. It all happens so quickly (her kitchen secret—cooking simultaneously in two or more pressure cookers). And an added plus is that the food comes to the table with most of its nutrients preserved.

Here's how this happens: As the food heats up, the tightly sealed lid of the pressure cooker prevents the steam from escaping into the air. The retention of this steam builds the pressure inside the cooker pot to fifteen pounds per square inch. (Some of the larger canning pressure cookers allow less pressure buildup—five and ten pounds per square inch.) This pressure raises the internal temperature of the pot, and the high temperature in turn cooks the food in the shortest time possible.

After the cooker is removed from the heat, the nutrient-rich steam condenses inside the pot, conserving all the nutrients in the cooked foods. In the normal course of pan cooking, these nutrients evaporate into the air. Just remember that for maximum nutrient retention, the steam should be given time to condense. If you release the lid too soon, some of the nutrients will be lost to the air.

Today's state-of-the-art pressure cookers are safe and easy to use and accidental kitchen disasters are really a thing of the past. (But just in case something seems amiss, remove the cooker from the heat and place it under running water. This immediately condenses the steam, releases the pressure, and stops further cooking.)

So go ahead, set aside your fears, and plan your next week's menu around this super-powerful gadget. Make soups, stews, curries, dried beans and lentils, vegetables, rice, and even some desserts (page 29) while you find other things to do with your free time.

All these recipes can also be made without the pressure cooker. They will just take a little more cooking liquid and a lot more time.

A "Curried" Beef Stew

To serve as a stew, pair with a tossed green salad and hot garlic bread. To present as a curry, serve it as the Indians would—with parantha or chapati breads, steamed basmati rice, yogurt raita, and a side of dry-cooked vegetables.

DO AHEAD:
Can be made up to 2 days in advance and refrigerated. It will thicken as it cools, so additional water (or broth) may be required when reheating.

NOTES:
You may have to brown the beef pieces in several batches. Add it in a single layer and turn as necessary.
If a thinner stew is desired, add more water and bring to a boil.

DO WE SMELL "CURRY" in this stew? If "curry" means Indian seasonings, yes, of course, we do.

1½ cups nonfat plain yogurt
4 cups water, beef, or chicken broth
3 tablespoons extra-virgin olive oil
2 pounds boneless stewing beef or top sirloin steaks, all fat removed and cut into 1½-inch pieces
1 tablespoon minced garlic
1 tablespoon peeled and minced fresh ginger
½ cup firmly packed minced fresh lemon basil leaves (or any other basil variety)
4 bay leaves
2 teaspoons dried thyme leaves
1 tablespoon ground coriander
1 teaspoon garam masala
¾ teaspoon salt, or to your taste
1 large russet potato, peeled and cut into 1-inch cubes
8 to 10 pearl onions, peeled, or 1 large onion, peeled and cut into 1-inch cubes
2 to 3 medium carrots cut into 1-inch pieces
2 medium parsnips, peeled and cut into 1-inch pieces
1 stalk celery, cut into ½-inch-long pieces
1 teaspoon dried fenugreek leaves
Chopped cilantro (fresh coriander) leaves and garam masala for garnish

Blend the yogurt and water until smooth; set aside. In a pressure cooker, heat the oil over moderately high heat. Add the beef, cook until brown on all sides, and remove to a bowl.

Add the garlic, ginger, basil, bay leaves, thyme, coriander, garam masala, and salt to the cooker and cook, stirring, for about 1 minute. Return the beef to the cooker and cook, stirring, over moderate heat for 3 to 5 minutes to thoroughly coat with the seasonings. Add the yogurt-and-water mixture. Secure the lid of the pressure cooker and cook over high heat for 3 minutes after the pressure regulator starts rocking. Remove from the heat and let the pressure drop by itself, 15 to 20 minutes.

Open the cover and add the potatoes, onions, carrots, parsnips, and celery. Secure the lid and cook over high heat for 1 minute after the pressure regulator starts rocking. Let the pressure drop by itself again, about 10 minutes. Open the cooker, add the dried fenugreek leaves and stir. Transfer to a serving bowl, garnish, and serve.

Minced Meat with Potato Wedges

THIS FRAGRANT ENTRÉE, MADE with ground meat and yogurt, has a creamy consistency and could be a chili with potatoes. My mother always made this dish with ground goat meat.

3 tablespoons vegetable oil

1 cup finely chopped onion

2 tablespoons peeled and minced fresh ginger

2 teaspoons minced garlic

2 cups finely chopped vine-ripened tomatoes (about 2 large tomatoes)

1 cup firmly packed finely chopped cilantro (fresh coriander) leaves, soft stems included

4 to 6 serrano peppers (optional), to your taste, skins punctured to prevent them from bursting

1 tablespoon ground coriander

2 teaspoons ground cumin

2 teaspoons dried fenugreek leaves

1 teaspoon garam masala

½ teaspoon ground turmeric

1 teaspoon salt, or to your taste

2 pounds extra-lean ground beef or lamb

3 small potatoes, peeled and each cut into 6 to 8 wedges

1½ cups nonfat plain yogurt, whisked until smooth

Garam masala and chopped cilantro leaves for garnish

In a pressure cooker, heat the oil over moderately high heat and cook the onions, stirring, until they are brown, 6 to 8 minutes. Mix in the ginger and garlic, and add the tomatoes, cilantro, and peppers and continue to cook, stirring as necessary, until all the juices from the tomatoes evaporate, 5 to 7 minutes. Add the coriander, cumin, fenugreek leaves, garam masala, turmeric, and salt, and mix in the ground meat and potatoes. Cook, stirring, over moderate heat until the meat turns brown, 5 to 7 minutes. Mix in the yogurt a little at a time while stirring constantly to prevent it from curdling. Secure the lid of the pressure cooker and cook over high heat until the pressure regulator starts rocking. Remove from the heat and let the pressure drop by itself, 10 to 12 minutes.

Open the cover and stir the contents. Transfer to a serving casserole, garnish with garam masala and cilantro, and serve.

Makes 8 servings

SERVING IDEAS:
Eat by the spoonful or with scoops of Indian breads or with tortillas, pitas, or focaccia, or serve over a bed of basmati rice. Dry out the sauce by cooking it a little longer, mash the potatoes, and serve rolled in Mexican tortillas with a handful of shredded lettuce, or, serve atop hamburgers and hot dogs. Try it as a pizza topping or pasta sauce.

DO AHEAD:
Can make 3 to 5 days in advance and refrigerate. Use it in one manner on the first day and another the next.

Spicy Meatballs in Caramelized Onion and Yogurt Sauce

Makes 6 to 8 servings

SERVING IDEAS:

This dish is great with Okra Bits with Potatoes and Tomatoes (page 138) or any other dry-cooked vegetable dish and Indian flat breads or a basmati rice pilaf. Serve over spaghetti, fettuccine, or steamed rice, or with warm bread rolls or biscuits.

DO AHEAD:

Freeze the uncooked meatballs in a single layer, then store in zipper bags for 2 to 3 months. They can go straight from the freezer to the pan. The dish can be cooked 3 to 5 days in advance and refrigerated.

STOVE-TOP VARIATION:

After adding the yogurt, cover the skillet and cook over high heat for the first 3 to 5 minutes, then over moderate heat until the meatballs are fork-tender and the sauce is very thick, another 10 to 15 minutes.

NO MATTER WHERE YOU live, meatballs spring up in some form or the other. Here Indian meatballs are simmered in a yogurt sauce.

2 pounds or more extra-lean ground beef or lamb
1 tablespoon minced fresh rosemary leaves or 1 teaspoon dried
1½ teaspoons salt, or to your taste
1 teaspoon freshly ground black pepper, or to your taste
2 tablespoons peanut oil
5 to 10 dried red chili peppers, to your taste
2 cups finely chopped onions
2 tablespoons peeled and minced fresh ginger
2 teaspoons minced garlic
1 cup loosely packed finely chopped cilantro (fresh coriander) leaves, soft stems included
1 teaspoon garam masala
2 cups nonfat plain yogurt, whisked until smooth
Tomato wedges and chopped cilantro leaves for garnish

In a large bowl, mix together the beef, rosemary, ½ teaspoon salt, and the pepper. Divide and shape the mixture into 35 to 40 one-inch balls. Set aside.

In a pressure cooker, heat the oil over moderately high heat and stir-fry the red chilies for 45 seconds. (Stand away from the skillet in case the chilies burst and accidentally fly toward your face.) Reduce the heat to moderate, add the onions, and cook, stirring occasionally, until they caramelize and turn dark brown, 10 to 12 minutes. Mix in the ginger, garlic, and cilantro, and add the meatballs and cook, stirring as necessary, until the meatballs are brown on all sides, 4 to 5 minutes. Stir in the garam masala and remaining 1 teaspoon salt, and add the yogurt a little at a time while stirring constantly to prevent it from curdling.

Secure the lid of the pressure cooker and cook over high heat for 1 minute after the pressure regulator starts rocking. Remove from the heat and let the pressure drop by itself, 10 to 12 minutes. Open the cover and stir the contents carefully. (Add more yogurt if you want a thinner sauce.)

Transfer to a serving dish, garnish with tomato wedges and cilantro, and serve.

Pastry-Topped Lamb Casserole

THIS PRESSURE-COOKED, THEN baked, boneless lamb casserole turns "gourmet" when we present it hiding under a sheet of golden puff pastry.

3 tablespoons peanut oil
2 teaspoons cumin seeds
2 cups finely chopped onions
4 serrano peppers, skins punctured to prevent them from bursting
2 tablespoons peeled and minced fresh ginger
2 teaspoons minced garlic
1 tablespoon ground coriander
1 teaspoon garam masala
½ teaspoon ground turmeric
½ teaspoon paprika
1 teaspoon salt, or to your taste
2½ pounds boneless leg of lamb, all fat removed and cut into 1-inch cubes
One 15-ounce can tomato sauce
2 cups nonfat plain yogurt, whisked until smooth
1 sheet from a 20-ounce package frozen puff pastry sheets, thawed for 20 minutes
1 large egg white beaten with 1 tablespoon water

Makes 8 servings

SERVING IDEAS:
Superb as a one-pot meal with a green salad or as part of a larger menu with dry-cooked vegetables, naans, and yogurt salads.

DO AHEAD:
Best when served within an hour of being made, while it is still hot. To make ahead of time, prepare the lamb up to 5 days ahead and refrigerate. Then reheat, transfer to a serving casserole, top with the puff pastry, and bake closer to serving time.

In a pressure cooker, heat the oil over moderately high heat and cook, stirring, the cumin seeds until they sizzle, 15 seconds. Add the onions and peppers and cook, stirring, until the onions turn golden, 5 to 7 minutes. Add the ginger, garlic, coriander, garam masala, turmeric, paprika, and salt, and mix in the lamb cubes. Reduce the heat to moderate and cook, stirring, until the lamb turns brown, 7 to 10 minutes. Add the tomato sauce and yogurt, stirring constantly to prevent the yogurt from curdling, and continue to cook for another 2 to 3 minutes.

Secure the lid of the pressure cooker and cook over high heat for 2 to 2½ minutes after the pressure regulator starts rocking. Remove from the heat and let the pressure drop by itself, 15 to 20 minutes. (The lamb should be tender; if not, then cook for another minute or two under pressure.) Open the cover, transfer to a large ovenproof casserole, and set aside.

Preheat the oven to 375°F. With a rolling pin, roll the pastry sheet out to about 2 inches larger than the top of the casserole. Cover the casserole with this sheet as you would with aluminum foil. Brush the top of the puff pastry with the egg white mixture, and prick with a fork all over to let the steam escape. Bake until the puff pastry turns golden, 20 to 25 minutes.

Remove from the oven and serve.

Embassy Chicken in Ginger-Cream Sauce

Makes 8 servings

SERVING IDEAS:

I once served this dish at a PTA luncheon (with more than a hundred parents) at my daughters' elementary school. Along with this were fresh lemonade, a side of cauliflower, bread rolls, and Punjabi Tapioca Pudding (page 292). At home, my daughters love it with naan or toasted sourdough bread slices.

DO AHEAD:

Can be made 2 to 8 hours in advance. Additional milk or broth will be needed when reheating, because the sauce thickens as it cools down.

The sauce and the chicken pieces can be prepared separately up to 5 days in advance and refrigerated. Do not mix until the day of serving. Bring the sauce to a boil (with additional milk or broth, if needed), then

EMBASSY, A POPULAR RESTAURANT in New Delhi, served a unique chicken dish that was a favorite in our family. I still remember those boneless chicken breasts, smothered in a lightly fragrant and smooth sauce, quickly disappearing as they were eaten with bite-size pieces of freshly made naan breads.

For the chicken:

8 to 10 boneless, skinless chicken breast halves (about 2½ pounds)

4 cups water

2 teaspoons minced garlic

1 tablespoon peeled and minced fresh ginger

1 tablespoon ground coriander

1 teaspoon ground cumin

1 teaspoon garam masala

¼ teaspoon freshly ground nutmeg

3 bay leaves

Salt and freshly ground black pepper to taste

For the ginger-cream sauce:

3 to 4 tablespoons safflower oil

2 tablespoons peeled and minced fresh ginger

1 small onion, finely chopped

¼ cup cornstarch

1 tablespoon ground coriander

1 teaspoon ground cumin

1 teaspoon paprika

½ teaspoon salt, or to your taste

3 cups reserved chicken broth

1 cup regular or low-fat milk

½ cup heavy cream or milk

A few tomato wedges and chopped cilantro (fresh coriander) leaves for garnish

Put all the ingredients for the chicken in a pressure cooker. Secure the lid of the pressure cooker and cook on high heat for 15 to 20 seconds after the pressure regulator starts rocking. Remove from the heat and let the pressure drop by itself, 10 to 12 minutes.

Open the cover, remove the chicken breasts from the broth, and set aside. (Cut the breasts into strips or pieces, if desired.) Pass the spicy broth through a sieve and reserve for making the sauce. There should be about 3 cups of broth.

To make the sauce, heat the oil in a large saucepan over moderate heat and cook the ginger and onion, stirring, until transparent, 3 to 5 minutes. Add the cornstarch and continue stirring until everything turns fragrant and golden, 5 to 7 minutes. Stir in the coriander, cumin, paprika, and salt, and mix in the reserved chicken broth and milk, stirring constantly to prevent the formation of lumps. (If the sauce seems too thin, dissolve 1 to 3 teaspoons additional cornstarch in another ½ cup of milk and add it to the sauce.)

When the sauce thickens (to a consistency like a thick custard), add the cream and simmer on moderately low heat until the oil separates to the sides, 25 to 30 minutes. Finally, mix in the cooked chicken pieces and simmer on moderately low heat for another 15 to 20 minutes to blend the flavors.

Transfer to a serving dish, garnish with tomato wedges and cilantro, and serve.

STOVE-TOP VARIATION: Boil the chicken ingredients together in a large pot until the chicken is tender, about 30 minutes.

mix in the the cooked chicken pieces and simmer on moderately low heat for another 15 to 20 minutes before serving.

Chicken Chili with Black Beans

Makes 8 servings

SERVING IDEAS:

Serve by itself by the bowlful or with hamburgers, tacos, and burritos. Also good over pizza and pasta. As an Indian main dish, pair with a side of vegetables, yogurt, and naan or parantha breads or a rice pilaf.

DO AHEAD:

Make up to 5 days in advance and refrigerate. If it seems too thick, reheat with additional yogurt or water.

THIS IS A CHILI with a difference. The meat is different and the beans are different, but it still is a chili made with the customary meat and bean combination. It cooks faster and is low in fat and cholesterol and high in taste and satisfaction.

For faster cooking, use canned black beans instead of dried.

1 cup dried black beans, picked over and rinsed

3 cups water

1 teaspoon salt, or to your taste

2 tablespoons extra-virgin olive oil

1 cup finely chopped onions

2 to 4 serrano peppers (optional), to your taste, chopped or left whole with the skins punctured to prevent them from bursting

1 tablespoon minced garlic

1 tablespoon peeled and minced fresh ginger

1 tablespoon ground coriander

1 teaspoon ground cumin

1 teaspoon paprika

1 teaspoon garam masala

¼ teaspoon ground turmeric

1½ pounds ground chicken breasts

One 15-ounce can tomato sauce

1 cup nonfat plain yogurt, whisked until smooth

1 teaspoon dried fenugreek leaves or oregano

½ cup firmly packed finely chopped cilantro (fresh coriander) leaves, soft stems included

Chopped cilantro and freshly ground black pepper for garnish

Put the black beans in a pressure cooker with the water and ½ teaspoon of the salt and boil, uncovered, over high heat for 1 to 2 minutes. Turn off the heat, cover the pressure cooker, and set aside for 1 to 2 hours. (You may stir once or twice.) Secure the lid of the cooker and cook over high heat for 2 minutes after the pressure regulator starts rocking. Remove the cooker from the heat and let the pressure drop by itself, 15 to 20 minutes. Open the cover and check the beans—they should be soft and creamy. (If not, then secure the lid and cook for another minute under pressure.)

In a medium, nonstick saucepan, heat the oil over moderately high heat and cook the onions, stirring, until brown, 5 to 7 minutes. Add the peppers, garlic, and ginger, and mix in the coriander, cumin, paprika, garam masala, turmeric, and the remaining ½ teaspoon salt.

Add the chicken and cook, stirring, until golden, 5 to 7 minutes on moderate heat. Break apart any lumps that form as the chicken firms up. Transfer to the pressure cooker and mix in the tomato sauce, yogurt, fenugreek leaves, and cilantro.

Secure the lid of the pressure cooker and cook for 1 minute after the pressure regulator starts rocking. Remove the cooker from the heat and let the pressure drop by itself, 10 to 12 minutes.

Open the cover and stir the contents. If the chili seems too dry, add some more water and boil again; if it has too much liquid, cook, uncovered, over moderate heat until it reaches the desired consistency. Transfer to a serving bowl, garnish with cilantro and pepper, and serve.

Pressured Risotto with Chipotle Peppers

SERVING IDEAS:

Present by itself with a hot soup and green salad, or as part of an Indian menu with a curry, vegetables, and yogurt raita.

DO AHEAD:

Can be made 3 to 5 days in advance and refrigerated. Remember, the risotto will thicken as it cools, so add more broth, water, or yogurt when reheating.

TO ME, RISOTTO IS an Italian *khitchere*, which in India is a soft and creamy dish made with basmati rice and lentils or vegetables. Risotto, on the other hand, is made with an Italian rice called Arborio, a starchy, short, round-grain rice that absorbs up to five times its weight in liquid and takes a long time to cook.

Authentic risotto is made by adding half a cup of liquid at a time and constantly stirring the rice until it is thick and creamy. When cooked in a pressure cooker, all the ingredients are added at the same time and cook for about 4 minutes after the pressure regulator starts rocking. Making risotto has never been easier.

Remove the chipotle peppers before stirring the cooked rice or they may break and make the risotto hot.

1 tablespoon extra-virgin olive oil
1 teaspoon cumin seeds
2 dried chipotle peppers
½ cup finely chopped whites from fresh green garlic or thoroughly washed leek whites plus 1 clove garlic
1½ cups Arborio rice
5 cups or more chicken broth (homemade, page 16, or canned; skim off fat)
½ teaspoon salt
½ cup nonfat plain yogurt, or more to taste, whisked until smooth
3 tablespoons minced fresh Italian parsley or cilantro (fresh coriander) leaves
2 tablespoons freshly grated Parmesan cheese
Garam masala for garnish

In a pressure cooker, heat the oil over moderately high heat and add the cumin seeds; they should sizzle upon contact. Immediately add the peppers and garlic whites and cook, stirring, until they are just golden, 2 to 3 minutes. Add the rice and cook, stirring, for 3 to 4 minutes, and mix in the chicken broth and salt.

Secure the lid of the cooker and cook over high heat for 4 minutes after the pressure regulator starts rocking. Remove from the heat and let the pressure drop by itself, 15 to 20 minutes. Open the cover and stir the risotto vigorously for 30 to 60 seconds. (The rice should be soft and creamy; if it is not, then add some more broth and cook for another minute or two, stirring, over high heat.) Stir in the yogurt, parsley, and Parmesan cheese.

Transfer to a serving casserole, garnish, and serve immediately.

Basmati "Risotto" with Wild Mushrooms

THE NATURAL FRAGRANCE OF basmati rice infuses every bite of this Indian "risotto."

1½ cups basmati rice, picked over
1 tablespoon extra-virgin olive oil
One 2-inch stick cinnamon
2 bay leaves
1 tablespoon peeled and minced fresh ginger
1 teaspoon minced garlic
1 cup diced wild mushrooms (morels, shiitakes, and/or chanterelles), fresh or
    reconstituted dried
3 cups water
1 teaspoon salt, or to your taste
½ cup firmly packed finely chopped cilantro (fresh coriander) leaves, soft stems
    included
Garam masala for garnish

Wash the rice in 3 to 4 changes of water, stirring lightly with your finger-tips, until the water runs almost clear. Set aside.

In a pressure cooker, heat the oil over moderately high heat and stir-fry the cinnamon and bay leaves for about 1 minute. Add the ginger and garlic and stir-fry until golden, 30 to 60 seconds. Add the mushrooms and rice and cook, stirring gently, until the moisture evaporates and the rice turns golden, 3 to 4 minutes.

Add the water and salt. Secure the lid of the pressure cooker and cook over high heat for 1 minute after the pressure regulator starts rocking. Remove from the heat and let the pressure drop by itself, 10 to 12 minutes. Open the cover, add the cilantro, and stir vigorously to break all the rice grains and make it creamy. Transfer to a serving casserole, garnish with the garam masala, and serve hot.

Makes 4 to 6 servings

SERVING IDEAS:
Though authentically served with lime or mango pickle and fresh homemade yogurt, I like it surrounded with a ring of sautéed or grilled vegetables or seafood and a simple yogurt raita salad.

DO AHEAD:
Make up to 5 days in advance and refrigerate. Reheat with additional water and top with a dollop of butter and a sprinkle of garam masala before serving; this gives a fresh-off-the-stove look and flavor.

Opo Squash with Tomatoes

Makes 6 to 8 servings

SERVING IDEAS:

Delicious with all sorts of dal and dried bean preparations. It also teams well with dry-cooked meat and vegetable dishes because it has a thin sauce.

DO AHEAD:

Like any other fresh vegetable dish, this is best when served immediately. However, it will keep for 3 to 5 days in the refrigerator.

STOVE-TOP VARIATION:

Add an extra 1/2 cup chopped tomatoes, cover, and cook over high heat in a skillet for 2 to 3 minutes, then over moderately low heat until the squash is tender, 25 to 30 minutes.

ALSO KNOWN AS MARROW, *louki,* or *ghia,* opo squash is a very popular summer vegetable in India. Though it is customarily presented as a simple side dish, it can be combined with other vegetables and transformed into elaborate entrées.

This fast and easy side dish can also be made with other types of summer squash, but cooking time will vary. The opo squash is probably the hardest variety of summer squash and thus requires a longer cooking.

3 tablespoons canola oil
1 large onion, cut in half lengthwise and thinly sliced
1½ pounds opo squash, peeled and cut into ¾-inch-long cubes
2 cups finely chopped vine-ripened tomatoes (about 2 large tomatoes)
½ teaspoon ground turmeric
2 teaspoons ground coriander
½ teaspoon salt, or to your taste
½ cup loosely packed finely chopped cilantro (fresh coriander) leaves, soft stems included
½ teaspoon freshly ground black pepper

In a pressure cooker, heat the oil over moderately high heat and cook the onion, stirring, until it starts to turn golden, 5 to 7 minutes. Stir in the squash, tomatoes, turmeric, coriander, and salt. Secure the lid of the pressure cooker and cook over high heat until the pressure regulator starts rocking. Remove from the heat and let the pressure drop by itself, 10 to 15 minutes.

Open the cover and stir in the cilantro. Transfer to a serving dish, garnish with the black pepper, and serve.

Curried Russet Potatoes with Fresh Peas

CALL IT *ALOO MATTAR* or *mattar aloo* in Hindi, this modest curry is a cinch to prepare after the first time around. Once you make this dish, you can make curries with all types of vegetables and meats because this recipe shows the basic curry-making procedure.

One 1½-inch piece fresh ginger, peeled and cut into thin slices
2 large cloves garlic, peeled
1 small onion, peeled and cut into 6 to 8 wedges
1 to 5 serrano peppers, to your taste, stems removed
½ cup firmly packed cilantro (fresh coriander) leaves, soft stems included
2 large, vine-ripened tomatoes, each cut into 8 wedges
3 tablespoons peanut oil
¼ cup nonfat plain yogurt, whisked until smooth
2 tablespoons ground coriander
2 teaspoons ground cumin
1 teaspoon dried fenugreek leaves
½ teaspoon paprika
½ teaspoon ground turmeric
1 teaspoon salt, or to your taste
2 large russet potatoes, peeled and cut into ¾-inch cubes
2½ cups shelled peas, preferably fresh (about 1½ pounds in pods)
3 cups water, or more as needed
Garam masala and finely chopped cilantro leaves for garnish

In the work bowl of a food processor fitted with the metal S-blade and the motor running, process the ginger, garlic, and onion until smooth by adding it through the feed tube. Remove to a bowl. Add the peppers, tomatoes, and cilantro to the food processor and process until smooth. Remove to another bowl and set aside.

In a pressure cooker, heat the oil over moderately high heat and add the onion mixture. (It may splatter from the onion juices, so be careful.) Cook, stirring, for 2 to 3 minutes, then reduce the heat to moderate and continue to cook, stirring until the onion mixture turns brown, 5 to 7 minutes. Add the tomato

SERVING IDEAS:
This everyday entrée can be served with any dry-cooked vegetable, yogurt raita, and Indian bread or rice.

DO AHEAD:
Can be made up to 5 days in advance and refrigerated. For a freshly cooked presentation, heat 1 tablespoon oil in a small saucepan, add ½ teaspoon cumin seeds and ¼ teaspoon paprika, stir briefly, and add it to the heated dish.

mixture, increase the heat to high and cook, stirring, until all the liquid from the tomatoes evaporates, 5 to 7 minutes. Mix in the yogurt in a thin stream, stirring constantly to prevent it from curdling. Add the coriander, cumin, fenugreek leaves, paprika, turmeric, and salt, then mix in the potatoes, peas, and water.

Secure the lid of the pressure cooker and cook over high heat for 1 minute after the pressure regulator starts rocking. Remove from the heat and let the pressure drop by itself, 15 to 20 minutes. Open the pressure cooker, stir the contents, and mash a few potatoes to thicken the gravy. (Add more water if you desire a thinner gravy.)

Transfer to a serving bowl, garnish with the garam masala and cilantro, and serve hot.

STOVE-TOP VARIATION: Add about ¾ cup extra water, cover the pan, and simmer over moderate to low heat until the potatoes are tender, 20 to 30 minutes.

Indo-Mexican Black Beans

BLACK BEANS LOOK LIKE oversized black urad beans. When prepared in the Indian manner, their taste is also very similar. Don't despair if the softened beans look too watery. The sauce will thicken after mashing part of the beans, cooking on moderately low heat for a while, and adding onions and tomato sauce.

2 cups dried black beans (about 1 pound), picked over
6 cups water
1 teaspoon salt, or to your taste
1 tablespoon peeled and minced fresh ginger
1 teaspoon freshly ground black pepper
2 tablespoons peanut oil
1 cup finely chopped red onions
1 tablespoon minced garlic
1½ tablespoons ground coriander
2 teaspoons ground cumin
1 teaspoon garam masala
½ teaspoon cayenne pepper (optional)
One 15-ounce can tomato sauce
½ cup loosely packed finely chopped cilantro (fresh coriander) leaves, soft stems
    included, for garnish

Wash and soak the beans in water to cover by 1 inch for 6 to 8 hours. Drain, rinse, and place in a pressure cooker with 5½ cups of the water and salt. Secure the lid of the cooker and cook for about 4 minutes after the pressure regulator starts rocking. Remove from the heat and let the pressure drop by itself, 15 to 20 minutes. Open the cover and test for doneness; they should be very tender. If not, cook under pressure for another minute. Mash about a third with the back of a ladle. Stir in the ginger and black pepper and simmer over moderately low heat for another 20 to 30 minutes.

In a small saucepan, heat the oil over moderately high heat and cook the onions, stirring, until golden, 4 to 6 minutes, then add the garlic. Cook for 1 minute and stir in the coriander, cumin, garam masala, and cayenne pepper. Mix in the tomato sauce, cook for 2 to 3 minutes, and transfer to the pressure cooker and mix with the cooked beans. Simmer over low heat for another 5 minutes. If you desire a thinner consistency, add some more water and bring to a boil again. To make the dish thicker, cook, uncovered, stirring, over high heat for a little longer. Transfer to a serving casserole, garnish with the cilantro, and serve hot.

Makes 6 to 8 servings

SERVING IDEAS:
Delicious with tacos, burritos, tostadas, quesadillas, and rice and exotic when served as part of an Indian buffet with freshly made naan or parantha breads.

DO AHEAD:
Cooked black beans stay fresh up to 5 days in the refrigerator. They will get thicker as they cool, so additional water will be required when reheating. They can be frozen for 2 to 3 months.

NOTE:
If the beans seem too thick after cooking, add ½ cup water.

Curried Red Beans

Makes 6 to 8 servings

SERVING IDEAS:

Keep the gravy thin and serve with steamed basmati rice, or make a thicker, creamier version and serve with parantha or chapati breads. A side of vegetables and yogurt raita can be served with both.

DO AHEAD:

Can be made up to 5 days in advance and refrigerated. Remember, the sauce will thicken as it cools, so add some water and bring to a boil again before serving.

RED BEANS HAVE A softer out skin, so the dish will be creamy.

2 cups dried red beans (about 1 pound), picked over
1 teaspoon salt, or to your taste
13 cups water
2 tablespoons corn oil
5 serrano peppers, skins punctured to prevent them from bursting
1 teaspoon minced garlic
½ cup minced scallion whites
2 cups finely chopped vine-ripened tomatoes
1 tablespoon peeled and minced fresh ginger
½ cup plus 3 tablespoons firmly packed finely chopped cilantro (fresh coriander) leaves, soft stems included
¼ teaspoon asafetida
1 tablespoon ground coriander
1 teaspoon ground cumin
¾ teaspoon ground turmeric
¼ cup nonfat plain yogurt, whisked until smooth
Garam masala for garnish

Put the red beans, salt, and 7 cups of the water in a pressure cooker, cover loosely, and bring to a boil over high heat. Turn off the heat, stir and let soak for 1 to 2 hours. (You may stir once or twice.) Or soak overnight in water to cover by 2 to 3 inches.

Drain and put in the pressure cooker with 6 cups of water and proceed with the recipe. Secure the lid of the cooker and cook for about 2 minutes after the pressure regulator starts rocking. Remove from the heat and let the pressure drop by itself, 15 to 20 minutes. Open the cover and test the beans for doneness; the beans should be very tender. If not, cook under pressure for another minute.

In a small saucepan, heat the oil over moderately high heat and cook the peppers, garlic, and scallion whites, stirring, until golden, 1 to 2 minutes. Add the tomatoes, ginger, and the ½ cup cilantro and cook, stirring occasionally, until all the liquid from the tomatoes evaporates, 8 to 10 minutes. Mix in the asafetida, and add the coriander, cumin, and turmeric and cook, stirring, for another minute. Add the yogurt a little at a time, stirring constantly to prevent curdling. Transfer from the skillet to the pressure cooker, mix with the cooked beans, and simmer, stirring occasionally, over low heat until the beans have a creamy consistency, another 15 to 20 minutes. Transfer to a serving casserole, garnish with the remaining cilantro and the garam masala, and serve.

Sizzling and Grilling Sensations

FIRST, IMAGINE TANTALIZING AROMAS arising from specially marinated meats and vegetables as they cook on the outdoor barbecue. Next, close your eyes and watch them as they appear before you—grilled to perfection, served over a bed of caramelized onion slices, tomato wedges, and serrano peppers.

The purpose of grilling is to quickly sear the outside surface of marinated meats and vegetables so that the inside remains tender and moist. This seared crust absorbs the flavors from the live coals and the finished food develops a phenomenal flavor.

My all-time favorite grilled foods are those prepared tandoori style—*tandoori* translates as "cooked in the tandoor," a barrel-shaped clay oven. Tandoori dishes—ranging from different kinds of meats, poultry, and seafood to vegetables and breads—have a distinctive, charbroiled characteristic that is hard but not impossible to recreate. Unfortunately, tandoors are not, for the most part, available in this country.

At the mention of tandoori foods, a distinctive lip-smacking, smoky, spicy, slighty tangy flavor comes to mind. The secret of this lies in the seasonings—an array of herbs, spices, and aromatic vegetables, such as ginger, garlic, and onion—and the marinades, made with an extraordinary blending of yogurt, lime juice, or vinegar, that are used. When the foods are allowed to steep in such fragrant marinades for long periods, sometimes up to 48 hours, they take on an exceptional flavor that is further enhanced when they are cooked in the super-high heat of the tandoor. As these foods cook, some of the marinade falls onto the hot coals, emitting a smoky aroma that clings to the food. This happens because the constricted space in the barrel retains the smoke for a long time, creating a "smoker" effect, cooking the foods in a cloud of smoke. (This does not happen over an open grill because the smoke dissipates into the air very quickly.)

Another feature that is unique to tandoori cooking is that all the foods (with the exception of breads) are first threaded on heavy-duty metal skewers (½- to ⅔-inch thick and 4 feet long) and then grilled. The tip of these skewers is placed deep in live coals. This instantly heats up the skewers and the heated skewers in turn cook the foods from the inside while the outside cooks simultaneously in the heat in the tandoor. The actual cooking time is thus reduced and the foods turn out very moist and succulent.

To bring this flavor to your home, use a covered grill and keep the lid down as much as possible or tent the foods with aluminum foil. Most of these tandoori-marinated foods can be cooked under the broiler also, about 8 inches away from the heat source, but the flavor will be slightly different. Stove-top griddles and cast-iron skillets and pans offer another alternative cooking method for tandoori-flavored foods. Just place the marinated foods in a preheated pan and cook on moderately high heat, turning them once or twice, until the outsides are seared and browned. Then baste the pieces, reduce the heat to moderately low, cover the pan, and cook, turning once or twice, until they become tender and are no longer pink inside and the vegetables are crisp-tender.

Another interesting indoor pan is the stove-top grill. The ridged, high-domed surface of this grill has numerous holes along its edges. It rests upon a metal pan that has a water ring. As the food grills, excess fat and juices flow through the holes into the drip pan's water ring. This reduces smoke and spattering, which means less mess to clean up. The flame reaches the ridged surface directly through the metal ring, and the foods can be seared quickly. Once seared, baste and cover the foods and grill, turning them a few times until the meats are no longer pink inside and the vegetables are crisp-tender.

The following tandoori-style delicacies, whether cooked on the barbecue, in the oven, or in a cast-iron skillet, are simple, healthful, and nutritious. Try them and you'll see why the word *tandoori* holds such a special place in our cuisine and in our hearts.

Chicken Tandoori

MARINATED IN NONFAT YOGURT with fragrant herbs and spices, threaded on a thick, 4-foot-long metal skewer, and traditionally grilled in a super-hot clay oven, this spectacular, brilliant-red chicken preparation came to India via the Mogul emperors. The Indians adopted it, and today tandoori chicken is considered an integral part of Indian cuisine.

The home-barbecued or oven-roasted version, though not the same as the authentically cooked tandoori chicken, is still excellent. This recipe also works well with small hen turkeys. (The red color is purely for visual impact and has no flavor, so I have not used any in this recipe. Use 2 to 3 drops of red or orange food color, if you so desire.)

Tandoori chicken can be served as an appetizer or a snack, as a summer barbecue with the suggested accompaniments, or as a main dish with dal, vegetables, yogurt, and naan bread.

At my request, our friends Kent and Sue Little and Rick Moreno (who are some of the most adventurous home cooks I know) tried this recipe in the smoker. The results were extraordinary and they swear that this is the best chicken they've ever had. Try it with the skin on or off.

I always make more chicken than I need, because leftovers are wonderful in sandwiches and casseroles and to make Traditional Chicken Curry (page 228).

8 pieces bone-in chicken breast halves and legs (2½ to 3 pounds) skin removed

2 tablespoons vegetable oil

⅓ cup plus 1 tablespoon fresh lime or lemon juice

2 teaspoons paprika

1 teaspoon salt, or to your taste

1 cup nonfat plain yogurt, whisked until smooth

1 tablespoon garlic ground to a paste in a mortar and pestle (about 5 to 6 large cloves)

1 tablespoon peeled fresh ginger ground to a paste in a mortar and pestle (about 1¼-inch piece ginger)

1½ teaspoons ground cumin

1 teaspoon garam masala

1 teaspoon ground dried fenugreek leaves

Thinly sliced scallions (white and pale green parts), chopped cilantro (fresh coriander) leaves, lime wedges, and serrano peppers for garnish

Makes 8 servings

SERVING IDEAS:
Chopped Spinach Salad with Cumin-Yogurt Dressing (page 48), Grilled Cumin- and Ginger-Glazed Skewered Vegetables (page 192), Grilled Gingerbread Naan (page 72), or garlic bread or Green Cilantro Chutney (page 257).

DO AHEAD:
The chicken pieces can be marinated and frozen. Thaw in the refrigerator before cooking. If making in large quantity, cover with aluminum foil and bake the chicken at 400°F until half done, then grill for the last 10 to 12 minutes to get a more authentic flavor.

SIZZLING
AND
GRILLING
SENSATIONS

continued

Make 1½-inch-deep cuts across each chicken piece—3 on each breast, 2 on each thigh, and 2 on each drumstick. Combine 1 tablespoon of the oil, ⅓ cup of the lime juice, the paprika, and salt and rub it over the chicken pieces, making sure to reach inside the cuts. Let marinate, covered with plastic wrap, for 30 to 60 minutes in the refrigerator.

Combine the yogurt, garlic, ginger, cumin, garam masala, and fenugreek leaves in a large bowl, and add the chicken, making sure to cover the pieces with the mixture. Cover the bowl with plastic wrap and marinate the chicken pieces for 12 and up to 48 hours in the refrigerator.

Remove the chicken from the marinade and discard the marinade. Combine the remaining 1 tablespoon each of oil and lime juice. Grill the chicken over medium-hot coals, turning and basting the pieces with the lime juice mixture a few times, the last time during the final 5 minutes of cooking, until the chicken is tender and no longer pink inside, 20 to 30 minutes, depending on the size.

To broil, put the chicken pieces on a broiler pan with a tray underneath to catch the falling juices and broil about 8 inches away from the heat source until the chicken is tender and no longer pink inside, 25 to 30 minutes. (Watch the heat carefully and if the pieces cook too fast, cover them with aluminum foil for 5 to 10 minutes to cook the insides properly.) Turn and baste the pieces a few times with the lime juice mixture. Or cover and bake on the center rack of a preheated 400°F oven until the chicken is tender and no longer pink inside, 30 to 35 minutes. Turn and baste the pieces a few times with the lime juice mixture.

Transfer to a platter, garnish with scallions, cilantro, lime wedges, and serrano peppers and serve.

Grilled Ginger and Lemon Chicken Drumsticks

YOU HAVE TASTED CHINESE, Thai, Italian, and American versions of lemon chicken. Here is another quick and easy recipe to add to your repertoire. This is also wonderful when cooked in a cast-iron pan, skillet, or griddle. Place everything in the pan and cook initially over moderately high heat for 5 to 7 minutes and then over medium heat until it is golden brown and fork-tender.

Place a few sprigs of rosemary over the hot coals for added flavor.

12 to 15 chicken drumsticks, skins removed
¼ cup fresh lime or lemon juice, or more to taste
2 tablespoons peeled and minced fresh ginger
1 tablespoon honey
½ cup loosely packed finely chopped cilantro (fresh coriander) leaves, soft stems included
2 tablespoons peanut oil
1 tablespoon roasted ground cumin (page 10)
¾ teaspoon salt, or to your taste
Freshly ground black pepper to taste
Tomato wedges and chopped cilantro leaves for garnish

Put the chicken in a bowl. Combine the lime juice, ginger, honey, cilantro, oil, cumin, salt, and pepper. Add to the bowl and mix until the chicken is fully coated with the mixture. Cover with plastic wrap and marinate the chicken for 12 to 24 hours in the refrigerator.

Remove the chicken from the marinade, discard the marinade, and grill the chicken over medium-hot coals until it is tender and no longer pink inside, 20 to 25 minutes. Turn the pieces occasionally to ensure even cooking.

Transfer to a platter, garnish with tomato wedges and chopped cilantro, and serve as a main dish.

Makes 4 to 6 servings

SERVING IDEAS:
Diced Tomato, Jicaina and Scallion Salad on Endive Boats (page 51), Minty Cottage Cheese Parantha Bread (page 60), or grilled or sautéed vegetables of your choice.

DO AHEAD:
See page 56.

VARIATION:
Try making this dish with skinless chicken thighs or breast halves or quarters.

Grilled Chicken Thighs Glazed with Cilantro Chutney

Makes 6 to 8 servings

SERVING IDEAS:

Present as an appetizer over sizzling sliced onions or as an entrée with naan breads, yogurt salad, and grilled or dry-cooked vegetables.

DO AHEAD:

Marinate up to 2 days in advance in the refrigerator, or freeze. Thaw, add the chutney up to 2 hours in advance, and grill closer to serving time.

THIS RECIPE IS INSPIRED by a dish made by Lalit Pant at his popular restaurant, Nawab of India, in Santa Monica. Lalit smears skinless, boneless chicken breast pieces with a green mint chutney and then grills them in the tandoor.

In this recipe, I use skinless chicken thighs, smother them with a green cilantro chutney, and then cook them over hot coals.

8 to 12 skinless chicken thighs (2 to 2½ pounds), skin removed
1 tablespoon vegetable oil
3 tablespoons white vinegar
1 tablespoon minced garlic
1 tablespoon peeled and minced fresh ginger
½ teaspoon salt
¾ cup Green Cilantro Chutney (page 257)
Shredded lettuce and tomato wedges for garnish

Make two or three deep 1½-inch cuts on each piece of chicken. Combine the oil, vinegar, garlic, ginger, and salt and rub it over the chicken pieces, making sure to reach inside the cuts. Cover with plastic wrap and let marinate for at least 12 and up to 48 hours in the refrigerator.

About 1 to 2 hours before grilling, add the chutney to the chicken pieces and mix it in with your fingers, making sure that each piece is well covered.

Grill the chicken over medium-hot coals until it is tender and no longer pink inside, 20 to 30 minutes. Turn the pieces occasionally to ensure even cooking. Transfer to a platter, lined with shredded lettuce. Garnish with tomato wedges and serve.

Chicken Tikka Kebabs

"TIKKAS" ARE PIECES OF skinless and boneless chicken breasts that are first marinated in a spicy lemony-garlicky yogurt marinade, then grilled in a tandoor. Combine them with a tomato-onion sauce and they become Chicken Tikka Masala (page 231).

2 pounds skinless, boneless chicken breasts, cut into 1½-inch cubes
⅓ cup nonfat plain yogurt, whisked until smooth
2 tablespoons fresh lime or lemon juice
1 tablespoon minced garlic
1 tablespoon peeled and minced fresh ginger
1 tablespoon ground coriander
1 teaspoon ground cumin
1 teaspoon garam masala
1 teaspoon paprika
½ teaspoon salt, or to your taste

To grill:
2 tablespoons melted butter or canola oil
2 tablespoons fresh lemon or lime juice
1 teaspoon roasted (page 10) ground cumin
1 teaspoon chaat masala
8 to 10 metal skewers or bamboo skewers, soaked at least 30 minutes in water
Shredded bronze leaf lettuce and halved cherry tomatoes for garnish

In a large bowl, combine the yogurt, lime juice, garlic, ginger, coriander, cumin, garam masala, and salt. Add the chicken pieces and combine to coat them well with the mixture. Cover the bowl with plastic wrap and marinate in the refrigerator for 12 to 24 hours. Prepare a basting mixture by heating the butter in a small saucepan over moderately high heat. Mix in the lemon juice, roasted cumin, and chaat masala. Set aside. Thread the marinated chicken on the skewers. Set aside the marinade.

Grill the chicken over medium-hot coals, turning the skewers occasionally until the chicken is tender and no longer pink inside, 15 to 20 minutes. During the last 5 minutes, baste with the lemon-butter mixture. To broil, chicken tikka kebabs can also be broiled in the oven, 10 to 12 inches from the source of heat. Baste and turn the tikkas over a few times.

Transfer to a platter lined with shredded lettuce. Garnish with tomato halves and serve.

SERVING IDEAS
Delicious as appetizers with any one or more chutneys of your choosing or as part of the main meal with sautéed onions, tomato wedges, serrano peppers, lemon wedges, and cilantro.

DO AHEAD:
Chicken tikka kebabs can be marinated and frozen; thaw in the refrigerator before cooking. The finished kebabs stay fresh, refrigerated, for 3 to 4 days. They can be frozen also; thaw, baste, and grill momentarily again before serving.

Silky Turkey Kebab Rolls

Makes 4 to 6 servings

SERVING IDEAS:

Cut into 1½-inch pieces and serve as snacks with Velvety Tamarind and Mango Sauce (page 248) and/or Yogurt-Cilantro Chutney (page 258).

DO AHEAD:

Pan-cook or broil the kebabs by placing the griddle 8 inches away from source of the heat, turning once with a spatula for 2 to 3 minutes, until they start to firm up. Then thread them onto skewers and grill. This step is especially useful if you prepare the rolls in advance (the uncooked meat mixture is soft and will fall off the skewers if it is kept for a long time).

BELONGING TO THE TANDOORI category, these silky-smooth, hot-dog look-alike kebabs are popularly served as hors d'oeuvres over a bed of sizzling onion slivers, lemon wedges, minced cilantro, and serrano peppers. Use these kebabs to make sandwiches with an Indian flavor along with grated or finely diced cucumbers, tomatoes, and scallions, and yogurt mint or cilantro chutney (instead of mayonnaise).

1 tablespoon peanut oil
2 tablespoons fresh lemon juice
1 teaspoon chaat masala
1 pound extra-lean ground turkey
1 tablespoon beaten egg
1 tablespoon peeled and minced fresh ginger
1 tablespoon minced garlic
¼ cup minced scallion whites (from 3 to 5 scallions)
1 to 3 serrano peppers (optional), to your taste, minced
2 teaspoons ground coriander
1 teaspoon ground dried fenugreek leaves
1 teaspoon ground dried oregano
1 teaspoon garam masala
½ teaspoon ground cumin
¾ teaspoon salt, or to your taste
¼ cup all-purpose flour, or more if required
12 to 15 metal skewers or bamboo skewers soaked at least 30 minutes in water
Lemon wedges, serrano peppers and finely chopped scallion greens for garnish

In a small bowl, combine the oil, lemon juice and chaat masala and set aside for the final basting. Put the turkey in a large bowl and mix in the egg, ginger, garlic, scallions, peppers, coriander, fenugreek, oregano, garam masala, cumin, and salt with a large spoon or your hands. (If the mixture seems too soft and sticky, add the flour.)

On a floured surface, roll the mixture into 12 to 15 long, thin hot-dog-shaped kebabs. Thread onto the skewers and grill over medium-hot coals, turning the kebabs several times until they become firm and golden, 7 to 10 minutes. Remove to a platter and baste with the reserved oil and lemon mixture, garnish with lemon wedges, peppers, and scallion greens, and serve.

Alternatively, heat 1 to 2 tablespoons oil in a nonstick or cast-iron skillet over moderately high heat and cook the kebabs on all sides until they are done. Baste and serve.

Grilled Saffron Seekh Kebabs

THIS IS ANOTHER HAND-me-down recipe from our mogul cuisine legacy (see Chicken Tandoori, page 177). *Seekh* is the Hindi word for skewers. These kebabs are made with a spicy ground-meat mixture that is pressed in the shape of hot dogs around metal skewers and then, traditionally, roasted in the tandoor. In this recipe they are grilled over hot coals.

⅓ teaspoon saffron threads
1 tablespoon milk
2 pounds extra-lean beef, lamb, or a combination
3 large cloves garlic, peeled
One 1-inch piece fresh ginger, peeled
1 small onion, peeled and cut into 4 to 6 pieces
1 teaspoon salt, or to your taste
1 teaspoon garam masala
15 to 20 metal skewers or bamboo skewers soaked at least 30 minutes in water
Lime or lemon wedges for garnish

Soak the saffron in the milk for 30 to 60 minutes. Place the meat in a large bowl.

In the work bowl of a food processor fitted with the metal S-blade or a blender, process the garlic, ginger, and onion together until smooth, stopping the machine to scrape down the side once or twice. Remove to the bowl containing the meat. Add the saffron milk, salt, and garam masala and mix well. Place in the refrigerator for 1 to 4 hours to marinate.

With moist fingers, divide the meat into 15 to 20 even portions and make hot-dog-shaped kebabs. Thread onto the skewers and grill over medium hot coals, turning frequently, until crispy and moist.

Transfer to a platter, squeeze some lime juice on them, and serve on a bed of sizzling onion rings or shredded lettuce.

Makes 6 to 8 servings

SERVING IDEAS:
Present as appetizers with Yogurt-Cilantro Chutney (page 258) or slice thinly and add to sandwiches, quesadillas, pasta, and pizza.

DO AHEAD:
These kebabs stay fresh in the refrigerator for 4 to 5 days. Cover and reheat in the microwave oven or in a preheated 400°F oven.

Grilled Sirloin Steaks

Makes 4 to 6 servings

SEE WHAT A MODERN tandoori-style marinade can do to sirloin steaks.

SERVING IDEAS:

For a steak and potato combination, pair with baked potatoes and Yogurt Raita Sauce with Crispy Minced Ginger (page 245) or serve with Vibrant Russet and Purple Potato Salad (page 52).

DO AHEAD:

Marinate the steaks up to 2 days in advance and grill just prior to serving. Leftovers are wonderful—sliced, in sandwiches, pita pockets, or rolled in tortillas.

¾ cup nonfat plain yogurt, whisked until smooth
¼ cup fresh lime or lemon juice
2 tablespoons minced garlic
2 tablespoons peeled and minced fresh ginger
¼ cup loosely packed minced fresh mint leaves or 1 tablespoon dried, ground
½ cup lightly packed minced fresh oregano leaves or 1 tablespoon dried, ground
¼ cup minced fresh rosemary leaves or 2 teaspoons dried, ground
1 tablespoon garam masala
¾ teaspoon salt, or to your taste
1 tablespoon peanut oil
1 teaspoon paprika, or to your taste
½ teaspoon cayenne pepper or crushed red pepper flakes
4 to 6 sirloin steaks (about 8 ounces each), all fat removed and rinsed

In a small bowl, combine the yogurt, lime juice, garlic, ginger, mint, oregano, rosemary, garam masala, and salt. In a small saucepan, heat the oil over moderate heat until hot but not smoking. Add the paprika and cayenne and immediately stir it into the yogurt mixture. Set aside about ¼ cup of this mixture in the refrigerator for basting purposes. Place the steaks in a flat baking dish, spread over the remaining yogurt mixture, and let marinate, covered with plastic wrap, for at least 12 and up to 48 hours in the refrigerator.

Remove the steaks from the marinade, discard the marinade, and grill over hot coals, turning and basting with the reserved yogurt mixture a few times, until the steaks reach the desired level of doneness. Or place on a broiler pan with a tray underneath to catch the dripping juices and broil about 8 inches from the heat source until the steaks reach the desired level of doneness. (Watch the heat carefully and if the pieces cook too fast, cover them with aluminum foil for 5 to 10 minutes to cook the insides properly.) Turn and baste the pieces a few times with the reserved yogurt mixture. Remove to a platter and serve.

The Indian Hamburger

IN THIS RECIPE, THE traditional American hamburger takes on the flavors of India. Just a simple addition of some Indian herbs and spices completely alters the character of an old-fashioned favorite even when it is served with popular fixings.

3 pounds extra-lean ground beef
1 tablespoon ground coriander
1 teaspoon ground cumin
1 teaspoon garam masala
½ teaspoon salt, or to your taste
2 tablespoons peeled and minced fresh ginger
¼ cup minced scallion greens (from 2 to 3 scallions)
½ cup firmly packed finely chopped cilantro (fresh coriander) leaves, soft stems
  included

In a large bowl, combine all the ingredients and mix thoroughly. Shape into 6 to 10 patties, each about 4 inches in diameter. (Remember, the patties will shrink as they cook.)

Put the patties on a grill over hot coals and cook to the desired level of doneness, 10 to 15 minutes. Turn once or twice and press the patties with a spatula to ensure that the insides get properly cooked.

The patties can be pan-fried by placing them in a nonstick or cast-iron skillet or on a stove-top griddle, and cooking them over moderately high heat until they become golden to golden brown on both sides, and are cooked through as you like them. Serve immediately on toasted hamburger buns.

Makes 6 to 10 hamburgers

SERVING IDEAS:
Serve on toasted hamburger buns with lettuce, slices of tomatoes, onions, cheese, and such condiments as mayonnaise, ketchup, mustard. Or try them with Green Cilantro Chutney (page 257) and grilled sliced onion, mushrooms, and tomatoes.

DO AHEAD:
Make the patties and freeze between sheets of waxed paper. Once frozen, transfer to plastic freezer bags. Thaw in the refrigerator (or microwave oven).

New Delhi Lamb Burger

Makes 6 to 10
hamburgers

SERVING IDEAS:

Serve romaine lettuce, slices of yellow or red tomatoes, onions, cheese, and condiments such as mayonnaise, ketchup, mustard. Or try with Quick Ginger, Apple, and Jalapeño Pepper Sauce (page 255) or Pureed Onion and Chipotle Pepper Sauce (page 249) and grilled vegetables of your choice.

DO AHEAD:

Make the patties and freeze between sheets of waxed paper. Once frozen, transfer to plastic freezer bags. Thaw in the refrigerator (or microwave oven).

MADE WITH GROUND LAMB instead of beef, this zippy burger has a flavor reminiscent of tandoori-style shish kebabs. And why not—both are made with lamb, enriched with similar spices, and cooked in or over direct flames.

3 pounds extra-lean ground leg of lamb
1 tablespoon peeled and minced fresh ginger
2 teaspoons minced garlic
¼ cup minced scallion greens (from 2 to 3 scallions)
1 to 4 minced jalapeño peppers (optional), to your taste, minced
2 tablespoons minced fresh mint leaves
1 tablespoon minced fresh rosemary leaves
1 tablespoon ground coriander
1 teaspoon ground cumin
1½ teaspoons garam masala
½ teaspoon salt, or to your taste

In a large bowl, combine all the ingredients and mix thoroughly. Shape into 6 to 10 patties, each about 4 inches in diameter. (Remember, the patties will shrink as they cook.)

Put the patties on a grill over hot coals and cook to the desired level of doneness, 10 to 15 minutes. Turn once or twice and press the patties with a spatula to ensure that the insides get properly cooked.

The patties can be pan-fried by placing them in a nonstick or cast-iron skillet, or on a stove-top griddle, and cooking them over moderately high heat until they become golden to golden brown on both sides, and are cooked through as you like them. Serve immediately on toasted hamburger buns.

Minty Grilled Pork Chops

SELECTING A MARINADE FOR these pork chops turned out to be more fun than I could have imagined. I opened my spice closet and started to think about the flavors I should choose. I seem to have ended up using all!

¾ cup nonfat plain yogurt, whisked until smooth

¼ cup balsamic vinegar

1 tablespoon minced garlic

1 tablespoon peeled and minced fresh ginger

½ cup firmly packed, finely chopped fresh mint leaves or 1 tablespoon dried, crumbled

¼ cup finely chopped fresh rosemary leaves or 1 teaspoon dried, crumbled or ground

2 teaspoons ground dried fenugreek leaves

Zest of 1 lemon, removed in strips with a vegetable peeler and minced

1 tablespoon ground coriander

2 teaspoons garam masala

1 teaspoon ground cumin

¾ teaspoon salt, or to your taste

6 to 8 pork loin chops (4 to 6 ounces each, about 2 pounds altogether), all fat removed and rinsed

Minced scallion greens and sprigs fresh mint and rosemary for garnish

In a small bowl, mix together all the ingredients except the pork chops and garnishes. Remove ¼ cup of the yogurt mixture to another small bowl and set aside in the refrigerator for basting. Place the pork chops in a large nonreactive baking dish, pour the remaining yogurt mixture over them, cover with plastic wrap, and let the chops marinate in the refrigerator for at least 12 and up to 48 hours.

Remove the pork chops from the marinade and grill over hot coals until seared from the outside, 3 to 4 minutes per side. Meanwhile, cut one 6- to 8-inch strip of aluminum foil to cover the length of the grill and place it on the back third of the grill. Put the seared pork chops on the foil, cover lightly with another piece of foil, and let them cook until they reach the required level of doneness. (This step allows the chops to remain moist while they cook properly from the inside.) Turn and baste occasionally with the reserved marinade.

Remove the pork chops to a platter and garnish with scallion greens and sprigs of mint and rosemary.

Makes 4 to 6 servings

SERVING IDEAS:
Reheat assorted naan breads on the front of the grill and serve them with Peppery Mashed Potatoes (page 137) and Yogurt Raita Sauce with Crispy Minced Ginger (page 245).

DO AHEAD:
Marinated pork chops can be refrigerated for up to 2 days or frozen for up to 1 month. Thaw, baste with the reserved marinade, and grill. Leftovers keep fresh for 3 to 4 days.

NOTE:
The front of the barbecue can be used to grill different vegetables and to heat any breads that are to be served with the meal.

Grilled Ahi Tuna with Honey and Crushed Carom Seeds

Makes 4 to 6 servings

SERVING IDEAS:

Present on a bed of shredded curly leaf or butter lettuce, topped with lightly sautéed red onions, diced red bell peppers, and lemon wedges, with a bowl of Yogurt Raita Sauce with Crispy Minced Ginger (page 245) on the side.

DO AHEAD:

Marinate the tuna up to a day in advance. Though the fish is best when served fresh, the leftovers are wonderful in salads and sandwiches.

CAROM SEEDS (THEY LOOK like celery seeds but have a strong thymelike flavor; see page 2) have a natural affinity to fish and I find that most of the grilled and pan-fried fish recipes benefit tremendously by its addition.

In India, we use a fish called pomfret. Frozen pomfret is available in Chinese, Korean, and some Asian markets and in specialty fish markets.

1½ to 2 pounds ahi tuna fillets (or sea bass, salmon, halibut or any other firm fish),
*   each ¾ to 1 inch thick, cut into 3-inch pieces*
1½ tablespoons honey
1 tablespoon minced garlic
1 tablespoon peeled and minced fresh ginger
1 teaspoon coarsely crushed carom seeds
1 tablespoon extra-virgin olive oil
1 teaspoon garam masala
1 teaspoon paprika
¼ teaspoon ground turmeric
¼ cup fresh lime or lemon juice
¾ teaspoon salt, or to your taste
Freshly ground black pepper to taste
1 to 2 tablespoons vegetable oil

Put the fish pieces in a large, nonreactive baking dish. Combine the honey, garlic, ginger, and carom seeds and rub both sides of each piece with this mixture. In a small, nonstick saucepan, heat the olive oil over moderately high heat and stir in the garam masala, paprika, and turmeric. Working quickly, mix in the lime juice, salt, and pepper and drizzle this mixture over the fish pieces. Cover with plastic wrap and let marinate in the refrigerator for at least 4 and up to 24 hours.

Cover the rack of your grill with heavy-duty aluminum foil, grease it with the vegetable oil, and poke a few holes in it to allow juices to drain.

Remove the fish from the marinade, discarding the marinade. Place the fish pieces on the foil, cover the grill with the lid or make a tent with additional aluminum foil, and grill until golden and flaky, 12 to 15 minutes. Turn once or twice with a spatula. Transfer to a platter and serve hot as suggested above.

Skewered Shrimp

THIS GRILLED SHRIMP RECIPE, made with a blend of Indian, Italian, and Asian seasonings, showcases how well a diverse group of flavors can combine to create new tastes.

For kitchen cooking, try the stove-top griddle or a cast-iron skillet.

4 to 5 large cloves garlic, peeled
One 1½-inch piece fresh ginger, peeled and cut into thin slices
¼ cup nonfat plain yogurt
1 large egg white
2 tablespoons fresh lime or lemon juice
1 teaspoon sesame oil
2 teaspoons dried oregano leaves, crumbled
¼ teaspoon ground turmeric
½ teaspoon paprika
½ teaspoon salt, or to your taste
Freshly ground black pepper to taste
1¼ pounds shelled and deveined jumbo shrimp (26 to 30 per pound), with tails on
8 to 10 metal skewers or bamboo skewers soaked at least 30 minutes in water

In a food processor or a blender, process the garlic and ginger together until minced. Add all the remaining ingredients, except the shrimp, and process again to mix.

Put the shrimp in a large, flat baking dish, pour the marinade on the shrimp, cover with plastic wrap, and let marinate in the refrigerator for at least 4 and up to 24 hours.

Remove the shrimp from the marinade, discarding the marinade, and thread onto the skewers. Grill over medium-hot coals until golden, 4 to 7 minutes. Turn the skewers once or twice. (If the shrimp stick to the grill, loosen them with a metal spatula.)

Makes 4 to 6 servings

SERVING IDEAS:
Partner with Yogurt and Roasted Cumin-Pepper Sauce (page 246) and A Medley of Roots (page 140), and serve with a basmati rice pilaf of your choice.

DO AHEAD:
Marinate the shrimp up to a day in advance. Shrimp tend to get tough when they are reheated; however, they can be grilled and refrigerated for 2 to 3 days and served cold in salads and sandwiches.

Shrimp Fajitas on a Griddle

Makes 8 servings

SERVING IDEAS:

Warmed tortillas, and any one or more of these sauces—Yogurt and Roasted Cumin-Pepper Sauce (page 246), Pureed Onion and Chipotle Pepper Sauce (page 249), Guacamole with Yogurt and Chaat Masala (page 256), Minty Sweet Pepper Chutney (page 262).

DO AHEAD:

Marinate the shrimp up to a day ahead. Chop all the vegetables and store in zipper bags for 2 to 3 days in the refrigerator. Make the dish closer to serving time.

SERVED ON SIZZLING-HOT platters with sautéed onion, colorful sweet peppers, mushrooms, and a choice of shrimp, chicken, beef or lamb, this Mexican speciality takes on a novel twist with the addition of Indian spices.

Pair it with any one or more of the suggested sauces and chutneys. However, my friend Anu Khatod says, "This dish has so much flavor, you don't need anything else."

1 pound medium-large shrimp (35 to 45 per pound), shelled and deveined

For the marinade:
¼ cup fresh lime or lemon juice
1 tablespoon walnut or peanut oil
1 tablespoon peeled and minced fresh ginger
2 teaspoons minced garlic
2 teaspoons chaat masala
1 teaspoon garam masala
1 teaspoon coarsely crushed carom seeds

For the fajitas:
3 tablespoons peanut oil
1 medium-size onion, cut in half lengthwise and thinly sliced
3 large bell peppers (1 each red, yellow, and green), seeded and cut into 2-inch-long julienne strips
2 cups small mushrooms, quartered
1 tablespoon roasted (page 10) ground cumin
2 teaspoons chaat masala
½ teaspoon paprika
1 teaspoon salt, or to your taste
¼ cup fresh lime or lemon juice
¼ cup lightly packed finely chopped cilantro (fresh coriander) leaves, soft stems included, for garnish

Put the shrimp in a large glass bowl. Add the marinade ingredients, coat the shrimp with the mixture, and marinate, covered with plastic wrap, in the refrigerator for at least 4 and up to 24 hours.

Put a large, nonstick rectangular pancake griddle or a large skillet over 2 burners of the stove (front to back) and heat the oil over moderately high heat. Cook the onion, stirring, until golden, 5 to 7 minutes. Turn off the back burner and slide the cooked onion toward the back of the griddle. Place the marinated shrimp in a single layer on the front of the griddle and cook, turning them once or twice, until pink and golden, 4 to 5 minutes. Slide them toward the onion. Place the bell peppers and mushrooms on the front of the griddle and cook, stirring until the peppers are crisp-tender, 3 to 4 minutes. Turn the heat on the back burner to moderately high heat and mix everything together. Top with the roasted cumin, chaat masala, paprika, salt, and lemon juice. Cook, stirring occasionally for another 2 to 4 minutes to blend the flavors. Garnish with the cilantro and serve with warmed tortillas and an array of salsas.

Grilled Cumin- and Ginger-Glazed Skewered Vegetables

Makes 8 servings

SERVING IDEAS:

I love these vegetables by themselves, but I must admit they are great over cooked pasta, couscous, or rice pilafs and with grilled meats, poultry, or seafood.

DO AHEAD:

Make the glaze up to 15 days in advance and refrigerate. Thread the skewers up to a day in advance and refrigerate. Baste and grill close to serving time. This dish is best when grilled fresh.

THE WARM SUMMER MONTHS bring with them an array of colorful yellow and red bell peppers and purple potatoes along with a variety of other delights that beg to be transformed into mouth-watering recipes.

This recipe is good with almost all types of vegetables—just make sure that each one is cut to a uniform size so that they will cook evenly. When you use baby potatoes, select those that are no larger than 1 inch in diameter. If you use larger potatoes cut them in half after boiling.

10 to 12 new baby potatoes, white, red, purple, gold or russet, boiled in water to
    cover until tender, drained, and left whole
10 to 12 yellow and green baby pattypan squash, each about 1 inch long
10 to 12 broccoli florets
10 to 12 cauliflower florets
15 to 20 pearl onions, peeled
15 to 20 small fresh shiitake mushrooms (about 1 inch each)
15 to 20 cherry tomatoes, about ½ inch in diameter
1 large red bell pepper, seeded and cut into 1-inch squares
1 large yellow bell pepper, seeded and cut into 1-inch squares
12 to 16 metal skewers or bamboo skewers, soaked for at least 30 minutes in water
¼ to ⅓ cup Roasted Cumin-Pepper Sauce (page 246), to your taste
2 to 3 cups shredded red romaine or any other lettuce

Thread all the vegetables onto the skewers. Baste with the sauce and grill over medium-hot coals until they get spotted and start to soften, 5 to 7 minutes. Turn the skewered vegetables as necessary.

Remove to a platter lined with shredded lettuce, drizzle some of the glaze over the vegetables, and serve with the remaining glaze on the side.

VARIATION: Add 10 to 12 baby Brussels sprouts in wintertime when they are plentiful.

Grilled Zucchini with Red Onion

FLAME ROASTED UNTIL BARELY tender, then grilled in a cast-iron griddle with slices of red onion and fragrant spices, this zucchini side dish is perfect on a hot summer day.

Any type of long, thin, straightneck variety of squash can be used. The flat round pattypan squashes also work well. Do not use the fatter varieties such as opo squash, marrow, or zucchini because the roasted flavor will not be as pronounced as in the thinner ones.

Serve over chopped greens and you have an instant summer salad.

15 to 20 pale-green zucchini, 1 by 4 to 5 inches, washed and dried (stem left intact)
1 large red onion, cut into half lengthwise and thinly sliced
2 tablespoons safflower oil
1 tablespoon ground coriander
1 teaspoon ground cumin
½ teaspoon salt, or to your taste
¼ teaspoon freshly ground black pepper
10 to 15 halved cherry tomatoes
1 tablespoon fresh lemon juice
A few sprigs of chopped cilantro (fresh coriander) leaves for garnish

Grill the zucchini over hot coals (about 450°F), or 6 inches under the broiler, turning them frequently until they are lightly charred on all sides. (Don't let them become soft.) Cut off and discard the stems and tips and slice each zucchini into 1-inch-thick diagonal slices. Set aside.

In a large, nonstick or a cast-iron skillet, heat the oil over moderately high heat and cook the onion, stirring, until it becomes golden, 5 to 7 minutes. Add the zucchini slices, cover the skillet and cook, turning once or twice, until they are crisp-tender, 4 to 5 minutes. Stir in the coriander, cumin, and salt and cook for 2 to 3 minutes, stirring a few times. Transfer to a serving dish and set aside.

Add the cherry tomatoes to the pan in which the zucchini slices were cooked and stir gently (or shake the pan) on moderate heat until they are slightly soft and glazed with the spices remaining in the pan, 2 to 3 minutes (season with more salt and pepper, if desired). Transfer to the zucchini dish and stir in the lemon juice. Garnish with cilantro and serve as a side dish.

Makes 8 servings

SERVING IDEAS:
Try as topping for pizza, combine it with cooked pasta, or partner it with all sorts of grilled fare.

DO AHEAD:
Best when served fresh. If made ahead, it gets watery and very soft, though it still tastes good. Grill the zucchini, cool, and refrigerate for 2 to 4 days. Cook the onions a few hours in advance. Slice the grilled zucchinis and combine with the onions in a skillet to reheat.

Grilled Kohlrabi and Turnips

SERVING IDEAS:

A perfect companion to grilled meat, chicken, or seafood, this dish is also wonderful with curries and dals.

DO AHEAD:

Slice the vegetables, mix with the oil, and refrigerate up to 2 days. Or cook the vegetables completely, cool, cover, and let them remain on the griddle for 3 to 4 hours. Reheat on the griddle before serving.

THIS DISH OFFERS AN alternate way of preparing these not-too-popular vegetables. The griddle I use in this recipe is one that has a ridged base, giving the impression that the vegetables have been grilled outdoors.

2 medium-large turnips, peeled, cut into half lengthwise, and cut into ¼-inch-thick pieces
2 medium-large kohlrabi, peeled, cut into half lengthwise, and cut into ¼-inch-thick pieces
1½ tablespoons peanut oil
2 teaspoons peeled and minced fresh ginger
1 teaspoon minced garlic
2 teaspoons ground coriander
½ teaspoon salt, or to your taste
Freshly ground black pepper to taste
Dried fenugreek, oregano, thyme, or parsley for garnish

Put the turnips and kohlrabi in a large bowl. Drizzle the oil over them and mix everything together with your hands, making sure the vegetables are fully coated.

Transfer the vegetables to a griddle with a ridged surface, place the griddle over moderately high heat, cover, and cook, turning the pieces once or twice until they are crisp-tender, 5 to 7 minutes. Uncover the griddle, and top the vegetables with the minced ginger, garlic, coriander, salt, and pepper (adding them one at a time or all at once), and cook, turning as necessary, until they are all marked with golden brown lines, 5 to 7 minutes. Garnish with a choice of herb or herbs and serve.

Griddle-Grilled Fennel Bulbs

THE ELEGANT SIMPLICITY OF grilled fennel bulbs can be given a new approach with just a variation in herbs and spices. Try the Indian savory spice blend called chaat masala for a taste you've never experienced before. Remember not to add extra salt because chaat masala already contains some.

2 fennel bulbs, trimmed, quartered lengthwise, and cut into ¼-inch-thick slices
   crosswise
1½ tablespoons safflower oil
1 teaspoon chaat masala
Chopped cilantro (fresh coriander) leaves to taste
1 tablespoon fresh lemon or lime juice

Put the sliced fennel in a large griddle with a ridged surface or a nonstick or cast-iron skillet in a single layer. Add the oil, cover the griddle, and cook over moderately high heat, turning once or twice, until the fennel becomes crisp-tender, 5 to 7 minutes.

Sprinkle the chaat masala and cilantro over them and cook, turning as necessary, until the juices dry up and the fennel turns golden, 3 to 4 minutes. Add the lemon juice and cook for another minute or two to blend the flavors. Transfer to a bowl or platter and serve.

Makes 4 servings

SERVING IDEAS:

The slightly firm bite of fennel provides a crunchy contrast to the delicate taste of grilled or sautéed seafood and tossed green salads.

DO AHEAD:

Can be made a few hours ahead of time. Let the fennel remain in the pan in which it cooked, and reheat before serving.

Grilled Eggplant Mush with Tomatoes and Peas

Makes 4 to 6 servings

SERVING IDEAS:

Present on the side with all sorts of curries, grilled or roasted meats, poultry, and seafoods, or in open-faced sandwiches or pita pockets, or as a dip for your favorite crackers or crudités.

DO AHEAD:

This dish, as well as the roasted eggplant pulp alone, stays fresh in the refrigerator for 4 to 5 days. It can be frozen for 3 to 4 months. Thaw and reheat in a microwave oven or over low heat.

YOU CAN CUT EGGPLANT into slices and grill them like everyone does, or you can grill them whole until tender, and then cook them in the way the Indians do at home—with lots of tomatoes and a sprinkling of peas.

To make a richer restaurant-style version, stir-fry some minced ginger and garlic with the onions and then add some garam masala and heavy cream during the last 5 to 7 minutes of cooking.

When selecting eggplants, choose the young eggplants (they contain fewer seeds and are sweeter) with shiny, unblemished skins. Remember, the smoky flavor will be more pronounced in smaller eggplants and they will also be easier and faster to grill.

3 small to medium-size eggplant (about 2 pounds total)
3 tablespoons vegetable oil
3 to 5 jalapeño peppers, to your taste, skins punctured to prevent them from bursting
1½ cups finely chopped onions
4 cups finely chopped vine-ripened tomatoes
1 cup frozen peas, thawed
1 cup lightly packed finely chopped cilantro (fresh coriander) leaves, soft stems included
1 teaspoon salt, or to your taste
Chopped cilantro for garnish

Lightly oil your hands and rub them over the surface of the eggplants. Then grill them, preferably over hot coals or over a direct flame (this gives the best flavor). Using kitchen tongs, turn frequently, until the skins are charred and the eggplants are tender, 10 to 15 minutes. Alternately, puncture the skins in a few places with the tip of a knife and bake in a preheated 400°F oven until tender, 35 to 40 minutes. Or place them 8 to 10 inches away from the broiler and turn frequently, with kitchen tongs, until the eggplants are tender and the skins are charred. Transfer to a bowl and set aside to cool.

Peel off the charred skins and discard. Mash the pulp with your hands, a fork, or in the food processor or blender until smooth. Mix in any juices that may have collected in the bowl. Set aside until needed.

In a large wok or saucepan, heat the oil over moderately high heat and cook the peppers and onion, stirring as necessary, until the onion turns golden, 5 to 7 minutes. Add the tomatoes and cilantro and continue to cook, stirring as necessary, until all the liquid from the tomatoes evaporates, 10 to 12 minutes. Then add the mashed eggplant and salt, reduce the heat to moderately-low, and continue to cook, stirring occasionally, for another 5 to 7 minutes. Add the peas and cook until they absorb the flavor of the dish, 5 to 7 minutes.

Transfer to a serving dish, garnish with the chopped cilantro, and serve hot as a side dish.

Flame-Roasted Corn on the Cob

Makes 8 servings

SERVING IDEAS:
Serve hot by themselves or on the side with Chicken Tikka Kebabs (page 181) or Grilled Saffron Seekh Kebabs (page 183).

DO AHEAD:
This corn is best served fresh.

COME THE MONSOON MONTHS in India, tender fresh corn floods the markets. Almost every street corner has a vendor sitting on the pavement beside a live fire that has been dulled with very small pieces of coal. Next to him is a pile of inviting fresh corn and wafting from the fire is the heavenly aroma of already roasted corn coated with fresh lime juice and masala.

8 ears fresh corn, husks removed but stems left intact
2 teaspoons chaat masala, or more to your taste
Pinch each of salt, freshly ground black pepper, and cayenne pepper
2 limes, cut into 6 to 8 wedges each

Put the ears of corn directly over the moderately-hot coals and roast, turning as each side gets cooked, until the whole ear is marked with black and brown spots.

Meanwhile, in a bowl, combine the chaat masala, salt, black and cayenne pepper. Take one lime wedge, press it into the chaat masala mixture (the spices will stick to the lime), and rub it all over the roasted corn. Squeeze the lime gently as you rub so some of the lime juice also coats the corn along with the spices.

Repeat with the remaining ears and serve. The roasted ears can be laid out on the picnic table with the spice mixture and lime wedges alongside and each person can take care of their own.

Roasting for Fun

ROASTING IS THE PROCESS of cooking foods with dry heat. This happens when meats, poultry, and vegetables are placed in a preheated oven to cook evenly on all sides by the circulation of heat inside the oven. In olden times, foods were roasted by piercing them with skewer-type rods (spits) and rotating them over an open flame to get a "rotisserie" effect. Today (unless you have a rotisserie), most of our home roasting is done in the oven. Indian roasting, on the other hand, is generally done in a tandoor (a clay oven; see page 175). Marinated or spiced meats and vegetables are threaded on skewers and then quickly roasted in the intense heat of burning coals as the heat circulates in the barrel-shaped tandoor. (Indian tandoori cuisine is actually a combination of grilling and roasting.)

Foods that are to be roasted are generally put on a broiler pan with a tray underneath to catch the drippings and juices. The foods themselves stay clear of all juices and don't get soggy. The flavor-laden drippings can then be used to make some of the best accompanying sauces. Sometimes I roast my foods on cookie sheets.

Roasting does take on a new meaning when Western techniques are combined with Indian seasonings.

Indian Turkey

Makes 20 to 25 half-pound servings

SERVING IDEAS:

Partner with Cran-berry-Orange Chutney (page 263), A Medley of Roots (page 140), and your favorite Thanks-giving fixings.

DO AHEAD:

Marinate the turkey up to a day in advance and roast fresh.

BASTED WITH FLAVORS FROM an authentic Indian kitchen and roasted in the familiar home oven, this turkey adds a new dimension to your traditional Thanksgiving meal. You'll want to start this the day before.

In this recipe, the bird is cooked without a stuffing. You can stuff this turkey with your favorite stuffing if you wish or use a cup or two of Simply Cumin Basmati or Herbal Basmati (page 270 or 271). For roasting a turkey without stuffing, allow 15 minutes per pound of turkey; for a stuffed turkey, increase the cooking time to 18 minutes per pound.

One 14- to 16-pound turkey, thawed if needed, washed, and patted dry with paper towels
10 to 12 large cloves garlic, peeled
One 2-inch piece fresh ginger, peeled and cut into thin slices
1 cup firmly packed cilantro (fresh coriander) leaves, soft stems included
½ cup firmly packed fresh mint leaves
1 cup plain nonfat yogurt, whisked until smooth
⅓ cup fresh lemon or lime juice
1 tablespoon ground coriander
1 tablespoon ground cumin
1 tablespoon ground dried fenugreek leaves
1 tablespoon garam masala
1½ teaspoons salt, or to your taste
2 tablespoons vegetable oil
1 tablespoon paprika
Shredded lettuce for garnish

Run your fingers carefully between the skin and the flesh of the turkey, starting at the neck opening and moving toward the tail and the thighs, to loosen the skin and create a pocket. (Be careful not to tear the skin.) Set aside.

In the work bowl of a food processor fitted with the metal S-blade and the motor running, process the garlic and ginger together until minced by adding them through the feed tube. Add the cilantro, mint, yogurt, lemon juice, corian-der, cumin, fenugreek, garam masala, and salt and process until everything is smooth, stopping the machine to scrape down the sides of the work bowl with a spatula a few times. Remove to a bowl and set aside.

In a small saucepan, heat the oil over moderately high heat until hot but not smoking. Remove from the heat, add the paprika, and immediately stir it into the bowl with the yogurt mixture. (Work quickly or the paprika will burn.)

Spread about one third of the mixture under the loosened turkey skin and rub another third over the skin and inside the cavity. (Reserve the remaining third in the refrigerator for basting the turkey as it cooks.) Cover the spiced turkey with plastic wrap and refrigerate overnight.

Preheat the oven to 325°F. Remove the turkey from the refrigerator, stuff the turkey if you wish to, fold the wings across the back, and tie them together with heavy kitchen string. Tie the drumsticks together and insert an instant-read meat thermometer into the thickest part of the thigh without touching the bone.

Put the turkey breast side up in a large roasting pan. Baste with the reserved marinade and roast, uncovered, basting every 35 to 45 minutes until the turkey is a rich brown color and the thermometer reads 180°F, 4½ to 5 hours. If the skin browns too fast, cover it with a piece of oil-basted muslin or tent loosely with heavy-duty aluminum foil.

Remove from the oven and allow the turkey to stand for 15 to 20 minutes before carving. Transfer to a serving platter, garnish with shredded lettuce, and serve with the chutney and root vegetables.

Thyme- and Ginger-Roasted Chicken

Makes 4 to 6 servings

SERVING IDEAS:

A saucy bean or lentil dish along with roasted or pan-sautéed vegetables and Indian flat breads all combine to transform this dish into a gastronomic delight.

DO AHEAD:

Marinate the chicken up to 24 hours in advance. Roast closer to serving time. The leftovers stay fresh for 3 to 5 days in the refrigerator.

UPON OUR RETURN FROM the farmers' market one Wednesday afternoon, my sister-in-law Asha Puri and I set out to make this delightful recipe. She wanted garlic, thyme, and lemon juice and I preferred ginger, cilantro, and balsamic vinegar. So in they all went, plus a few more.

This recipe can also be made with skinless chicken. Tent with heavy-duty aluminum foil after the chicken turns brown.

One 3- to 3½-pound chicken, washed and patted dry
6 large cloves garlic, peeled
One 1½-inch piece fresh ginger, peeled and cut into thin slices
1 to 4 serrano peppers, to your taste, stems removed
½ cup loosely packed fresh thyme sprigs, tough stems removed, or 1 tablespoon dried
½ cup loosely packed cilantro (fresh coriander) leaves, soft stems included
1 tablespoon minced fresh rosemary leaves or 1 teaspoon dried
⅓ cup yogurt cheese (page 79) or nonfat sour cream
2 tablespoons balsamic vinegar
1 tablespoon fresh lime or lemon juice
2 teaspoons dried fenugreek leaves
1½ teaspoons garam masala
1 teaspoon salt, or to your taste
½ teaspoon freshly ground black pepper, or to your taste
Shredded lettuce and garam masala for garnish

Run your fingers carefully between the skin and flesh of the chicken, starting at the neck opening and moving toward the tail and the thighs, to loosen the skin and create a pocket. (Be careful not to tear the skin.) Carefully, with the tip of a knife, make a few gashes in the meat under the skin. This ensures that the marinade will penetrate deeper. Set aside.

In a food processor fitted with the metal S-blade and the motor running, process the garlic, ginger, and peppers together until minced by adding them through the feed tube. Add the remaining ingredients (except the garnish) and process again until smooth, stopping the machine to scrape down the sides of the work bowl with a spatula a few times.

Spread about half of the mixture under the loosened chicken skin, making sure it reaches inside the gashes, and rub the other half over the skin and inside the cavity. Cover with plastic wrap and marinate the chicken for at least 12 and up to 24 hours in the refrigerator.

Preheat the oven to 400°F. Put the chicken breast side down in a roasting pan (a heavy metal tray or ovenproof casserole) on the center rack of the oven. Roast until the skin turns golden, 35 to 40 minutes. Reduce the heat to 375°F, turn the bird over, and roast, basting occasionally with the pan juices, until the breast side turns rich brown in color, another 20 to 25 minutes.

Remove from the oven and allow the chicken to stand for 7 to 10 minutes before carving. Transfer to a serving platter, garnish with shredded lettuce and garam masala, and serve.

Roasted Cornish Game Hens

Makes 4 servings

SERVING IDEAS:
Serve Indian style with Curried Russet Potatoes with Fresh Peas (page 171) and whole-wheat tortillas or basmati rice.

DO AHEAD:
Marinate the hens up to 24 hours in advance. Roast closer to serving time. Leftovers stay fresh for 3 to 5 days in the refrigerator.

"ARE YOU SURE YOU want to combine yogurt with balsamic vinegar and not lemon juice?" was the reaction I got from Kent and Sue Little, my friends and recipe testers, when they first read this recipe and reluctantly agreed to try it.

Imagine my delight when they came back and said, "Neelam, this recipe is a real winner. Give us more like this one."

4 Cornish game hens (1¼ to 1½ pounds each)
⅔ cup nonfat plain yogurt
3 tablespoons balsamic vinegar
1 tablespoon minced garlic
1 tablespoon peeled and minced fresh ginger
1 tablespoon minced fresh rosemary leaves
1 teaspoon dried fenugreek leaves
1 teaspoon garam masala
½ teaspoon coarsely crushed carom seeds
½ teaspoon cayenne pepper or paprika, or to your taste
1 teaspoon salt, or to your taste
Shredded lettuce and garam masala for garnish

With a toothpick or wooden skewer, poke the game hens in several places. Place in a large bowl. Combine the remaining ingredients (except the garnishes), add to the bowl, and mix until the game hens are fully coated with the mixture. Cover with plastic wrap and marinate for at least 12 and up to 24 hours in the refrigerator.

Preheat the oven to 400°F. Put the hens breast side down in a roasting pan (a heavy metal tray or ovenproof casserole) on the center rack of the oven. Roast until the skin turns golden, 35 to 40 minutes. Reduce the heat to 375°F, turn the birds over, and roast, basting occasionally with the pan juices, until the breast side turns rich brown in color, another 20 to 30 minutes.

Remove from the oven and transfer to a serving platter, garnish with shredded lettuce and garam masala, and serve.

Marinated Rack of Baby Lamb

FOR YOU LAMB LOVERS, here is an innovative creation—racks of baby lamb marinated in a cardamom-laced pesto-style blend of roasted nuts, basil, mint, and rosemary, then roasted under the oven broiler.

15 to 20 almonds
10 to 12 cashew nuts
2 tablespoons pine nuts
10 to 12 green cardamom pods
Seeds from 4 black cardamon pods
2 teaspoons fenugreek seeds
6 to 8 large cloves garlic, peeled
One 2½-inch piece fresh ginger, peeled and cut into thin slices
¼ cup firmly packed fresh basil leaves
½ cup firmly packed fresh mint leaves
¼ cup loosely packed fresh rosemary leaves
½ cup nonfat plain yogurt
¼ cup fresh lime or lemon juice
¼ cup fresh orange juice
1 tablespoon extra-virgin olive oil
2 teaspoons garam masala
1 teaspoon salt, or to your taste
4 to 6 racks of baby lamb (8 to 10 ounces each)
Fresh mint and rosemary sprigs for garnish

In a spice or coffee grinder or with a mortar and pestle, grind the almonds, cashews, pine nuts, cardamom pods and seeds, and fenugreek seeds together to a fine powder. Remove to a small nonstick skillet and dry roast the blend, stirring gently over moderate heat until golden and fragrant, 4 to 6 minutes.

In the work bowl of a food processor fitted with the metal S-blade and the motor running, process the garlic and ginger together until minced by dropping them through the feed tube. Add the basil, mint, and rosemary, start the machine, and pour the yogurt, lime and orange juice and oil through the feed tube in a thin stream. Process until pureed, stopping the machine to scrape down the sides of the work bowl with a spatula a few times. Mix in the ground-nut mixture, garam masala, and salt.

Makes 4 to 6 servings

SERVING IDEAS:
Serve the whole racks as an entrée with Indo-Mexican Black Beans (page 173) and parantha or naan breads. To serve as hors d'oeuvres, cut the cooked racks into individual chops and serve over a bed of fresh parsley greens with chilled beer or wine.

DO AHEAD:
Marinate the racks of lamb up to 48 hours in advance. The actual roasting doesn't take too long. This dish is best when served fresh, though leftovers are wonderful as snacks. The nut marinade is extremely delicious, so collect whatever remains in the tray and serve it over rice the next day.

continued

Put the racks of lamb in a large glass casserole dish and, with your fingers, coat both sides of each rack with the yogurt-nut mixture. Cover the dish with plastic wrap and marinate in the refrigerator for 12 and up to 48 hours (the longer the better).

Preheat the oven to 500°F. Remove the racks from the casserole, place on a heavy-duty cookie sheet, and bake on the lowest shelf in the oven until the bottom sides of the racks are done and the tips of the bones turn golden, 6 to 8 minutes.

Change the oven setting to "broil." Remove the cookie sheet from the bottom shelf and place it 8 to 10 inches from the source of the broiler heat. Broil until the racks become brown and fragrant, 10 to 15 minutes. (You may reposition the racks but do not turn them over; the marinade of nuts is heavy and tends to fall off if the pieces are turned.)

Transfer to a platter, garnish with rosemary and mint sprigs, and serve.

Peppery Pork Loin Chops with Ginger, Cilantro, and Tarragon

THESE PORK CHOPS, ENCRUSTED with zesty cracked peppercorns and baked in a pool of fresh tomatoes and exotic seasonings, are simple enough to be served every day and festive enough to be a part of large buffets.

Six to eight 5- to 6-ounce boneless pork loin chops (about ¾ inch thick)
2 tablespoons cracked black peppercorns, or to your taste
½ teaspoon salt, or to your taste
5 large cloves garlic, peeled
One 1½-inch piece fresh ginger, peeled and cut into thin slices
½ cup loosely packed cilantro (fresh coriander) leaves, soft stems included
¼ cup loosely packed fresh tarragon leaves
2 large vine-ripened tomatoes, coarsely chopped
Garam masala and chopped cilantro (fresh coriander) leaves for garnish

Place the pork chops in a large, nonstick skillet and sprinkle both sides of each chop generously with cracked peppercorns and a touch of salt. Cook over high heat, pressing down with a spatula (to ensure that the peppercorns adhere to the chops) and turning once or twice, until both sides are brown, 2 to 3 minutes per side. Remove to a casserole dish in a single layer, cover, and set aside.

Preheat the oven to 400°F. In the work bowl of a food processor fitted with the metal S-blade and the motor running, process the garlic and ginger together until minced by dropping them through the feed tube. Add the cilantro, tarragon, and tomatoes and process until pureed. Transfer to the casserole with the pork chops, making sure that all the chops are coated with this mixture.

Cover and bake in the center of the oven until the chops are fork-tender, 25 to 30 minutes. Remove from the oven. If the sauce seems too thin, transfer it to the skillet in which the pork chops were browned and reduce over moderately high heat until it becomes quite thick, 3 to 5 minutes. Return to the casserole with the pork chops.

Garnish with garam masala and chopped cilantro and serve.

Makes 4 to 6 servings

SERVING IDEAS:
Pan-sautéed mixed vegetables and stir-fried rice or couscous are perfect partners to these great-tasting pork chops.

DO AHEAD:
These chops do taste best when they are fresh. You could, however, pan-cook the chops, cover them with the sauce, and set them aside for up to 4 hours. Bake them just prior to serving.

Sunil's Cumin-Baked Sea Bass with Marinara Sauce

Makes 4 to 6 servings

SERVING IDEAS:

Serve with Wilted Red Swiss Chard with Sautéed Goat Cheese (page 46) or Tomato, Jicama, and Scallion Salad on Endive Boats (page 51) along with garlic bread or a mixed basmati and wild rice pilaf.

DO AHEAD:

This fish is best when served fresh. The sauce can be made 3 to 5 days in advance and the fish can be marinated up to 24 hours ahead of time. Then the actual baking and assembly are quick and easy.

SUNIL VORA OF THE Clay Pit restaurant never refuses to give me any recipe I ask for. Here is one of his favorite fish recipes. I tried it with green lingcod and it was wonderful.

6 fillets fresh sea bass (6 to 8 ounces each)
4 to 6 large cloves garlic, peeled
One 1½-inch piece fresh ginger, peeled and cut into thin slices
1 teaspoon curry powder
1 teaspoon ground cumin
½ teaspoon cayenne pepper, or to your taste
½ teaspoon salt, or to your taste
¼ cup fresh lime or lemon juice
1 recipe Sunil's Marinara Sauce (page 253)

Wash the fillets and place them in an overproof casserole. In a mortar and pestle or a mini food processor or chopping by hand, process the garlic and ginger together until minced. Remove to a bowl and mix in the curry powder, cumin, cayenne, salt, and lime juice. Rub each fillet on both sides with this mixture, cover the casserole with plastic wrap, and marinate the fish in the refrigerator for at least 2 and up to 24 hours.

Preheat the oven to 425°F. Remove the plastic wrap and place the casserole in the center of the oven. Bake until the fillets become white and flaky, 10 to 15 minutes, depending on the thickness of the fillets. To make the tops golden, place under the broiler for a minute or two.

Transfer to a warm serving platter, drizzle some marinara sauce over the pieces, and serve with the remaining sauce on the side.

Honey-Roasted Tuna

HERE IS ANOTHER RECIPE from Sunil Vora's (of The Clay Pit restaurant in Los Angeles) special collection. Sunil suggests serving this fish without any sauce.

2 pounds fresh tuna or any other firm fish (four 8-ounce fillets or 8 to 12 thinner fillets)
4 to 6 large cloves garlic, peeled
One 1½-inch piece fresh ginger, peeled and cut into thin slices
3 tablespoons fresh lime or lemon juice
2 tablespoons honey
1 tablespoon extra-virgin olive oil
1 tablespoon chopped fresh dill or dried mixed Italian herbs
2 teaspoons Chinese chili paste or red chili flakes in oil, or to your taste
1 teaspoon ground cumin
½ teaspoon garam masala
½ teaspoon salt, or to your taste

Wash the fillets and place them in an ovenproof casserole. In a mortar and pestle or a mini food processor or chopping by hand, process the garlic and ginger together until minced. Remove to a small bowl and mix in the remaining ingredients. Rub each fillet on both sides with this mixture, cover the casserole with plastic wrap, and marinate the fish in the refrigerator for at least 2 and up to 24 hours.

Preheat the oven to 425°F. Remove the plastic wrap, place the casserole in the center of the oven, and bake until the fillets become white and flaky, 10 to 15 minutes, depending on the thickness of the fillets. To make the tops golden, place under the broiler for a minute or two.

Transfer to a warm serving platter and serve.

Makes 4 to 6 servings

SERVING IDEAS:
Present on a bed of Couscous Pilaf with Cilantro-Glazed Cherry Tomatoes (page 288) and Chopped Spinach Salad with Cumin-Yogurt Dressing (page 48). As a starter, this fish is stunning with Yogurt-Cilantro Chutney (page 258).

DO AHEAD:
This dish is best when served fresh. Marinate the fish up to 24 hours ahead of time.

Oven-Roasted Root Vegetables

Makes 8 servings

SEE WHAT LEMON JUICE and chaat masala can do to everyday root vegetables.

Toss everything in a roasting pan, turn on the oven, and take a nap. Just remember: The roasting time varies with the size of the vegetables, so cut them into similar-size pieces. This recipe can be made with any one or a combination of different types of roots.

SERVING IDEAS:

These vegetables are exotic accompaniments to summer barbecues and fall entertaining. Serve with any grilled or roasted chicken, lamb, or seafood preparation.

2½ to 3 pounds mixed yams, sweet, purple, Yukon Gold, and russet potatoes, taro root, parsnips, turnips, beets, and carrots, peeled and cut into 1-inch pieces
12 to 15 pearl onions, peeled
1 to 2 tablespoons extra-virgin olive oil
1 tablespoon minced garlic
1 tablespoon peeled and minced fresh ginger
½ cup firmly packed minced fresh dill
1 to 3 serrano or jalapeño peppers (optional), to your taste, minced
1 teaspoon salt, or to your taste
½ teaspoon freshly ground black pepper, or to your taste
½ cup loosely packed finely chopped cilantro (fresh coriander), leaves, soft stems included
2 tablespoons fresh lime or lemon juice
1 teaspoon chaat masala, or more to your taste

DO AHEAD:

This dish stays fresh for 3 to 5 days in the refrigerator. Serve hot, cold, or at room temperature.

Preheat the oven to 400°F. Put the vegetables in a large roasting pan or casserole dish. Toss (preferably with your fingers) with oil, garlic, ginger, dill, jalapeño peppers, salt, and black pepper.

Cover and roast in the center of the oven until the vegetables are tender, 50 to 60 minutes. Stir once or twice. (If you wish to brown them, uncover and place under the broiler for a minute or two.)

Remove from the oven, add the cilantro, lemon juice, and chaat masala, toss well, and serve.

Oven-Roasted Eggplant Ovals

Makes 6 to 8 servings

"CAN'T YOU DO SOMETHING else with these eggplant slices?" asked my husband, Pradeep, when I packed him a roasted eggplant sandwich for lunch.

What, may I ask, is "something else"? I've already served them as part of formal Italian and Indian buffets, as a vegetarian pizza topping, chopped in a salad of baby greens, in lunch bag sandwiches and pita pockets, and in Mexican quesadillas . . . and he asks for something different!

SERVING IDEAS:

Serve as a side dish with curried dals and beans or partner them with pizza, pasta, or plain sourdough rolls.

1 or 2 eggplants (about 1½ pounds total)
2 tablespoons extra-virgin olive oil
3 to 4 large cloves garlic, peeled
One ½-inch piece fresh ginger, peeled and cut into thin slices
1 serrano pepper (optional), stem removed
3 tablespoons fresh lime or lemon juice
1 tablespoon dried mixed Italian herbs, crumbled
1 teaspoon coarsely ground carom seeds
¾ teaspoon salt, or to your taste
Shredded lettuce as needed

DO AHEAD:

This dish stays fresh for 5 to 7 days. Serve hot, cold, or at room temperature.

Cut the eggplant into ½-inch-thick slices. Using 1 tablespoon of the oil, baste each slice and place oiled side down in a single layer on a cookie sheet.

Preheat the oven to 450°F. In a mortar and pestle or a mini food processor or chopping by hand, process the garlic, ginger, and pepper together until minced. Remove to a bowl and mix in the lime juice, the remaining tablespoon oil, the Italian herbs, carom seeds, and salt. Brush this mixture evenly over the tops of the eggplant slices and roast in the center of the oven until the eggplant slices are soft and golden, 15 to 20 minutes.

With a metal spatula, remove them slice by slice to a platter lined with shredded lettuce and serve.

Roasted Stuffed Japanese Eggplants

Makes 4 to 6 servings

SERVING IDEAS:

Offer as a side dish with curries or grilled fare, on open-face sandwiches, in pita pockets with a yogurt sauce or chutney, or over pizza and pasta.

DO AHEAD:

This dish stays fresh for 5 to 7 days in the refrigerator. Serve it hot, cold, or at room temperature.

GET THE FRESHEST AND the best eggplants you can find, even if it means going an extra mile to the nearest farmers' market or produce stand.

10 to 12 long, thin Japanese eggplants (about 1½ pounds)
2 tablespoons extra-virgin olive or canola oil
1 tablespoon minced garlic
1 tablespoon ground coriander
1 teaspoon ground cumin
1 teaspoon mango powder
½ teaspoon carom seeds
½ teaspoon paprika
¼ teaspoon ground turmeric
½ teaspoon salt, or to your taste
Fresh parsley sprigs for garnish

Wash and wipe dry each eggplant, then cut lengthwise up to the stem, leaving the stem intact.

Preheat the oven to 350°F. In a small bowl, combine the remaining ingredients (except the parsley) until a paste is formed. With a spoon or your fingers, stuff each eggplant with this mixture, then place them on a well-greased ovenproof platter or casserole dish and roast until the eggplants are soft and sizzling, 40 to 45 minutes. Turn them once after about 25 minutes.

Garnish with parsley sprigs and serve as a side dish.

Roasted Tomato-Basil-Stuffed Portobello Mushrooms

OF LATE, A LARGE variety of mushrooms has been flooding the produce markets. The portobello is the largest mushroom I've seen (sometimes six inches in diameter) or cooked with. I've grilled it with a touch of extra-virgin olive oil and spices on hot coals, roasted it alone or in combination with other vegetables, sautéed it with different greens, and added it to curries and casseroles, and I've always been impressed with the way it holds its shape and flavor.

Here I stuff these giant-size caps with spicy chopped tomatoes, potatoes, and fresh basil and then roast them until they are tender and juicy. The diced potatoes absorb most of the mushroom juices as they are released, leaving a perfectly textured sauce.

2 large or 4 small to medium-size portobello mushrooms (about 1 pound)
2 cups finely chopped fresh tomatoes (about 2 large)
1 small potato, peeled and finely diced
1 cup loosely packed finely chopped fresh basil leaves
1 serrano pepper (optional), finely chopped
2 tablespoons canola oil
1½ tablespoons minced garlic
1½ tablespoons ground coriander
1 teaspoon salt, or to your taste
¼ teaspoon freshly ground black pepper, or to your taste
Freshly grated Parmesan cheese for garnish

Cut off the tips of the mushroom stems and then wash and dry each mushroom. Remove the stems and chop finely.

In a bowl, combine the remaining ingredients (except the Parmesan), then mix in the chopped stems. Mound the mixture evenly in the mushroom caps.

Preheat the oven to 350°F. Place the portobello caps on a well-greased ovenproof platter or casserole dish and roast in the center of the oven until fork-tender and the sauce looks done, 25 to 30 minutes. There is no need to turn them.

Garnish with Parmesan cheese and serve.

Makes 4 to 6 servings

SERVING IDEAS:
Serve them over a bed of fluffy basmati rice or on a platter of cooked pasta of your choice. Or cool and serve over a bed of torn greens—the tomato sauce makes a lovely salad dressing.

DO AHEAD:
This will stay fresh for 3 to 5 days in the refrigerator and can be served hot, cold, or at room temperature.

Herb-Roasted New Potatoes

Makes 6 to 8 servings

SERVING IDEAS:

Serve as a first course with Green Cilantro Chutney (page 257) and a glass of merlot or on the side with a saucy pasta dish or a curry.

DO AHEAD:

Can be made 2 to 3 days in advance and reheated, preferably on a cookie sheet in a single layer or in the microwave oven.

THIS RECIPE IS GOOD with all types of baby potatoes—purple, Yukon Gold, and russet—and with larger ones when they are cut into thick slices, wedges, or ¾-inch cubes.

Try it with different combinations of fresh greens and herbs—fenugreek, watercress, basil, lemon basil, dill, lemon verbena, oregano, thyme, etc.

Poblano peppers are deep green, about two inches wide at the stem end, and slightly tapering with pointed tips. This mildly hot variety comes from Mexico and is sometimes called pasilla.

One 1½-inch piece fresh ginger, peeled and cut into thin slices
1 to 5 jalapeño peppers, to your taste, stems removed
1 large poblano pepper, seeded and coarsely chopped
½ cup firmly packed cilantro (fresh coriander) leaves, soft stems included
½ cup firmly packed fresh dill sprigs or 1 tablespoon dried
½ cup firmly packed fresh Italian parsley leaves or 1 tablespoon dried
¼ cup firmly packed fresh mint leaves or ½ tablespoon dried
2 tablespoons fresh thyme leaves or 1 teaspoon dried
24 to 30 baby (1-inch) new white potatoes, halved or quartered lengthwise (about 2 pounds)
2 tablespoons extra-virgin olive oil
1 teaspoon salt, or to your taste
½ teaspoon freshly ground black pepper, or to your taste
2 to 4 tablespoons fresh lime or lemon juice, to your taste
Garam masala and fresh dill sprigs for garnish

In a food processor fitted with the metal S-blade and the motor running, process the ginger and peppers together until minced by dropping them through the feed tube. Add all the herbs and process until minced, stopping the machine to scrape down the sides of the work bowl with a spatula a few times. Set aside.

Preheat the oven to 375°F. Put the potatoes in a large mixing bowl and add the oil, salt, black pepper, and the processed herb mixture. Toss with your fingers or salad spoons, making sure that all the potatoes are well coated with the mixture.

Transfer to a lightly greased cookie sheet in a single layer (use two cookie sheets if one is not large enough) and roast in the center of the oven until the potatoes are tender, 30 to 40 minutes.

Turn the oven dial to "broil" and broil the potatoes 6 to 8 inches from the source of heat until golden, 2 to 4 minutes.

Transfer to a serving platter, gently mix in the lime juice, garnish with garam masala and dill sprigs, and serve. (If the potatoes stick to the cookie sheet, loosen with a metal spatula.)

Restuffed Baked Potatoes

Makes 4 to 6 servings

SERVING IDEAS:

Offer as appetizers, on a bed of shredded greens with a saucy yogurt chutney, or as a part of a light lunch with a hearty soup and salad.

DO AHEAD:

Assemble the potatoes and refrigerate for up to 24 hours. Bake closer to serving time. Or place the stuffed potatoes on freezer trays and freeze individually. When frozen, transfer to freezer bags and freeze for 3 to 4 months. They can go straight from the freezer to the oven.

SOMETIMES CALLED TWICE-BAKED because they are baked two times—once whole and then after being stuffed—these potatoes can be made with an array of different vegetables.

8 large russet potatoes, well washed, individually covered with aluminum foil and baked in a 400°F oven until tender, about 45 minutes
3 tablespoons butter, melted
½ cup extra-firm tofu, patted dry with paper towels and coarsely mashed
2 tablespoons frozen peas, thawed, drained, and coarsely mashed
2 tablespoons minced morel or shiitake mushrooms, fresh or reconstituted
1 to 3 serrano peppers (optional), to your taste, minced
2 tablespoons finely chopped cilantro (fresh coriander) leaves, soft stems included
2 teaspoons peeled and minced fresh ginger
1 teaspoon chaat masala, or to your taste
¼ teaspoon salt, or to your taste
Freshly ground black pepper to taste
2 tablespoons fresh lime or lemon juice
½ cup grated mild Cheddar cheese, or more to your taste
Minced fresh chives for garnish

Cut the baked potatoes in half lengthwise and scoop out the softened inside pulp, leaving about ¼ inch on the skin, to form a cup. Baste the outside skin of each potato cup with melted butter and place on a cookie sheet.

Preheat the oven to 400°F. Mash the scooped-out pulp and set aside. In a medium-size bowl, combine ¾ cup of the mashed potatoes with all the remaining ingredients (except the cheese and chives). Stuff each potato cup with equal amounts of this mixture. Top evenly with the grated cheese and bake in the center of the oven until the cheese melts and forms a golden crust, 15 to 20 minutes. Garnish with minced chives and serve.

Curries with Flavor

TAKE ONE BITE OF a well-made Indian curry and you'll be hooked for life. Eat one that is not so good and say farewell to a dish that could be a lifetime palate pleaser. So important is the first bite that it is almost worth waiting for the right "curry" to come along. This wait may end at a friend's house, at a good Indian restaurant, or in your own kitchen—with a true and tried recipe in your hands.

Before the experiments in your own kitchen start, let me explain the meaning of the word *curry*, a word that evokes strong love-hate emotions in people, yet very few people truly understand it. They mistakenly think of curries as hot and spicy dishes, enriched with curry powder and lots of oil. If you are one of those, I urge you to think again.

"Curry," in Indian terminology, means a gravy (or a sauce) and "curries" are entrées that contain a gravy or a sauce. The final dish gets its name from the vegetable or meat that is cooked in the sauce. So a chicken curry is essentially a saucy dish containing pieces of chicken that have cooked in that sauce from beginning to end. As they cook, they absorb from and impart to each other flavor, resulting in an outstanding dish.

The major difference between a gravy as we know it in the Western world and a curry is that a "gravy" is made separately and served on the side with cooked meats and vegetables, whereas a "curry" is made by braising the meats and vegetables in the sauce itself. (Dishes made without any sauce are called "dry-cooked.")

There is no set of rules dictating the use of any specific spices or curry powder, for that matter. In fact, Indians don't use curry powder at all—they add their favorite spices by the spoonfuls, making curries that are unique to their families. Everyday home curries are robust and full of flavor yet mild enough to be enjoyed by children and adults alike. (For added heat at mealtimes, we serve chutneys and pickles or chopped or whole green chili peppers on the side to be added to the individual's taste.)

An authentic Indian curry sauce is made with *bhuna hua* (stir-fried) ground (or finely chopped) onion, garlic, ginger, and tomatoes; this is called a wet masala. It is fried over moderate to low heat until it turns a rich gold color (sometimes dark brown) with no visible specks of any white from the onion (if there is, the curry will have a raw taste). Added to this cooked wet masala is an array of herbs and spices (called dry masala) and some cooking liquid—usually water, yogurt, or buttermilk, and occasionally broths and juices. Indian curries do not require any starchy thickeners like flour, corn-starch, or arrowroot.

In my opinion, a stew is a variation of a curry. The method of preparation and seasonings are dif-ferent but the final product looks very similar. The first time I saw a freshly made stew, I mistook it for a thin curry with meat and vegetables. I started to look around for chapati breads and basmati rice, only to realize that I was not at an Indian home or restaurant.

So if most of the curries are made by stir-frying, roasting, or braising and they look like stews, why is there such a mystery about curries? By choice, perhaps—if curries remain exotic dishes, only to be eaten when someone else makes them, then maybe we won't have to cook them ourselves. However, as time goes by and cultures and cuisines intermingle, the novelty of curries will soon wear off and more and more people will find themselves craving these super-sumptuous, delightfully satis-fying dishes.

Remember, there's lots of room to be creative in the world of curries. So, play around with herbs, spices, and seasonings from other cuisines and invent new curries every time you stand in front of your stove—after all, curries are just dishes with a sauce.

For those of you who love curries, here are some more recipes for your files, and to those of you who hate them, my humble request—please take them to your kitchens and give them another chance.

Yogurt-Braised Lamb Chops with Whole Spices

WHEN WHOLE SPICES ARE stir-fried, they become incredibly aromatic, and this fragrance permeates the foods in an exceptional manner. Here, we stir-fry a bunch of whole spices, combine them with ginger, yogurt, and more spices and then simmer the lamb until the meat almost melts off the bone.

3 tablespoons vegetable oil
3 bay leaves, preferably fresh
One 3-inch stick cinnamon
15 to 20 cloves, to your taste
15 to 20 black peppercorns, to your taste
10 green cardamom pods, pounded lightly to break the skins
8 black cardamom pods, pounded lightly to break the skins
4 to 8 dried hot red peppers, to your taste
1 medium-large onion, cut in half lengthwise and thinly sliced
1½ teaspoons cumin seeds
1 tablespoon ground coriander
1 tablespoon peeled and minced fresh ginger
1 tablespoon minced garlic
1 teaspoon salt, or to your taste
1½ cups nonfat plain yogurt, whisked until smooth
10 to 12 bone-in lamb chops (about 3 pounds), all fat removed and chops washed
Garam masala and chopped cilantro (fresh coriander) leaves for garnish

In a large saucepan, heat the oil over medium heat and cook the bay leaves, cinnamon, cloves, peppercorns, cardamom pods, and peppers, stirring, until they are golden and highly fragrant, 2 to 3 minutes. Add the onion and cook, stirring, until it turns dark brown (almost caramel colored), 10 to 12 minutes. Mix in the cumin seeds, coriander, ginger, garlic, and salt, and add all the yogurt in a thin stream, stirring constantly to prevent it from curdling. Add the lamb chops, cover the pan, and increase the temperature to high. Bring to a boil and cook for 2 to 3 minutes, then reduce the heat to moderate, and cook until the lamb chops are tender and the sauce almost clings to the meat, 30 to 40 minutes. Carefully turn the lamb chops over a few times to ensure proper cooking.

Add ½ cup or more whisked yogurt or water if you prefer a thinner gravy or uncover the pan and cook on high heat to dry out the extra juices. Before serving, remove any extra oil that floats to the surface. Transfer to a serving dish, garnish with the garam masala and cilantro, and serve hot.

Makes 6 servings

SERVING IDEAS:

Although all types of vegetable side dishes are wonderful with this, my favorite is Grilled Eggplant Mush with Tomatoes and Peas (page 196). Yogurt raita, chutneys, rice, and breads make the menu complete.

DO AHEAD:

This is one of those dishes that actually tastes better the next day; it stays fresh, refrigerated, for 3 to 5 days.

NOTE:

To avoid accidentally biting into the whole spices in the completed dish, remove them from the pan after the initial stir-frying, tie them in a piece of cheesecloth (like a bouquet garni), then return them to the pan and finish cooking the dish.

Boneless Lamb Chops in Fragrant Saffron-Cardamom Sauce

Makes 4 to 6 servings

SERVING IDEAS:

Keep the gravy thick and serve it with bite-size pieces of Indian flatbreads, or make a thinner sauce and team with a basmati rice pilaf. A yogurt raita and simple salad of chopped tomatoes and cucumbers dressed with lime juice and chaat masala are also wonderful companions.

DO AHEAD:

Stays fresh in the refrigerator for 4 to 5 days. Reheat with additional yogurt or milk if required. Garnish and serve.

ENRICHED WITH GROUND NUTS, cardamom pods, and saffron, this lamb dish is placed high in the hierarchy of nonvegetarian curries from India. The truly authentic version of this curry is made with goat chops (called *chaampein* in Hindi) and contains heavy cream, but to make it easier on the heart, I've added nonfat yogurt instead.

Don't let the long list of ingredients intimidate you, because once you gather them together, the dish is a cinch to make.

½ teaspoon saffron threads
¼ cup milk (any kind)
10 to 12 raw cashew nuts, to your taste
10 to 12 raw almonds, to your taste
15 cloves
15 black peppercorns
3 to 5 black cardamom pods, to your taste
7 to 10 green cardamom pods, to your taste
1 tablespoon ground coriander
1 teaspoon ground dried fenugreek leaves
½ teaspoon ground turmeric
¼ teaspoon ground nutmeg
1 teaspoon salt, or to your taste
3 tablespoons peanut oil
1½ cup finely chopped onions
2 teaspoons minced garlic
1 tablespoon peeled and minced fresh ginger
1½ cup finely chopped vine-ripened tomatoes
2 cups nonfat plain yogurt, whisked until smooth
8 to 10 bone-in lamb chops (about 2 pounds), all fat removed and chops washed
Chopped cilantro (fresh coriander) leaves and garam masala for garnish

Soak the saffron threads in the milk and set aside for 30 minutes or longer to infuse.

In a spice or coffee grinder or with a mortar and pestle, grind the cashew nuts, almonds, cloves, peppercorns, and cardamom pods into a fine powder. Remove to a bowl, mix in the coriander, fenugreek leaves, turmeric, nutmeg, and salt and set aside.

In a large, nonstick saucepan, heat the oil over moderately high heat and cook the onions, stirring, until they turn brown, 10 to 12 minutes. Add the garlic, ginger, and reserved ground spices and stir until fragrant, 2 to 3 minutes. Mix in the tomatoes and cook, stirring, until all the liquid from the tomatoes dries up, 5 to 7 minutes.

Add all the yogurt in a thin stream, stirring constantly to prevent it from curdling. Add the lamb chops, cover the pan, and increase the heat to high. Cook for the first 2 to 3 minutes, then reduce the heat to moderately low and cook until the lamb chops are tender and the sauce is thick, 30 to 40 minutes. Carefully turn the lamb chops over a few times to ensure proper cooking.

Mix in the saffron milk and cook for another 2 to 5 minutes, depending on the type (thick or thin) of gravy desired. (Add ½ cup more yogurt or milk if you prefer a thinner gravy or uncover the pan and cook on high heat to dry out the extra juices.) Before serving, remove any extra oil that floats to the surface. Transfer to a serving platter, garnish with cilantro and garam masala, and serve hot.

Curried Boneless Leg of Lamb with New Potatoes

Makes 8 servings

SERVING IDEAS:

Present on a bed of steamed basmati rice or with freshly made parantha breads and a side of the vegetable of your choice.

DO AHEAD:

Here is a dish that tastes better the next day, so if you can, make it 1 to 2 days in advance. (It stays fresh 3 to 5 days in the refrigerator.) If the sauce becomes thick, reheat with additional whisked yogurt or water.

THE SECRET TO COOKING a perfect lamb curry is the proper combination of all the masala ingredients. The long marination with fragrant herbs and spices counters the gamey smell of the lamb, and the final dish comes to the table succulent and tender, ready for instant consumption.

To make it easy, have your butcher remove all the fat and cut the lamb into small pieces. At home, trim off any remaining fat before cooking.

3 to 3½ pounds boneless leg of lamb, all fat removed, cut into 1½-inch pieces, and washed
¼ cup fresh lemon juice
1 tablespoon minced garlic
1 tablespoon peeled and minced fresh ginger
3 teaspoons garam masala
1 teaspoon paprika
1 teaspoon salt
2 tablespoons peanut oil
1½ cups finely chopped onions
1½ tablespoons minced fresh rosemary leaves or 1 teaspoon dried
1 tablespoon ground coriander
½ teaspoon ground turmeric
½ teaspoon salt, or to your taste
2 cups finely chopped vine-ripened tomatoes (2 large)
6 to 8 new potatoes, white, red, purple, Yukon Gold, or russet, (1 to 1¼ pounds), cut in half
1 cup nonfat plain yogurt, whisked until smooth
1 teaspoon ground dried fenugreek leaves (optional)
Chopped cilantro (fresh coriander) leaves and garam masala for garnish

Put the lamb pieces in a large bowl. Mix together the lemon juice, garlic, ginger, 2 teaspoons of the garam masala, and the salt, add to the bowl, and mix until the lamb is fully coated with the mixture. Cover with plastic wrap and marinate the lamb in the refrigerator for at least 12 and up to 48 hours.

In a large, nonstick saucepan, heat the oil over moderately high heat and cook the onions, stirring, until they turn dark brown, 10 to 12 minutes. Add the rosemary, coriander, the remaining teaspoon of garam masala, turmeric, and salt. Mix in the tomatoes and cook, stirring occasionally, for 4 to 5 minutes (the liquid should not evaporate completely). Add the potatoes and marinated lamb plus all its marinade. Increase the heat to high and bring to a boil. Reduce the heat to moderate, cover the pan, and cook, stirring often, until most of the liquid evaporates and the gravy is very thick, 20 to 25 minutes.

Add all the yogurt in a thin stream, stirring constantly to prevent it from curdling, and continue to cook the lamb until it is fork-tender and the gravy is thick, 10 to 15 minutes. Stir occasionally. Mix in the fenugreek leaves. Add ½ cup or more whisked yogurt or water if you prefer a thinner gravy or uncover the pan and cook on high heat to dry out the extra juices.

Transfer to a serving platter or casserole, garnish with cilantro and garam masala, and serve hot.

Ground Meat–Stuffed Tomato Cups in Creamy Tomato Sauce

Makes 6 to 8 servings

SERVING IDEAS:

Present with a side of dry-cooked green vegetables (such as okra, zucchini, broccoli, asparagus), a basmati rice pilaf, and Indian or other breads.

DO AHEAD:

Make a few hours ahead of time or assemble it up to 2 days in advance and bake just prior to serving.

THOUGH I HAD EATEN this dish a number of times in India, I had forgotten about it until one evening when Lalit Pant served it as part of an elaborate dinner at his restaurant, Nawab of India in Santa Monica, California. Lalit, thanks for a reintroduction to this priceless centerpiece recipe.

For a vegetarian version, use crumbled paneer cheese or tofu instead of ground meat.

2 tablespoons vegetable oil
1 cup finely chopped onions
1 cup finely chopped vine-ripened tomatoes
2 cups extra-lean ground beef or lamb
1 tablespoon finely chopped fresh rosemary leaves
1 tablespoon ground coriander
½ teaspoon ground cumin
1 teaspoon garam masala
¾ teaspoon salt, or to taste
½ cup firmly packed finely chopped cilantro (fresh cilantro) leaves, soft stems included
3 to 5 finely serrano peppers (optional), to your taste, chopped
½ cup nonfat plain yogurt, whisked until smooth
10 medium-size vine-ripened tomatoes, cut in half lengthwise and pulp removed (with a grapefruit or regular spoon) and reserved
¼ cup grated mild Cheddar or Monterey Jack cheese
1 recipe Creamy Tomato Sauce (page 252)
Chopped cilantro leaves for garnish

In a medium saucepan, heat the oil over moderately high heat and cook the onions, stirring occasionally, until golden, 5 to 7 minutes. Add the tomatoes and cook, stirring occasionally, until all the liquid evaporates, 3 to 5 minutes. Add the ground meat and cook, stirring occasionally, until the meat turns golden, 5 to 7 minutes. Stir in the rosemary, coriander, cumin, 1/2 teaspoon of the garam masala, and the salt and cook 4 to 5 minutes, until the meat is brown. Add the cilantro, peppers, and yogurt and cook 4 to 5 more minutes, stirring occasionally, until all the juices dry up.

Fill each tomato half with the cooked meat, top with Cheddar cheese, and set aside.

Preheat the oven to 400°F. Place the stuffed tomatoes in a large serving casserole in a single layer and pour the tomato sauce around it. Cover and bake in the center of the oven until the tomatoes are slightly soft and the cheese on top melts, about 15 minutes. Uncover the casserole and spoon some sauce over each tomato. Cover and cook until the tomatoes are quite soft but still retain their shape, 5 to 10 more minutes.

Garnish with cilantro and the remaining ½ teaspoon garam masala and serve as a main or side dish.

Curried Top Sirloin in Yogurt and Roasted Spices

Like any other saucy dish, this recipe is enticing with flat breads and rice pilafs. For added flavor, present a yogurt raita and some chutneys on the side.

DO AHEAD:

Here is a dish that is superb when freshly made, but even more flavorful a day or two later. Leftovers stay fresh for 3 to 5 days in the refrigerator.

MADE TRADITIONALLY WITH GOAT meat (mutton), this recipe is irresistible with beef also.

2 tablespoons blanched almond slivers
2 tablespoons unsweetened shredded coconut
1 tablespoon coriander seeds
2 teaspoons cumin seeds
1 teaspoon poppy seeds
1 teaspoon black peppercorns
¼ teaspoon cloves
5 green cardamom pods
Seeds from 2 black cardamom pods
1 to 3 dried hot red peppers (optional), to your taste, broken
3 tablespoons extra-virgin olive oil
1½ cups finely chopped onions
1 tablespoon minced garlic
1 tablespoon peeled and minced fresh ginger
2 cups finely chopped vine-ripened tomatoes
1 cup loosely packed finely chopped cilantro (fresh coriander) leaves, soft stems included
½ teaspoon paprika
½ teaspoon ground turmeric
1 teaspoon salt, or to your taste
2 pounds top sirloin steak, all fat removed and cut into 1½-inch pieces
1½ cups nonfat plain yogurt, whisked until smooth
½ cup orange juice or water, or as needed
Chopped cilantro leaves and garam masala for garnish

Put the almonds, coconuts, spices, and peppers in a large skillet and roast over moderately high heat, shaking the pan occasionally, until they are fragrant and golden. Cool and grind them into a powder in a spice or coffee grinder. Set aside.

In a large, nonstick saucepan, heat the oil over moderately high heat and cook the onions, stirring, until dark brown, 10 to 12 minutes. Stir in the garlic and ginger. Add the tomatoes and cilantro and cook, stirring as necessary, until most of the juices from the tomatoes evaporate, 7 to 10 minutes. Add the paprika, turmeric, salt, and the reserved ground spices and stir to mix. Add the sirloin pieces, reduce the heat to moderately low and cook, stirring, for 5 to 7 minutes, to absorb the flavors. Add all the yogurt in a thin steam, stirring constantly to keep it from curdling. Mix in the orange juice, cover the pan, and cook until the gravy is thick and the meat pieces are fork-tender, 20 to 25 minutes. (Add more juice or water if the dish or curry becomes too dry.)

To prepare this recipe using a pressure cooker, brown the onion in the pressure cooker, and add the remaining ingredients, including the orange juice as instructed in the above paragraph. Secure the lid of the cooker and cook over high heat for about 2 minutes after the pressure regulator starts rocking. Remove the cooker from the heat and let the pressure drop by itself, 10 to 12 minutes.

Remove to a serving dish, garnish with cilantro and garam masala, and serve.

Traditional Chicken Curry

SERVING IDEAS:
Pair with a side dish of dry-cooked vegetables, yogurt raita, and a basmati rice pilaf or with any Indian bread.

DO AHEAD:
Can be made 4 to 5 days in advance and refrigerated. Reheat with additional whisked yogurt or some water.

NOTE:
You can use boneless chicken pieces along with some "chicken-less" bones to get the same flavor as using bone-in chicken. In that case, remember to discard the bones before serving the dish.

MY MOTHER RUBBED HER chicken with a ground paste of raw papaya to tenderize it, which added a subtle flavor to the chicken and reduced the cooking time remarkably. Papayas contain papain, an enzyme that breaks down the protein in meats. This "papaya treatment" is not necessary with American chickens.

A rich and flavorful curry is made by cooking the chicken pieces with the bone left in.

3 tablespoons vegetable oil
One 3-inch stick cinnamon
3 to 4 bay leaves, to your taste
2 cups finely chopped onions
2 teaspoons minced garlic
2 tablespoons peeled and minced fresh ginger
2 cups finely chopped vine-ripened tomatoes (about 2 large tomatoes)
2 tablespoons ground coriander
2 teaspoons dried fenugreek leaves
1½ teaspoons garam masala
½ teaspoon ground turmeric
1½ teaspoons salt, or to your taste
1 teaspoon freshly ground black pepper, or to your taste
1 cup nonfat plain yogurt, whisked until smooth
10 to 12 mixed chicken pieces (drumsticks, thighs, and quartered breasts, about 2½ pounds), skin removed
Garam masala and a few sprigs cilantro (fresh coriander) for garnish

In a large, nonstick saucepan, heat the oil over moderately high heat and cook the cinnamon stick and bay leaves, stirring, for 30 to 40 seconds, until fragrant. Add the onions and continue to cook until the onion turns medium brown, 7 to 10 minutes. Stir in the garlic and ginger, and add the tomatoes. Cook, stirring, until all the liquid evaporates, 7 to 10 minutes. Mix in the coriander, fenugreek leaves, garam masala, turmeric, salt, and pepper. Add all the yogurt in a thin stream, stirring constantly to prevent it from curdling.

Finally, add the chicken pieces, cover, and cook over high heat for about 5 minutes. Reduce the heat to moderately high and cook until the chicken is tender, 20 to 30 minutes. Turn the pieces over a few times to ensure even cooking. (If the dish seems too dry, add some more yogurt or water and continue to cook until the chicken is done.)

Transfer to a platter, garnish with garam masala and cilantro, and serve.

Sushi Mysoor's Chicken Curry with Coconut Milk

MY DAUGHTERS, SUMITA AND Supriya, always sang praises of the chicken curry prepared in their friend Sapna's home. It was only after I got the recipe and made it myself that I realized how good it was.

Sapna's mother, Sushi, a native of Bangalore, India, makes this dish fiery hot with a lot of dried red chilies, but this version is a lot milder. So go ahead, add the chilies to your heart's desire, and have fun.

This curry can also be made with lamb and beef.

3 tablespoons peanut oil
One 2-inch piece fresh ginger, peeled and cut into thin slices
4 to 6 large cloves garlic, to your taste, peeled and coarsely chopped
2 to 5 dried hot red peppers (optional), to your taste
2 large onions, coarsely chopped
2 tablespoons ground coriander
¾ teaspoon ground cinnamon
¾ teaspoon ground cloves
½ teaspoon cayenne pepper, or to your taste
1 teaspoon paprika
1 teaspoon salt, or to your taste
3 large, vine-ripened tomatoes, coarsely chopped
1 cup loosely packed fresh dill or cilantro (fresh coriander) leaves
3½ pounds chicken pieces (drumsticks, thighs, wings, quartered breasts) or
    2½ pounds halved or quartered boneless breasts or thighs, skin removed
¾ to 1 cup coconut milk, to your taste
Chopped fresh dill or cilantro for garnish

In a large saucepan, heat 2 tablespoons of the oil over moderately high heat and cook the ginger, garlic, hot red peppers and onions, stirring, until they start to turn golden, 5 to 7 minutes. Transfer to a food processor or blender and process, scraping down the side of the work bowl a few times, until smooth. (If the onion mixture is not smooth, mix in a few pieces of tomato and process again.) Add the coriander, cinnamon, cloves, cayenne, paprika, and salt and process once again until well mixed. Remove to a bowl and set aside. In the same work bowl, process the tomatoes and dill until finely chopped. Set aside.

Put the chicken pieces (in one or two batches) in the pan in which the

SERVING IDEAS:
Best when served with steamed basmati rice and Mixed Vegetables with Fresh Curry Leaves (page 141). A bowl of chilled melons or sliced mangoes add a welcome, soothing touch, especially if you make the curry hot, like I do.

DO AHEAD:
Can be made 3 to 5 days ahead of time, refrigerated, and reheated with additional water if required.

onions were cooked, add the remaining 1 tablespoon oil, and cook over moderately high heat, turning them once or twice, until they are golden, 4 to 7 minutes. Add the reserved onion mixture, reduce the heat to moderate, and cook, stirring, until it is fragrant and brown, 5 to 8 minutes. Mix in the coconut milk and cook for a few minutes. Add the tomatoes and cook over moderately high heat until the chicken is tender and the gravy is thick, 15 to 20 minutes. (Add ½ cup or more water and bring to a boil once again if you prefer a thinner gravy.) Garnish with chopped dill or cilantro, transfer to serving dish, and serve.

Chicken Tikka Masala

THIS DISH CALLS FOR simmering pregrilled Chicken Tikka Kebabs (page 181) in a garlicky tomato-onion sauce. The simmering allows perfect bonding between the sauce and the kebabs.

4 to 5 cloves garlic, to your taste, peeled
1 large onion, peeled and cut into 8 wedges
2 to 6 serrano or jalapeño peppers (optional), to your taste, stems removed
One 1½-inch piece fresh ginger, peeled and cut into thin slices
4 to 5 large, vine-ripened tomatoes, coarsely chopped
1 cup loosely packed cilantro (fresh coriander) leaves, soft stems included
3 tablespoons peanut oil
1 tablespoon coriander
2 teaspoons ground cumin
1 teaspoon paprika
2 teaspoons ground dried fenugreek leaves
1¼ teaspoons garam masala
½ teaspoon salt, or to your taste
¼ cup nonfat plain yogurt, whisked until smooth
¾ to 1 cup milk or half-and-half, to your taste
1 recipe Chicken Tikka Kebabs (page 181)
Chopped cilantro for garnish

In the work bowl of a food processor fitted with the metal S-blade and the motor running, process the garlic, onion, and peppers until smooth by dropping them through the feed tube. Remove to a bowl. In the same bowl, process the ginger, tomatoes, and cilantro until smooth. Set aside.

In a large, nonstick saucepan, heat the oil over moderate heat and cook the pureed onion-garlic mixture, stirring, until fragrant and golden brown, 7 to 10 minutes. Add the pureed tomato mixture and cook, stirring as necessary, until all the liquid evaporates, 10 to 15 minutes. Mix in the coriander, cumin, paprika, fenugreek leaves, 1 teaspoon of the garam masala, and the salt, and add the yogurt in a steady stream, stirring constantly to prevent it from curdling, until it is absorbed into the sauce. Finally, add the milk, increase the heat to high, and bring to a boil.

Carefully mix in the grilled chicken tikka kebabs and simmer over moderately low heat for 5 to 10 minutes to blend the flavors. The sauce should be of medium consistency. Add some extra milk or water if it seems too thick or cook, uncovered, over high heat to thicken the sauce. Garnish with the remaining ¼ teaspoon garam masala and cilantro and serve.

Makes 8 servings

SERVING IDEAS:
A must with home-made or purchased naan breads and a salad of chopped dark-green lettuce, cucumber, and scallion whites dressed with Yogurt and Roasted Cumin-Pepper Sauce (page 246). Serve a side of vegetables and rice for a more elaborate meal.

DO AHEAD:
When refrigerated separately, the kebabs stay fresh for 3 to 5 days, and the sauce 5 to 7 days. Combine and simmer a few hours or just before serving. The sauce can also be frozen for about 2 months.

Diced Chicken with Fresh Peaches

A salad of bitter greens (arugula, radicchio, watercress, and endive) topped with an olive oil and balsamic vinegar dressing and all types of Indian flatbreads complement the fruity flavors of this dish. Also delicious cold (and at room temperature) in sandwiches, burritos, and quesadillas.

DO AHEAD:

Can be made 3 to 5 days in advance and refrigerated. For a variation, make the sauce separately and serve with grilled meats, chicken, or seafood.

EVERY OTHER YEAR MY peach tree sheds tons of ripe and fragrant peaches. These aromatic delights instantly bruise as they fall to the ground, but they have a flavor that is hard to find. It is these peaches that I use in this recipe—a recipe that is finger lickin' good.

If you don't have a tree, buy the ripest peaches you can find in the market. Sometimes I puree my own peaches and freeze them for future use.

3 tablespoons peanut oil
1½ cups finely chopped onions
3 large cloves garlic, thinly sliced
One 1¼-inch piece fresh ginger, peeled and cut into julienne strips
1 tablespoon ground coriander
1 teaspoon garam masala
½ teaspoon ground cumin
1 teaspoon salt, or to your taste
1 teaspoon freshly ground black pepper, or to your taste
2½ pounds skinless, boneless chicken tenders, tendons removed and each cut in half
6 to 8 fresh tree-ripe peaches, peeled, pitted, and pureed in a blender or food processor (about 2 cups)
¼ cup fresh lemon juice
1 cup loosely packed finely chopped cilantro (fresh coriander) leaves, soft stems included

In a large, nonstick skillet, heat the oil over moderately high heat and cook the onions, stirring, until they are golden, 5 to 7 minutes. Add the garlic and ginger and continue to cook until they are brown, 2 to 3 minutes. Mix in the coriander, garam masala, cumin, salt, and ½ teaspoon of the pepper, and add the peach puree and the chicken. Cover the pan and cook, stirring occasionally, over moderately high heat for 5 to 7 minutes to absorb flavor. Reduce the heat to moderately low and cook until the chicken is tender and most of the liquid dries up, 10 to 12 minutes. Uncover the pan, add the lemon juice and cilantro, increase the heat to moderately high and cook, stirring occasionally, until all the liquid dries up, 5 to 7 minutes.

Transfer to a serving dish, garnish with the remaining ½ teaspoon pepper, and serve.

Chicken Breasts in Cashew-Garlic Sauce

WHILE LABORIOUS, THE ROAD to this favorite is not impossible.

1 cup raw cashew pieces

3½ cups water

One 1½-inch piece fresh ginger, peeled and cut into thin slices

5 large cloves garlic, peeled

½ cup plus 2 to 4 tablespoons nonfat plain yogurt, whisked until smooth

3 tablespoons vegetable oil

4 to 6 black cardamom pods, to your taste, pounded lightly to break the skin

One 1-inch stick cinnamon

5 serrano peppers, skins punctured to prevent them from bursting

1½ cup finely chopped onions

1 tablespoon ground coriander

1 teaspoon garam masala

1 teaspoon salt, or to your taste

8 to 10 bone-in chicken breast halves (3 to 3½ pounds), skin removed and each cut in half or left whole

Garam masala and chopped cilantro (fresh coriander) leaves for garnish

Makes 6 to 8 servings

SERVING IDEAS:
  Pair this saucy dish with a side of grilled or pan-cooked vegetables and parantha or naan breads. Or pair it with any basmati rice pilaf with vegetables.

DO AHEAD:
  Can make 3 to 5 days in advance, refrigerate, and reheat with additional water or yogurt, if required.

Soak the cashew pieces in 1 cup of the water for 1 hour or longer. Drain. In a food processor or blender, puree the soaked cashews, ginger, and garlic until smooth. (Add 2 to 4 tablespoons yogurt or water if required for blending.) Set aside.

In a large, nonstick saucepan, heat the oil over moderately high heat and cook, stirring, the cardamom pods, cinnamon, and peppers until they sizzle, 30 to 40 seconds. Add the onions and cook, stirring occasionally, until they turn medium to dark brown, 7 to 10 minutes. Add the cashew-garlic paste and continue to cook, stirring, until the mixture turns brown, 5 to 7 minutes.

Mix in the coriander and garam masala, and add the remaining ½ cup yogurt in a steady stream, stirring constantly to prevent it from curdling. Add the salt and chicken breasts. Cook, stirring, for 3 to 4 minutes, and add the remaining 2½ cups water and bring to a boil. Reduce the heat to moderate and simmer until the chicken is tender and the sauce is thick and creamy, 25 to 30 minutes. (Add more water or whisked yogurt if you prefer a thinner sauce.)

Transfer to a serving dish, garnish with the garam masala and cilantro, and serve hot.

Halibut in Tamarind Sauce

Makes 4 to 6 servings

HALIBUT BRAISED IN TAMARIND sauce offers a quick-cooking curry.

SERVING IDEAS:

Delicious with steamed basmati rice or buttered hot whole-wheat tortillas. Serve a dry-cooked vegetable dish on the side.

DO AHEAD:

The tamarind extract can be made up to a week in advance and refrigerated. The dish is best when served fresh, but it keeps 2 to 3 days in the refrigerator.

NOTE:

Follow the same procedure if using compressed tamarind. Simply dissolve the tamarind concentrate in 1 cup water.

¼ pound fresh tamarind pods or one 2-inch cube compressed tamarind or 2 tablespoons tamarind concentrate
1½ cups hot water
2 pounds halibut (or sea bass, tuna, cod, or any other firm fish) fillets, ¾ to 1 inch thick, cut into 1½-inch-long pieces
2 to 3 tablespoons white vinegar or fresh lime or lemon juice, to your taste
1½ tablespoons minced garlic
1½ tablespoons peeled and minced fresh ginger
2 teaspoons ground cumin
½ teaspoon ground turmeric
1 teaspoon salt, or to your taste
Freshly ground black pepper to taste
3 tablespoons olive oil
1 teaspoon mustard seeds
2 to 4 serrano peppers, to your taste, whole with skins punctured or minced
1 tablespoon dried thyme
3 large, vine-ripened tomatoes (about 1¼ pounds), pureed in a food processor or blender or finely chopped
Chopped cilantro (fresh coriander) leaves and garam masala for garnish

Remove the hard shell and rootlike covering from the tamarind pods, then soak in 1 cup of the hot water for 2 to 4 hours or longer (up to 2 days); gently rub with your fingers as they soak. Sieve the pods, add the remaining water to the pulp, mix with your fingers, and extract some more juices. Set aside.

Place the fish in a flat nonreactive dish. Combine the vinegar, garlic, ginger, cumin, turmeric, ½ teaspoon of the salt, and pepper. Pour over the fish and mix until coated. Cover with plastic wrap and refrigerate for 2 to 4 hours.

In a large, nonstick saucepan, heat the oil over moderately high heat. Add the mustard seeds and immediately cover the skillet or the seeds fly out as they pop. When the popping subsides (about 30 seconds), remove the cover and add the peppers, thyme, and tomatoes. Raise the heat to high, cook, stirring, until most of the juices from the tomatoes evaporate, 5 to 7 minutes.

Mix in the marinated halibut, the remaining ½ teaspoon salt, and the tamarind extract and cook until the fish just starts to flake, 8 to 10 minutes. Remove to a platter, garnish with cilantro and garam masala, and serve.

Shrimp Vindaloo

VINDALOO MEANS "WITH VINEGAR," and this sauce, containing vinegar and lots of ground red chilies, is a specialty curry from southern India. We reserve this fiery dish only for the well-seasoned palate that can tolerate its chilied heat. (To make the dish less hot, use paprika instead of the red chilies and add it along with the other dried spices.)

Authentic vindaloo can also be made with chicken, beef, lamb, pork, or potatoes. (All these take longer to cook, so adjust the cooking time—let them remain in the pan when you add the tomatoes.)

Lalit Pant of Nawab of India, a popular restaurant in Santa Monica, California, says, "The longer the marination, the better the vindaloo."

2 to 5 dried red peppers, to your taste, stems removed
3 tablespoons white vinegar
5 to 7 large cloves garlic, to your taste, peeled
One 1½-inch piece fresh ginger, peeled and cut into thin slices
1 large onion, peeled and cut into 6 to 8 wedges
2 teaspoons ground cumin
1½ teaspoons dry mustard
1½ teaspoons garam masala
1 teaspoon salt, or to your taste
¾ teaspoon ground turmeric
1¼ pounds jumbo shrimp, shelled and deveined, with tails removed
2 large, vine-ripened tomatoes, (about 1 pound) each cut into 6 to 8 wedges
2 to 3 tablespoons peanut oil
30 to 40 fresh curry leaves (optional), to your taste, finely chopped
Chopped cilantro (fresh coriander) leaves and garam masala for garnish

Soak the peppers in the vinegar for 30 to 40 minutes or longer. In the work bowl of a food processor and with the motor running, process the peppers until minced by dropping them in through the feed tube. Similarly, add the garlic, ginger, and onion and process until finely chopped. Mix in the vinegar in which the chilies were soaked, the cumin, mustard, garam masala, salt, and turmeric and process to combine.

Put the shrimp in a large bowl, coat completely with the vinegar-onion mixture, cover the bowl with plastic wrap, and refrigerate 4 to 6 or up to 24 hours.

In the same unwashed food processor bowl, process the tomatoes until smooth. Remove to a bowl and refrigerate until needed.

continued

Makes 4 to 6 servings

SERVING IDEAS:
Pair this super-hot dish with steamed basmati rice, or serve as part of a larger menu with naan breads or sourdough rolls and a side of dry-cooked vegetables.

DO AHEAD:
Best when served fresh; however, if you make it with lamb, chicken, pork, or potatoes, it can be made 3 to 5 days in advance and refrigerated.

In a large, nonstick saucepan, heat the oil over moderately high heat and cook the curry leaves, stirring, until golden, 30 to 50 seconds. (Stand away from the pan—the moisture from the curry leaves may cause the oil to splatter.) Add the marinated shrimp plus the marinade and cook until the shrimp are barely firm, 3 to 4 minutes. Remove the shrimp to a bowl. Add the pureed tomatoes to the same pan and cook until most of the liquid has dried up and the sauce is thick, 5 to 7 minutes.

Return the shrimp to the pan and cook for another 3 to 5 minutes to blend the flavors. Transfer to a bowl, garnish with chopped cilantro and garam masala, and serve.

Spinach with Tofu or Paneer Cheese

REMEMBER THE DAYS WHEN we ate our spinach only because Mom said it was good for us? Well, today, we have a choice; we don't absolutely have to eat our spinach—unless we really want to.

2 bunches spinach (1¼ pounds), trimmed of tough stems and thoroughly washed
2 bunches watercress (½ pound), trimmed of tough stems and thoroughly washed
3 tablespoons vegetable oil
One 2-inch stick cinnamon
3 bay leaves
1 cup finely chopped onions
1½ tablespoons peeled and minced fresh ginger
2 teaspoons minced garlic
2 cups finely chopped vine-ripened tomatoes (2 large tomatoes)
1 tablespoon ground coriander
1¼ teaspoons garam masala
1 teaspoon salt, or to your taste
⅓ teaspoon ground turmeric
½ cup half-and-half or nonfat plain yogurt, whisked until smooth
1 pound extra-firm tofu or 1 recipe Homemade Paneer Cheese (page 44), cut into
    ¾-inch cubes
Tomato wedges for garnish

Cook the spinach and watercress (with whatever water is still clinging to their leaves) in a large nonstick saucepan over moderate heat until wilted, 3 to 4 minutes. Cool and process in a food processor until smooth. Set aside.

In another large, nonstick saucepan, heat the oil over moderately high heat and cook the cinnamon, bay leaves, and onions, stirring, until the onions are golden, 3 to 5 minutes. Add the ginger and garlic and cook for another 2 minutes, and add the tomatoes and cook until all the liquid from the tomatoes evaporates, 7 to 10 minutes. Remove the bay leaves and discard, stir in the coriander, 1 teaspoon of the garam masala, the salt, and turmeric, then mix the spinach and cook for 3 to 5 minutes.

Reduce the heat to moderate, add the half-and-half and tofu, and cook for 5 to 7 minutes to heat through and blend the flavors. Stir occasionally and very carefully so as not to break the pieces.

Transfer to a serving dish, garnish with the remaining ¼ teaspoon garam masala and the tomato wedges, and serve hot.

Makes 6 to 8 servings

SERVING IDEAS:
Try with chapati or parantha breads or corn tortillas. Or serve as part of a larger menu with a grilled or saucy meat or chicken dish and a side of dry-cooked vegetables.

DO AHEAD:
Make enough, as this dish stays fresh, refrigerated, for 3 to 5 days. For a freshly cooked look, heat 1 tablespoon oil in a small saucepan until hot but not smoking, remove from the heat, add ½ teaspoon paprika, and immediately top the heated spinach with this mixture. Garnish and serve.

Potatoes in Minty Onion Curry

Makes 8 servings

SERVING IDEAS:

This entrée is terrific with Mixed Vegetables with Fresh Curry Leaves (page 141) or Grilled Eggplant Mush with Tomatoes and Peas (page 196), plain yogurt, and chapati breads or a simple pilaf.

DO AHEAD:

Can be made 3 to 5 days in advance and refrigerated. The curry ingredients (masala) can be cooked and frozen for 2 to 3 months. Thaw the masala, add the potatoes and water, and finish cooking the dish. This dish will thicken as it cools, so adjust the water accordingly, especially if you cook it ahead of time.

EVERYONE LOVES POTATOES, SO why not give them a taste they will savor for a long time.

The curry-making technique here is entirely different—we stir-fry the chopped onions, garlic, and ginger until they are dark brown, then puree and add them to the curry.

For a variation in flavor, throw in some basil, oregano, dill, or any other fragrant herbs of your choice along with (or instead of) the herbs that are already included in this recipe.

4 medium-size, vine-ripened tomatoes, coarsely chopped
½ cup firmly packed cilantro (fresh coriander) leaves, soft stems included
¼ cup firmly packed fresh mint leaves
2 tablespoons fresh thyme leaves
3 tablespoons peanut or safflower oil
1 large onion, cut in half lengthwise and thickly sliced
3 large cloves garlic, peeled
One 1½-inch piece fresh ginger, peeled and cut into thin slices
¼ cup nonfat plain yogurt
2 tablespoon ground coriander
1 teaspoon ground cumin
2 teaspoons ground dried fenugreek leaves
1½ teaspoons garam masala
½ teaspoon ground turmeric
1 teaspoon salt, or to your taste
10 to 12 small russet potatoes (about 2½ pounds), peeled and cut in half lengthwise
3 to 3½ cups water or more, as needed
Chopped cilantro (fresh coriander) or mint leaves for garnish

Place the tomatoes, cilantro, mint, and thyme in the work bowl of a food processor or blender, process until smooth, and remove to a small bowl. Do not wash the food processor.

In a large saucepan, heat the oil over moderately high heat and stir-fry the onion, garlic, and ginger together until the onions are dark brown (almost caramel colored), 10 to 12 minutes. Tilt the pan at an angle to separate the oil from the mixture. Leave the oil in the pan and remove the onion mixture to the food processor. Add the yogurt and process until smooth. Remove to another bowl and set aside.

Transfer the reserved tomato puree to the pan in which the onions were stir-fried and cook over moderately high heat, stirring, until all the liquid from the tomatoes evaporates, 5 to 7 minutes. Add the coriander, cumin, fenugreek leaves, 1 teaspoon of the garam masala, turmeric, and salt, and cook for 1 minute. Mix in the onion-yogurt mixture and potatoes, reduce the heat to moderate, and cook, stirring, for 4 to 5 minutes to thicken slightly. Add the water, raise the heat to high, and bring to a boil. Cover the pan, reduce the heat to moderate, and simmer until the potatoes are tender and the sauce is thick and creamy, 25 to 30 minutes.

Transfer to a serving casserole, garnish with the remaining ½ teaspoon garam masala and the cilantro, and serve.

Curried Chinese Long Beans with Red Potatoes

Makes 8 servings

SERVING IDEAS:

This simple everyday curry is best with a side of another vegetable, a yogurt raita, and chapati breads or whole-wheat tortillas.

DO AHEAD:

Can be made 3 to 5 days in advance and refrigerated.

SOMETIMES KNOWN AS "YARD-long" or "asparagus" beans, Chinese long beans are deep green, stringless, round, and very long (12 to 18 inches). If you can't find them, use any stringless variety.

2 tablespoons safflower oil
1 teaspoon cumin seeds
2 teaspoons ground coriander
¼ teaspoon ground turmeric
¼ teaspoon garam masala
¾ teaspoon salt, or to your taste
1 tablespoon peeled and minced fresh ginger
2 cups peeled, seeded, and finely diced vine-ripened tomatoes
1 cup loosely packed finely chopped cilantro (fresh coriander) leaves, soft stems included
1 pound Chinese long beans, trimmed and cut into ⅓-inch-long pieces
4 to 5 baby red potatoes, peeled and quartered
2 to 2½ cups water, as needed
½ teaspoon mango powder for garnish
2 tablespoons chopped cilantro leaves for garnish

In a large, heavy wok or saucepan, heat the oil over moderately high heat and add the cumin seeds, which should sizzle upon contact with the hot oil. Quickly add the coriander, turmeric, garam masala, salt, and ginger and cook, stirring, for about 30 seconds. Add the tomatoes and cilantro, reduce the heat to moderate and cook, stirring occasionally, until most of the liquid evaporates, 5 to 7 minutes. Add the beans, potatoes, and 2 cups of the water, cover the pan, raise the heat to high and boil for 2 to 3 minutes. Reduce the heat to moderately low and continue to cook until the potatoes are tender and the gravy is thick, 15 to 20 minutes. (If a thinner gravy is required, add some more water and bring to a boil again.)

Transfer to a serving dish, garnish with the mango powder and cilantro, and serve.

Curried Pink Lentils and Yellow Mung Beans with Sautéed Spinach

PINK LENTILS AND YELLOW mung beans are members of the dal (legume) family which includes various types of dried peas and beans. Both these varieties are quick cooking and easy to digest. They do not need endless hours of soaking and simmering, and are loaded with complex carbohydrates and protein.

Cover the pan partially, allowing the steam to escape. This dal produces a froth that rises to the top and spills over. This happens only if the pan is covered tightly. If the steam is allowed to escape, this does not happen. In a tightly covered pan, the steam and froth have no escape, so they push open the lid.

1 cup dried pink lentils, picked over and washed
1 cup dried yellow mung beans, picked over and washed
6 cups water, or more if needed
5 fresh serrano or dried hot red peppers
½ teaspoon ground turmeric
1 teaspoon salt, or to your taste
3 tablespoons canola oil
1 cup finely chopped onions
1 teaspoon cumin seeds
1 tablespoon peeled and minced fresh ginger
1 teaspoon minced garlic
1 small bunch fresh spinach, trimmed of tough stems, thoroughly washed, and finely shredded
1 tablespoon ground coriander
½ teaspoon paprika

Put the lentils, beans, water, peppers, turmeric, and salt in a large saucepan and bring to a boil, uncovered, over high heat. Reduce the heat to low, cover the pan partially, and simmer, stirring occasionally, until soft and creamy, 20 to 25 minutes. Transfer to a serving dish, cover, and keep hot.

In a medium saucepan, heat the oil over moderately high heat and cook the onions, stirring, until golden, 5 to 7 minutes. Add the cumin seeds, which should sizzle upon contact with the hot oil. Mix in the ginger and garlic. Cook, stirring, for another minute or two and then add the spinach. Cook, stirring, until the spinach wilts, 2 to 4 minutes, stir in the coriander and paprika.

Transfer everything to the hot dal and mix lightly with a fork.

Makes 6 to 8 servings

SERVING IDEAS:

Present as a main dish with any dry-cooked vegetable side dish, yogurt raita, and rice or bread. Or pair it with grilled meats, poultry, or seafood. Make it a little soupy and serve as a nutritious soup with a green salad and rolls.

DO AHEAD:

Can be made 4 to 6 hours ahead of time and reheated in the microwave oven. (Do not stir when you reheat, as that will cause the topping to completely mix with the dal.) Or you can cook the dal and spinach 2 to 3 days ahead of time and store separately in the refrigerator, then heat both separately, mix lightly, and serve. Remember, the dal will thicken as it cools and more water may be needed while reheating.

Garbanzo Beans in Tomato-Yogurt Curry

HERE'S ONE OF MOTHER'S recipes that's easy to make and is perfect for entertaining.

One 1½-inch piece fresh ginger, peeled and cut into thin slices
5 large cloves garlic, peeled
1 medium-size onion, peeled and cut into 6 to 8 wedges
2 to 5 jalapeño peppers (optional), to your taste, stems removed
3 large, vine-ripened tomatoes, cut into 8 wedges each
1 cup loosely packed cilantro (fresh coriander) leaves, soft stems included
1 cup lightly packed fresh basil leaves
2 cups nonfat plain yogurt
1½ cups water, or more as needed
3 tablespoons vegetable oil
1 tablespoon ground coriander
1 teaspoon ground cumin
1 teaspoon ground dried fenugreek leaves
½ teaspoon ground turmeric
½ teaspoon paprika
½ teaspoon salt, or to your taste
Four 15½-ounce cans garbanzo beans, drained and rinsed
1 large russet potato, boiled in lightly salted water to cover until tender, drained, peeled, and cut into ¾-inch dice
Garam masala and chopped cilantro leaves for garnish

In a food processor fitted with the metal S-blade, process the garlic, ginger, and onions until smooth by dropping them through the feed tube. Set aside.

In the same processor, process the peppers, tomatoes, cilantro, and basil until smooth. Remove to a separate bowl and set aside. Then process the yogurt and water together until well combined and set aside.

In a large, nonstick saucepan, heat the oil over moderately high heat and cook the onion mixture, stirring, until it turns into a rich golden color, 5 to 7 minutes. Add the tomato mixture and continue to cook, stirring, until all the juices from the tomatoes dry up, 6 to 8 minutes. Add the coriander, cumin, fenugreek leaves, turmeric, paprika, and salt and stir for about 1 minute. Stir in the yogurt mixture, raise the heat to high, and bring to boil. Reduce the heat to moderate, add the garbanzo beans and potato dice, and cook, stirring very carefully, until the beans are very soft and the gravy is thick, 5 to 7 minutes. Remove to a serving bowl. Garnish and serve.

A Sauce and the Chutney Bowl

THE AMERICAN HERITAGE DICTIONARY defines a sauce as "a flavorful liquid dressing or relish served as an accompaniment to food," and "something that adds zest, flavor or piquancy to something else." And that, indeed, is what sauces are all about. Made with an infinite variety of ingredients, some smooth, some chunky, sometimes cooked with vegetables and at others times grilled with meats and seafood, tangy and sour, savory and spicy, hot or cold, sauces are always full of flavor and unconditionally eager to add spirited companionship to all sorts of dishes.

Chutneys, like relishes, are condiments that belong to another group of lively perker-uppers without which mealtimes would be incomplete. They come packed with a spice rack full of tantalizing flavors that radically affect the taste of our foods. Made with vegetables, fruits, fresh herbs, and fragrant spices—sweet, tart, salty, spicy, fiery hot, or mild—freshly blended into one big mush or cooked and preserved, they are all part of the *chat-patti* (savory lip-smacking) family of palate pleasers.

Even though, at times, there is a certain overlap in their definition, sauces and chutneys are uniquely different. Sauces are those special somethings that go hand in hand with the preparation of everyday foods. How can we make a stew or a curry without a sauce or serve plain, "unsaucy" spaghetti and meatballs? Chutneys, on the other hand, are those sprightly guests who live in our pantry and refrigerator and visit us only when we are in the mood for explosive fun and bursts of concentrated flavor.

With this introduction, I bring to you a number of sauces and chutneys that will add a brand-new character and pizzazz to your meals. Partner them with vegetables and chips, grilled and pan-fried foods, pizza or pasta, Mexican, Italian, or American foods and experience a lifetime of joyful eating.

A word about yogurt and yogurt raita sauces in Indian cuisine: Indians customarily serve yogurt (*dahi*) in some form or the other with all their meals. It can reach the table as plain, unadorned, freshly made, and naturally sweet yogurt, or enriched with an array of herbs, spices, vegetables, fruits, and special lentil or *besan* (garbanzo bean flour) dumplings. This value-added enhanced version instantly attains a new identity—it can no longer be called yogurt. It is now a raita. In America, my students and friends refer to raitas as a sauce—and in a broad sense, most of them are. A raita is a smooth sauce when we add only some herbs and spices to adorn it. The addition of chopped or grated uncooked vegetables like cucumber, tomatoes, scallions or onions, zucchini, bell peppers, carrots, beets, or turnips, or boiled potatoes, grilled eggplants, and summer squashes, steamed spinach, and other greens, along with spices and fresh herbs like mint, cilantro, and parsley transforms these smooth sauces into chunky ones that can essentially be presented as side dishes.

Yogurt and yogurt raitas are soothing and nutritious, provide relief on hot summer days, cool the palate when we eat hot and spicy foods, and last, but not the least, fortify our bodies with some friendly bacteria that get our digestive juices flowing.

Yogurt Raita Sauce with Crispy Minced Ginger

REFRESHING TO THE PALATE and nurturing to the stomach, this low-fat yogurt raita sauce is one of the most user-friendly sauces of the Indian cuisine.

3½ cups nonfat plain yogurt
½ cup minced scallion whites
½ cup minced fresh mint leaves
½ teaspoon salt, or to your taste
½ teaspoon freshly ground black pepper, or to your taste
1 tablespoon peanut oil
2 tablespoons peeled and minced fresh ginger
1 tablespoon minced fresh chives or scallion greens for garnish

Put the yogurt in a serving dish and beat with a fork or a whisk until smooth. Mix in the scallions, mint, salt, and pepper.

In a small skillet, heat the oil over moderately high heat and cook the ginger, stirring, until golden, 1 to 2 minutes. Transfer the ginger and oil to the yogurt and mix lightly. Garnish with the chives and serve chilled.

VARIATION: Add 1 teaspoon minced garlic or cumin, caraway, celery, or mustard seeds instead of the ginger. (Cover the pan after adding the mustard seeds—they tend to pop and fly off.)

Makes about 4 cups

SERVING IDEAS:
This versatile sauce replaces sour cream and butter when served with baked potatoes. As a side dish, it pairs well with summer barbecues and winter curries.

DO AHEAD:
Stays fresh in the refrigerator for 5 to 7 days. Don't add the scallions until ready to serve.

Yogurt and Roasted Cumin-Pepper Sauce

Makes about 3½ cups

SERVING IDEAS:

Sensational with bar-becued chicken, seafood, and lamb and with Mexican tacos, tostadas, and fajitas. It also makes a great dressing for green or grilled salads and rice pilafs.

DO AHEAD:

Make 3 to 4 hours in advance and store in the refrigerator. Or com-bine everything, except the scallions and gar-nish, and refrigerate 2 to 4 days, adding them just prior to serving.

OFFSET THE SUMMER'S HEAT with this flavor-laden raita sauce.

To make a more elaborate version, mix in one or more of the following: chopped tomatoes, grated cucumbers, jicama, turnips, or zucchini, diced boiled potatoes, or chopped fresh or frozen spinach.

2 teaspoons cumin seeds
½ to 1 teaspoon black peppercorns
3½ cups nonfat plain yogurt
1 serrano pepper (optional), minced
½ cup minced scallions (white and light green parts)
¼ cup loosely packed finely chopped cilantro (fresh coriander) leaves, soft stems included
2 tablespoons minced fresh mint leaves
½ teaspoon salt, or to your taste
⅛ teaspoon paprika or cayenne pepper for garnish

Put the cumin seeds and peppercorns in a small, nonstick skillet over mod-erately high heat and toast them until the cumin seeds turn a few shades darker and the peppercorns start to pop, 1 to 2 minutes. Shake the pan as you toast them. Cool and coarsely grind them in a spice grinder or with a mortar and pes-tle. Set aside.

Put the yogurt in a serving dish and beat with a fork or a whisk until smooth. Mix in the pepper, scallions, cilantro, mint, and salt.

Setting aside about ½ teaspoon of the cumin-peppercorn mixture for gar-nish, stir the remaining mixture into the yogurt. Garnish with remaining ½ tea-spoon cumin-peppercorn mixture and the paprika and serve.

Yogurt-Tahini Sauce

CALL IT A SAUCE, a dip, or a marinade, the complex flavors in this blended mixture of tahini and yogurt are really a knockout.

Tahini is a paste (or "butter") made with sesame seeds. It is available in Middle Eastern markets and health food stores and in some supermarkets.

¾ cup nonfat plain yogurt
2 tablespoons tahini
2 large cloves garlic, minced or pressed
One 1-inch piece fresh ginger, peeled and minced or ground
2 tablespoons fresh lemon juice
¼ teaspoon sesame oil
½ teaspoon freshly ground black pepper, or to your taste
¾ teaspoon salt, or to your taste
2 tablespoons minced cilantro (fresh coriander) leaves

In a small bowl, mix everything together until smooth. Taste and adjust the seasonings and refrigerate until needed.

Makes about 1 cup

SERVING IDEAS:
Great with chopped raw or lightly steamed vegetables and grilled chicken and seafood. Mix in some more yogurt and honey and it turns into a delicious salad dressing. Or add to pita pockets with garbanzo beans and lots of diced tomatoes and lettuce.

DO AHEAD:
Can be made up to a week in advance and refrigerated.

Velvety Tamarind and Mango Sauce

Makes about 4 cups

SERVING IDEAS:

Drizzle over yogurt raitas and salads, present as a dipping sauce with appetizers and tandoori fare, or mix in some diced ripe bananas (or peaches and apricots) and raisins and serve as a condiment with meals.

DO AHEAD:

An ideal do-ahead sauce—it stays fresh for about 2 months in the refrigerator and can be frozen for almost a year. Freeze in smaller containers, then thaw, stir to mix, and use as needed. If the consistency is not smooth, boil again.

THIS DARK-BROWN, SWEET-and-sour sauce of smooth and velvety consistency is called *sonth* in India. There it is most popularly served as a spiky sauce over special chaats and chaat salads (page 33) but I find that it also lends itself beautifully to an array of American appetizers and grilled fare.

Jaggery is an unrefined medium-brown cane sugar that comes in big round blocks or in broken lumps. It is available in Indian and Middle Eastern markets. Tamarind powder is also available in Indian markets.

1 pound jaggery or 1 cup firmly packed dark brown sugar
3 cups water
1 cup tamarind powder, sifted to remove lumps
2 tablespoons chaat masala
2 teaspoons ground ginger
2 teaspoons ground roasted (page 10) cumin seeds
2 teaspoons salt, or to your taste
½ teaspoon black salt

Coarsely pound the jaggery pieces and put in a large, nonstick saucepan. Add the water and stir to mix. (It will still remain quite lumpy.) Cook over moderately high heat, stirring occasionally, until the lumps dissolve completely, 3 to 4 minutes. Remove from the heat and mix in the remaining ingredients. Return to the stove, raise the heat to moderately high, and bring to a boil. Reduce the heat to moderate and cook, stirring occasionally, for 3 to 5 minutes. Add up to an additional ½ cup water if the sauce looks too thick. (Always bring the mixture to a boil after you add the water or the sauce will spoil quickly.)

Adjust the seasonings, transfer to a bowl, and refrigerate until needed.

Pureed Onion and Chipotle Pepper Sauce

CHIPOTLE PEPPERS ARE SMOKE-dried jalapeño peppers from Mexico and they impart a flavor that no other pepper can. And I don't just mean the heat—it's their outstanding smoky aroma, which can be intoxicating.

I can handle very hot foods, but this sauce is *muy pica* even for me. To mellow it down, boil both the chilies with the onions, but puree only one of them (or half of one). Or add some chopped fresh tomatoes, cilantro, and yogurt and adjust the seasonings to suit your palate.

1 large onion, peeled and cut into 8 pieces
1 or 2 dried chipotle peppers (do not substitute), to your taste
3 large cloves garlic, peeled
2 black cardamon pods, pounded with a pestle until completely broken apart
2 bay leaves, broken into small pieces
1¼ cups water
1 large, vine-ripened tomato, cut into 6 wedges
¼ cup nonfat plain yogurt
½ teaspoon salt, or to your taste
1 tablespoon vegetable oil

Put the onion, peppers, garlic, cardamom pods, bay leaves, and water in a medium saucepan, cover, and bring to a boil over high heat. Reduce the heat to moderate and continue to boil until all the water evaporates and the onion pieces start to caramelize on the bottom, 10 to 12 minutes.

Transfer to the work bowl of a food processor or blender, add the tomato, yogurt, and salt and process until smooth.

In a saucepan, heat the oil over moderately high heat until hot but not smoking. Put the sauce into the saucepan and bring to a boil. Reduce the heat to moderately low and simmer for 3 to 5 minutes. Remove to a serving bowl and serve hot.

Makes about 1 cup

SERVING IDEAS:
Use as a condiment with grilled meat, chicken, fish, fajitas, or chips, or over pasta, pizza, or sautéed vegetables. Or present as a dipping sauce with crudités, corn chips, and deep-fried finger foods.

DO AHEAD:
Can hold up to 7 days in the refrigerator or freeze for 2 to 3 months.

Roasted Red Lipstick Pepper Sauce with Chipotle Peppers

Makes about 2 cups

SERVING IDEAS:

Try making your next loaf of bread with this sauce (adjust the quantity of liquid) or serve as a dip with chopped vegetables and corn chips, on the side with barbecued meats and steamed vegetables, or as a topping over pieces of paneer or fresh mozzarella cheese.

DO AHEAD:

Can be refrigerated 3 to 5 days or frozen for 2 to 3 months.

THE FIRST TIME I saw red lipstick peppers at my farmers' market in Santa Monica, I did not know what to expect. The first bite unfolded their sweet secret. Brilliantly red in color, looking like oversized jalapeño peppers (1½ to 3 inches across at the stem end and 3 to 5 inches in length), lipstick peppers are available only during the short summer months. If you cannot find them, use red bell peppers instead. To mellow the fiery bite of this sauce, mix in some nonfat sour cream. Canned chipotle peppers in adobo sauce are available in most supermarkets.

1 pound red lipstick peppers or 2 large red bell peppers
2 large cloves garlic, peeled
One 1-inch piece fresh ginger, peeled and cut into 3 to 4 thin slices
½ cup firmly packed cilantro (fresh coriander) leaves, soft stems included
¼ cup firmly packed fresh mint or basil leaves or 2 teaspoons dried
1 canned chipotle pepper
1 tablespoon fresh lemon or lime juice, or more to your taste
½ to ¾ teaspoon salt, to your taste
½ teaspoon freshly ground black pepper, or to your taste
¼ to ½ cup nonfat plain yogurt, to your taste, whisked until smooth
Chopped cilantro for garnish
Garam masala for garnish

Wash the peppers and then roast them over an open flame, on a grill, or under a broiler until charred on all sides. Remove to a bowl, cover the bowl with plastic wrap, and set aside for 15 to 30 minutes. (This allows the peppers to sweat and cool down, making them easy to peel. Roasted peppers can remain unpeeled for 5 to 7 days in the refrigerator.) Peel the peppers, removing as much of the charred skin as possible. (Do not wash them in water because this leaches out most of the juices and flavor from the peppers. Rinsing your hands as you go along is adequate.) Remove the stems, coarsely chop the peppers, and set aside in a bowl. Strain the accumulated juices and add that to the bowl.

In the work bowl of a food processor or blender, process the roasted peppers, garlic, ginger, cilantro, mint, pepper, and lemon juice together until smooth. Add the salt, pepper, and yogurt and blend again until smooth. Taste and adjust the seasonings. Transfer to a serving bowl. Garnish and serve.

Pasta Sauce with Roasted Japanese Eggplants and Peppers

THIS SKILLFUL MINGLING TINGLES your taste buds as you gobble up your pasta.

Makes 6 to 7 cups

2 to 4 Japanese eggplants (½ to ¾ pound)
1 large red bell pepper
1 large poblano pepper
2 tablespoons olive oil
1 tablespoon minced garlic
½ to 1 teaspoon minced serrano peppers, to your taste
½ teaspoon cayenne pepper (optional)
4 to 5 medium-size, vine-ripened tomatoes, coarsely chopped
1 tablespoon mixed dried basil and oregano
1 teaspoon ground dried fenugreek leaves
One 15-ounce jar tomato sauce
½ teaspoon salt, or to your taste
¼ cup half-and-half, nonfat sour cream, or nonfat plain yogurt, whisked until
   smooth
½ cup firmly packed chopped fresh basil leaves, or more to your taste

SERVING IDEAS:
  Enjoy with pasta, lasagna, or pizza or make quick pizza bagels or toasts. Simmer pieces of paneer cheese, tofu, or fresh mozzarella cheese in it or pair with all sorts of freshly grilled fare.

DO AHEAD:
  Can be made 5 to 7 days ahead of time and refrigerated. It also freezes very well up to 3 months.

NOTE:
  Do not wash peeled eggplants and peppers in water because this leaches out most of the juices and flavor from the eggplants and peppers. Rinsing your hands as you go along is adequate.

Roast the eggplants and peppers over an open flame or under a broiler until charred on all sides. Remove to a bowl, cover with plastic wrap, and set aside for 15 to 30 minutes. (This allows the peppers to sweat and cool down, making them easy to peel. Roasted eggplants and peppers can remain unpeeled for 3 to 5 days in the refrigerator.) Peel the eggplants and peppers, removing as much of the charred skin as possible. Remove the stems of the eggplants and the stems and seeds of the peppers, coarsely chop, and put in the work bowl of a food processor or blender. Strain all the accumulated juices and add them to the bowl. Process the eggplants and peppers together until smooth. Set aside.

In a medium saucepan, heat the oil over moderately high heat and cook the garlic, stirring, until it just starts to turn golden, 45 to 60 seconds. Mix in the minced serrano peppers and cayenne pepper, add the tomatoes, basil, and oregano, and fenugreek leaves and cook, stirring, until the tomatoes are soft, 1 to 2 minutes. Add the eggplant and pepper puree and cook, stirring, for a minute or two. Mix in the tomato sauce and salt and bring to a boil. Add the half-and-half and fresh basil and simmer for 2 to 4 minutes before serving.

Creamy Tomato Sauce

Makes about 4 cups

SERVING IDEAS:

Team with stuffed potatoes, zucchini, or eggplant or pair with grilled seafood, chicken, pasta, or rice pilafs. Or make a quick entrée by simmering pieces of leftover turkey or chicken, tofu, paneer cheese, or lightly steamed or microwaved vegetables in it for a few minutes.

DO AHEAD:

Can be made 3 to 5 days in advance and refrigerated; or be frozen for 2 to 3 months.

ONE SIMPLE VEGETABLE (OR should I say, fruit)—tomato—and how it dominates the cooking scene, be it Indian or Italian. Here is a spectacular sauce that takes the best from both cuisines.

3 large, vine-ripened tomatoes (1½ to 2 pounds), coarsely chopped
4 to 6 large cloves garlic, to your taste, peeled
One 1¼-inch pieces fresh ginger, peeled and cut into thin slices
½ teaspoon salt, or to your taste
½ teaspoon freshly ground black pepper, or to your taste
1½ cups water
¼ cup finely chopped fresh basil leaves
2 to 3 tablespoons cornstarch dissolved in ¾ cup water
½ cup heavy cream or half-and-half
1 tablespoon canola oil
1 to 2 serrano peppers, to your taste, halved or quartered lengthwise
1 tablespoon ground coriander
½ teaspoon ground cumin
½ teaspoon paprika
¼ teaspoon garam masala
Chopped fresh basil leaves for garnish

Put the tomatoes, garlic, ginger, salt, pepper, and water in a large saucepan. Cover and cook over moderately high heat for 5 to 7 minutes, then reduce the heat to moderate and cook until the tomatoes are completely softened, 15 to 20 minutes. Cool and pass through a food mill or puree in a blender or food processor. (To make it smooth, puree, then pass through a sieve.) Return the sauce to the saucepan.

Add the basil and bring the sauce to a boil over moderately high heat. Stir in the cornstarch-and-water slurry. Reduce the heat to low, add the cream, and simmer the sauce for 2 to 4 minutes to blend flavors.

Meanwhile, heat the oil in a small saucepan over moderately high heat and stir-fry the peppers for about 1 minute, until golden. (Stand away from the pan while you are doing this in case the chilies burst and accidentally fly toward your face.) Mix in the coriander, cumin, paprika, and garam masala, immediately remove the pan from the heat, and transfer the contents to the sauce. Stir to mix and remove the sauce from the heat. Garnish with the chopped fresh basil and serve.

Sunil's Marinara Sauce

THIS SAUCE COMES TO us with the compliments of Sunil Vora of The Clay Pit, an Indian restaurant in Los Angeles. Sunil prefers to blanch, seed, and then chop the tomatoes, but to make the recipe easier and faster, I simply chop them.

2 tablespoons extra-virgin olive oil
1 cup finely chopped onions
1 teaspoon dried oregano
1 teaspoon dried basil
3 cups finely chopped vine-ripened tomatoes (3 large tomatoes)
½ teaspoon salt, or to your taste
¼ cup lightly packed finely chopped cilantro (fresh coriander) leaves, soft stems
    included

In a medium, nonstick saucepan, heat the oil over moderately high heat and cook the onions, stirring, until golden, 3 to 5 minutes. Add the oregano, basil, tomatoes, and salt and cook until the tomatoes soften and the sauce is thick, 10 to 12 minutes. Add the cilantro and cook for another minute. Remove to a serving bowl and serve with Sunil's Cumin-Baked Sea Bass with Marinara Sauce (page 208).

Makes about 2 cups

SERVING IDEAS:
Magnificent with cooked pasta, pizza, baked fish, and chicken as well as Indian parantha breads, paneer cheese, and tandoori fare.

DO AHEAD:
Stays fresh for 5 to 7 days in the refrigerator and freezes well for about 3 months.

Tangy Plum Sauce

CELEBRATE THE SUMMER WITH this light and refreshing sauce made with pureed tree-ripened plums and lots of fresh ginger. Also, try making it with peaches, nectarines, apricots, mangoes, and other fragrant fruits of the summer months.

SERVING IDEAS:

Delicious served as a dip with Indian and Chinese appetizers. Add some whisked yogurt and it becomes a perfect salad dressing. Drizzle over roasted vegetables, use as a marinade for fillets of fish, or cook until very thick and use as a last-minute glaze.

DO AHEAD:

Stays fresh in the refrigerator for 4 to 5 days and in the freezer for 2 to 3 months.

One 1½-inch piece fresh ginger, peeled and cut into thin slices
2 to 4 serrano peppers (optional), to your taste, stems removed
1 to 1½ pounds firm plums, pitted and coarsely cut into small pieces (peeled or unpeeled)
½ cup loosely packed cilantro (fresh coriander) leaves, soft stems included
2 to 4 tablespoons fresh lime or lemon juice, to your taste
1 tablespoon sesame seeds, toasted (page 34)
½ teaspoon sesame oil
½ teaspoon salt, or to your taste
½ teaspoon freshly ground black pepper, or to your taste
Garam masala for garnish

In the work bowl of a food processor fitted with the metal S-blade and the motor running, drop the ginger and peppers through the feed tube and process until minced. Add the plums, cilantro, lemon juice, sesame seeds, sesame oil, salt, and pepper and process, stopping to scrape down the sides a few times, until minced.

Transfer to a serving bowl, garnish with the garam masala, and serve.

Quick Ginger, Apple, and Jalapeño Pepper Sauce

PUREED APPLES, GINGER, AND jalapeño peppers are simmered in citrus juices to make this slightly tangy, savory sauce that will enslave your taste buds forever.

One 2-inch piece fresh ginger, peeled and cut into thin-slices

2 to 4 jalapeño peppers, to your taste, stems removed

2 small MacIntosh apples (or any other tart apple), cored, peeled, and cut into 1-inch pieces

4 small, vine-ripened (or canned) Roma tomatoes, quartered

3 tablespoons corn oil

1 cup firmly packed finely chopped cilantro (fresh coriander) leaves, soft stems included

1½ tablespoons ground coriander

¾ teaspoon salt, or to your taste

½ teaspoon freshly ground black pepper, or to your taste

½ cup fresh lemon juice

1 cup fresh orange juice

1 tablespoon minced fresh chives or garlic chives for garnish

In the work bowl of a food processor fitted with the metal S-blade and the motor running, drop the ginger and peppers through the feed tube and process until minced. Add the apples and tomatoes and process, stopping to scrape down the sides of the work bowl a few times, until minced.

In a medium, nonstick saucepan, heat the oil over moderate heat and cook the apple mixture, stirring, until it is fragrant and golden and all the juices evaporate, 12 to 15 minutes. Mix in the cilantro, and add the coriander, salt, and pepper. Stir for 30 seconds. Mix in the lemon and orange juices and bring to a boil. Simmer for a minute or two to blend flavors and remove to a bowl. Garnish with chives and serve hot or chilled.

Makes about 2 cups

SERVING IDEAS:

Present on the side with any type of grilled meat, poultry, or seafood, as a spread in hamburgers and sandwiches, over cooked pasta, or as a pizza sauce. I love to stuff it in romaine lettuce leaves and snack on them.

DO AHEAD:

Stays fresh for 5 to 7 days in the refrigerator, or frozen for 2 to 3 months. In fact, the flavors improve as time goes on.

Guacamole with Yogurt and Chaat Masala

I FOUND OUT A long time ago that yogurt prevents guacamole from discoloring. It also increases the volume, enhances the taste, and fortifies it with protein and calcium.

2 large avocados, peeled, pitted, and mashed with a fork (about 1½ cups)
½ cup nonfat plain yogurt, whisked until smooth
½ cup finely chopped vine-ripened tomatoes
¼ cup minced scallion whites
1 tablespoon peeled and minced fresh ginger
1 to 3 serrano peppers, to your taste, minced
½ cup firmly packed finely chopped cilantro (fresh coriander) leaves, soft stems included
3 to 4 tablespoons fresh lime or lemon juice, to your taste
1 teaspoon chaat masala, or to your taste
1 teaspoon salt, or to your taste
Chopped cilantro for garnish

Put the mashed avocados in a large serving bowl and mix in the remaining ingredients, except the garnish. Taste, adjust the seasonings, and refrigerate until ready to serve. Garnish with cilantro and serve.

SERVING IDEAS:

Present with tacos, tostadas, quesadillas, and fajitas. It adds an intriguing touch to sandwiches and pita pockets and pizzas (add it after the pizza has been cooked). Also a perfect partner to corn or potato chips and freshly cut vegetables.

DO AHEAD:

Can be stored and refrigerated up to 4 days ahead. To freeze, omit the yogurt and freeze in airtight containers for 2 to 3 months. Thaw, mix in the yogurt, garnish, and serve.

Green Cilantro Chutney

THIS SPELLBINDING PUREE OF "greens"—cilantro, mint, peppers, and scallions—is a must in every home.

3 to 5 serrano peppers, to your taste, stems removed
1 fresh poblano pepper, seeded and cut into 4 to 6 pieces
2 cups coarsely chopped scallion greens
3 cups firmly packed cilantro (fresh coriander) leaves, soft stems included
½ cup firmly packed fresh mint leaves
¼ cup fresh lime or lemon juice
1 teaspoon sugar
1 teaspoon salt, or to your taste
½ teaspoon freshly ground black pepper
Cilantro or mint leaves for garnish

In the work bowl of a food processor fitted with the metal S-blade and the motor running, drop the peppers and scallions through the feed tube and process until smooth. Add the cilantro and mint (in 2 or 3 batches, adding more as each batch gets pureed) and with the motor running, pour the lime juice in a fine stream and blend until smooth. Add the sugar, salt, and black pepper and process, stopping to scrape down the sides of the work bowl a few times, until minced. Transfer to a bowl, adjust the seasonings, garnish with cilantro, and serve.

Makes about 2½ cups

SERVING IDEAS:
This can be a condiment with the main meal, a dip for snacks and appetizers, a glaze for different meats (see Grilled Chicken Thighs Glazed with Cilantro Chutney, page 180), a sandwich spread, a spunky pizza sauce, and a salad partner—the list is endless.

DO AHEAD:
Stays fresh in the refrigerator 10 to 15 days and in the freezer for up to 6 months. Freeze in ice cube trays and transfer to freezer bags after frozen.

Yogurt-Cilantro Chutney

Makes about 2¹/₂ cups

SERVING IDEAS:
  This versatile chutney can be used inter-changeably with Green Cilantro Chutney (page 257).

DO AHEAD:
  Stays fresh in the refrigerator for 6 to 8 days.

THIS SAUCY CHUTNEY IS basically a cilantro chutney enriched with yogurt and additional spices. It can double as a zesty side dish if more yogurt is added to it.

5 jalapeño peppers, stems removed
6 scallions, each cut into 3 to 4 pieces
2 cups firmly packed cilantro (fresh coriander) leaves, soft stems included
3 tablespoons fresh lime or lemon juice, or more to your taste
1 teaspoon chaat masala, or to your taste
1 teaspoon sugar
1 teaspoon salt, or to your taste
½ teaspoon freshly ground black pepper, or to your taste
1½ cups nonfat plain yogurt, whisked until smooth
½ teaspoon paprika and a few sprigs cilantro for garnish

In the work bowl of a food processor fitted with the metal S-blade and the motor running, drop the peppers and scallions through the feed tube and process until smooth. Add the cilantro, and with the motor running, pour the lemon juice in a fine stream, and process, stopping to scrape down the sides of the work bowl a few times, until minced. Add the chaat masala, sugar, salt, and pepper and combine. Taste and adjust the seasonings.

Put the yogurt in a serving bowl, mix in the processed chutney, adjust the seasonings, and refrigerate until needed. Garnish with paprika and cilantro sprigs and serve.

Jalapeño and Basil Pesto-Style Chutney

THE TITLE TELLS IT all. Pesto is a pureed blend of garlic, pine nuts, olive oil, and fresh basil leaves. Chutney is a puree of hot peppers, scallion greens, fresh herbs, and lemon juice. Together, this tangy mixture makes a superb pesto-style chutney.

3 tablespoons pine nuts
3 to 4 large cloves garlic, to your taste, peeled
5 jalapeño peppers, stems removed
6 scallions, each cut into 3 to 4 pieces
1½ cups firmly packed chopped fresh basil leaves
1 cup firmly packed, chopped cilantro (fresh coriander) leaves, soft stems included
2 tablespoons olive oil
3 tablespoons fresh lime or lemon juice, or more to your taste
1 teaspoon chaat masala, or more to your taste
1 teaspoon sugar
1 teaspoon salt, or to your taste
½ teaspoon freshly ground black pepper, or to your taste
Fresh basil leaves for garnish

In the work bowl of a food processor fitted with the metal S-blade and the motor running, drop the pine nuts, garlic, peppers, and scallions through the feed tube and process until smooth. Add the basil and cilantro, then start the machine, add the oil and lemon juice in a fine stream, and process until smooth. (Scrape down the sides of the work bowl a few times with a spatula.) Add the chaat masala, sugar, salt, and pepper and combine. Taste and adjust the seasonings. Transfer to a serving bowl and refrigerate until needed. Garnish with basil leaves and serve.

Makes about 2½ cups

SERVING IDEAS:
Like Green Cilantro Chutney (page 257) this pesto-chutney is wonderful with an array of appetizers, sandwiches, pizzas, pastas, and grilled fare.

DO AHEAD:
Stays fresh in the refrigerator 10 to 15 days and in the freezer for up to 6 months. Freeze in ice cube trays and transfer to freezer bags after frozen.

Italian Parsley and Mango Chutney

Makes about 2 cups

SERVING IDEAS:

Serve interchangeably with Green Cilantro Chutney (page 257) with all sorts of appetizers, sandwiches, and crudités or as a condiment with the main meal.

DO AHEAD:

Stays fresh in the refrigerator for 6 to 8 days.

WHEN I ASKED MY greengrocer for regular parsley, he looked at me disdainfully and said, "I don't sell that stuff, I only have Italian parsley—it has more flavor." Yes, the flavor is wonderful and so is the texture of this smooth, pesto-style chutney that comes packed with the goodness of parsley (rich in vitamin C and iron) and citrusy cilantro, and contains no oil or nuts.

1 to 5 serrano peppers (optional), to your taste, stems removed
1 small, extra-firm mango (about ½ pound), peeled, seeded, and cut into small
   pieces
2 to 3 cloves garlic, to your taste, peeled
6 scallions, each cut into 3 to 4 pieces
1 cup firmly packed fresh Italian parsley leaves
1 cup firmly packed cilantro (fresh coriander) leaves, soft stems included
½ cup nonfat plain yogurt, or more to your taste, whisked until smooth
2 to 4 tablespoons fresh lemon or lime juice, to your taste
1 tablespoon ground roasted (page 10) cumin seeds
½ teaspoon freshly ground black pepper, or to your taste
½ teaspoon black salt
1 teaspoon salt, or to your taste
Few sprigs fresh Italian parsley for garnish

In the work bowl of a food processor fitted with the metal S-blade and the motor running, drop the peppers, mango, garlic, and scallions through the feed tube and proceed process until smooth. Add the parsley and cilantro, then start the machine, add the yogurt and lemon juice through the feed tube, and process until smooth. (Stop the machine and scrape down the sides of the work bowl a few times with a spatula.)

Add the cumin seeds, pepper, black salt, and salt and process once again. Taste and adjust the seasonings. Transfer to a serving bowl and refrigerate until needed. Garnish with parsley leaves and serve.

Garlicky Cashew and Almond Chutney

Makes about 2 cups

IT'S SNOWY WHITE, LOOKS like ground coconut chutney, and tastes like fresh, unripe nuts taken straight off the trees and spiked with heavenly flavors and a squeeze of fresh lime.

When the almonds are soaked in water, they absorb moisture, become soft, slip their skins easily, and capture some of their original essence. This centuries-old practice is supposed to transform the almonds into super-powerful health foods that strike a balance with the heat in the body, while enriching the cells in the brain. That is why my mother gave us a few soaked, skinned almonds with our milk every morning. My husband got his almonds dipped in honey.

30 shelled raw almonds
1 small clove garlic, peeled
One 1-inch piece fresh ginger, peeled and cut into thin slices
1 serrano or jalapeño pepper (optional), stem removed
30 to 35 raw cashews
2 tablespoons fresh lime or lemon juice
½ teaspoon salt, or to your taste
½ teaspoon freshly ground white or black pepper, or to your taste
1 cup nonfat plain yogurt, whisked until smooth
Chopped cilantro (fresh coriander) or mint leaves for garnish

Soak the almonds in water to cover for 8 to 12 hours at room temperature. Drain and remove the brown skins. Set aside.

In the work bowl of a food processor fitted with the metal S-blade and the motor running, drop the garlic, ginger, pepper, almonds, and cashews through the feed tube and process until minced. Add the lime juice, salt, and pepper and process again until smooth.

Put the yogurt in a serving bowl and stir in the puree. Garnish with cilantro and serve.

SERVING IDEAS:

As perfect with finger foods as it is with sandwiches, grilled and oven-roasted meats, poultry, and seafood. For a variation, sauté the ground-nut mixture in 1 tablespoon oil until golden, and then mix into the yogurt.

DO AHEAD:

Make the puree and store in the refrigerator for up to 7 days. Mix with the yogurt only when needed.

Minty Sweet Pepper Chutney

Makes about 1 cup

SERVING IDEAS:

I like to add 1 to 2 teaspoons of this to stir-fried vegetables, greens, or shrimp. Add to the hot oil before mixing in the vegetables or as a final touch to the cooked dish. Add some red or green peppers and make a fiery version, then present it with pizza (instead of red pepper flakes) or mix it with pureed tomatoes to make an unusual salsa.

DO AHEAD:

Stays fresh for 10 to 15 days in the refrigerator and can be frozen for 2 to 3 months.

RED BELL PEPPERS ARE combined with garlic, ginger, and fresh mint to make this breath-taking chutney.

2 large red bell peppers
One 1-inch piece fresh ginger, peeled and cut into thin slices
3 large cloves garlic, peeled
½ cup firmly packed fresh mint leaves
1½ teaspoons salt, or to your taste
1 teaspoon coarsely ground carom seeds
1 to 3 teaspoons cayenne pepper (optional), to your taste
1 teaspoon coarsely ground black pepper
¼ cup fresh lemon juice

Cut each pepper in half and remove the stems, seeds, and white membranes. Then cut into 1-inch cubes.

In the work bowl of a food processor fitted with the metal s-blade and the motor running, drop the ginger and garlic through the feed tube and process until minced. Then add the mint and red pepper pieces and process until smooth. Add the salt, carom seeds, cayenne, black pepper, and lemon juice and process again to mix. Refrigerate at least 24 hours before using.

Cranberry-Orange Chutney

ORANGE ZEST, THE THIN, fragrant, glossy outer skin of the orange, is used as a spice to add new flavor to an old favorite. With a vegetable peeler, remove the very thin outer layer from an orange, making sure that you do not remove any white pith.

Zest of 2 large oranges
One 1½-inch piece fresh ginger, peeled and cut into thin slices
2 to 5 serrano peppers (optional), to your taste, stems removed
1 tablespoon vegetable oil
10 black cardamom pods, pounded lightly to break the skins
One 3-inch stick cinnamon
1 tablespoon fennel seeds
½ teaspoon nigella seeds
1 teaspoon coarsely ground fenugreek seeds
Two 12-ounce packages fresh or frozen cranberries
2 cups water
2 cups orange juice, preferably fresh
3½ cups sugar
1½ teaspoons salt, or to your taste
5 tablespoons white vinegar, or more to your taste
1 tablespoon blanched almond slivers, toasted (page 34), for garnish
1 tablespoon pine nuts, toasted (page 34), for garnish

In the work bowl of a food processor fitted with the metal S-blade and the motor running, drop the orange zest, ginger, and peppers through the feed tube and process until minced. Set aside.

Heat the oil in a large, heavy stainless steel or other nonreactive saucepan over moderately high heat and cook the cardamom pods, cinnamon, fennel, nigella, and fenugreek seeds, stirring, until fragrant, 45 to 60 seconds. Stir in the orange zest mixture, and add the cranberries, water, orange juice, sugar, and salt. Raise the heat to high and bring to a boil. Cook, stirring, until everything turns slightly thick, 5 to 7 minutes. Watch carefully for accidental spills.

Reduce the heat to moderate, add the vinegar, and continue to cook until the chutney is quite thick, another 7 to 10 minutes. The chutney will continue to thicken as it cools. Transfer to a bowl and set aside until cold. Garnish with the toasted nuts and serve.

Makes about 6 cups

SERVING IDEAS:
Charming not only with Thanksgiving and Christmas dinner, but everyday roasted and grilled foods. Also great on hot toasted bread, in plain yogurt, or with any rice pilaf.

DO AHEAD:
This preserved chutney can be stored in the refrigerator for over a year.

Mango, Apple, and Peach Chutney

Makes about 2½ cups

Serving Ideas:

Present as a savory fruit spread on hot buttered toast or as a condiment with any meal. Combine with plain yogurt or pureed roasted peppers to make a wonderful salad dressing or sauce for grilled seafood, chicken, or vegetables. Also excellent with freshly made chapatis and paranthas.

Do Ahead:

Stays fresh for over 1 year at room temperature. It does not need to be refrigerated until opened.

THIS COMPLEX SWEET, TART, and aromatic chutney is a take-off on the traditional mango chutney.

1 large, extra-firm, unripe green mango (about ¾ pound)
1 large Granny Smith or any other tart apple (about ½ pound)
2 to 3 extra firm, unripe peaches (about ½ pound)
1 tablespoon peanut oil
1 teaspoon minced garlic
1 teaspoon ground fenugreek seeds
¼ teaspoon asafetida
1 teaspoon black peppercorns
20 cloves
One 3-inch stick cinnamon
5 black cardamom pods, pounded lightly to break the skins
½ teaspoon nigella seeds
1½ teaspoons salt, or to your taste
2 cups sugar
6 tablespoons white vinegar

Peel, seed, and cut the mango into large pieces, then grate it with the apple and peaches. This can be done by hand or in a food processor fitted with the grating disk.

In a large, heavy, stainless steel or other nonreactive saucepan, heat the oil over moderately high heat and cook the garlic and fenugreek, stirring, until golden, 1 to 2 minutes. Add the asafetida, peppercorns, cloves, cinnamon, cardamom pods, and nigella seeds and stir for another minute. Mix in the grated fruits, salt, and sugar. Raise the heat to high and bring to a boil, stirring, for 4 to 5 minutes. (The sugar will melt and there will be enough liquid.) Reduce the heat to moderately low and simmer until the chutney becomes slightly thick, 15 to 20 minutes. Mix in the vinegar and continue to simmer until the syrup is thick and golden like honey, another 15 to 20 minutes. (Don't allow the chutney to become too thick, because it will thicken further as it cools.)

Let the chutney cool completely, then put it in sterile glass jars. Store in a cool place. The color of the chutney deepens with the passing of time, but that does not affect the taste. Always use a dry spoon when ladling it out, as added moisture will cause the chutney to spoil faster.

Yogurt Cheese–Herb Mayonnaise

THIS MAYONNAISE IS A health-promoting blend of eggs, fruit, yogurt, herbs, and spices. (Discard the yolks and add 2 extra egg whites, if you so desire.)

I cook the turmeric in hot oil before adding it to the mayonnaise for two reasons. One, so it doesn't taste raw, and more important, because cooked turmeric imparts a brilliant yellow color, which raw turmeric does not.

¾ cup yogurt cheese (page 79)
1 tablespoon fresh lime or lemon juice
1 large clove garlic, peeled
One ½-inch piece fresh ginger, peeled and cut into thin slices
1 to 3 serrano or jalapeño peppers, to your taste, stems removed
3 large hard-boiled eggs, shells removed
¼ cup lightly packed chopped cilantro (fresh coriander) leaves, soft stems included
½ to 1 teaspoon dry mustard, to your taste
1 teaspoon salt, or to your taste
½ teaspoon freshly ground black pepper, or to your taste
1 tablespoon canola oil
½ teaspoon ground turmeric

Put the yogurt cheese and lime juice in a medium serving bowl and mix well with a wire whisk or fork.

In the work bowl of a food processor fitted with the metal S-blade and the motor running, drop the garlic, ginger, peppers, and eggs through the feed tube and process until minced. Add the cilantro, mustard, salt, and pepper and process until everything is well mixed. Taste and adjust the seasonings. Put in the bowl with the yogurt cheese and combine thoroughly.

In a small saucepan, heat the oil over moderate heat until hot but not smoking. Remove from the heat, add the turmeric, and immediately pour the contents into the mayonnaise bowl. Stir to mix and refrigerate until needed.

Makes about 1½ cups

SERVING IDEAS:
Call it a mayonnaise, chutney, sauce, or sandwich spread, this versatile recipe serves the purpose of all of them.

DO AHEAD:
This will stay fresh for 3 to 5 days in the refrigerator.

Soy-Pickled Jalapeño Peppers

Makes about ½ cup

SERVING IDEAS:

Especially delicious in Cream-Style Chicken Corn Soup with Pickled Jalapeño Peppers (page 20), but also intriguing with deep-fried appetizers (Samosa Egg Rolls or Potato and Vegetable Cutlets, page 95 or 97), stir-fried noodles, and steamed basmati rice. I also like to use it to make paneer cheese (page 44). I boil the milk and then add this pickle, instead of yogurt, to curdle it.

DO AHEAD:

Make this pickle ahead of time—it stays fresh for 1 to 2 months in the refrigerator.

THIS SPUNKY PICKLE, MADE with jalapeño peppers, soy sauce, and vinegar, is served in Chinese restaurants throughout India. Beware, it is very hot, so use sparingly. I once added one super-hot habanero pepper to it and it turned out so hot that even my brother Virender Bhalla, who can generally handle very hot foods, almost touched the sky.

¼ cup white vinegar
2 tablespoons soy sauce
4 to 6 jalapeño peppers, to your taste, quartered lengthwise and thinly sliced
1 teaspoon salt
1 teaspoon freshly ground black pepper

In a bowl or a bottle, combine all the ingredients and refrigerate until ready to use.

Wild for Rice

"AND WHAT ABOUT A *pullao* [pilaf]?" my father would say when my mother recited the party menu and forgot to mention the rice. Have you ever wondered what mealtimes would be without rice? Rice—the humble staple the world over, the grain we take for granted.

So let's wear our chef's hat as we attempt to broaden our repertoire with this much-loved, but generally neglected, staple that comes in a variety of shapes, sizes, and flavors—fragrant white or brown basmati, long- or short-grain, sticky or sweet, Chinese, brown or wild, or the exclusive rice grown in Texas and California called Texmati and Calmati respectively.

Before we go on, let's also remind ourselves that we consume most of our rice in its least nourishing form—as milled and polished white rice, minus the nutrient-rich bran and germ. Its simple elegance and health-promoting potential are enhanced with every new ingredient that is added to it and its flavor heightened with the herbs and spices of your choice.

Served as an accompaniment, entrée, or one-pot meal, rice is just wonderful, because rice is, well, rice.

ON BASMATI RICE

Basmati rice is the unique, highly fragrant long-grain rice that is India's special gift to the rest of the world. It grows only in the foothills of the Himalayas, where the ideal soil and climatic conditions produce the best possible basmati. Efforts to reproduce it elsewhere in the world have not been successful.

Because of its increasing popularity, I've devoted a large part of this chapter to dishes made with basmati rice. Just in case you are unable to find it, use the regular fortified, long-grain rice (but don't wash it or you will lose most of the water-soluble nutrients). Remember, basmati rice is very similar to long-grain rice and can be used to make all your favorite recipes—whether they are Indian, Middle Eastern, American, Mexican, or Oriental.

ON COOKING BASMATI RICE

Basmati rice may contain some tiny stones and impurities, so the first step is to remove them. Then wash the rice in three to four changes of water to remove the excess starches and soak it for at least thirty minutes (and up to twelve hours) before cooking it—this gives the grain a chance to absorb moisture and expand to its optimum length. As a result, the rice cooks much faster and the final dish comes to the table light and fluffy, with each grain long and separate.

Always use a little less than twice the amount of water, especially if rice is to be soaked. Then use the soaking water to cook the rice so all the water-soluble vitamins that may have leached into the water are returned to the rice. Cook the rice, uncovered, over high heat until it comes to a boil. Then reduce the heat to the minimum level, cover the pan, and finish cooking the rice. Do not stir the cooked rice because the grains may break and stick together. Use a spatula to transfer the rice to a platter. (In India, we have special rice-serving spoons, large, oval-shaped, flat spoons with a short handle.)

Basmati rice may be precooked and reheated. My trick is to cook the rice partially (until it absorbs most of the water), transfer it to a serving casserole, and set aside for up to eight hours. Then reheat it in the microwave oven for two to four minutes on high power or in a preheated 300°F oven for twenty to twenty-five minutes. Allow cooked rice to rest for about five minutes before serving.

Each cup of uncooked rice yields 2½ to 3 cups of cooked rice and serves two to four people, depending on the rest of the menu.

Steamed Basmati Rice

A SPELLBINDING AROMA ARISES from the pan and spreads through the house when I steam this naturally fragrant rice. For golden steamed rice, add ½ teaspoon ground turmeric along with the salt. For added interest, throw in some capers.

Try making a quick dessert with leftover steamed, unsalted basmati. Add some milk and sugar and bring to a boil in the microwave oven or over direct heat. Sprinkle some ground cinnamon and cardamom seeds over the top and serve hot.

2 cups basmati rice, picked over
3¾ cups water
1 teaspoon salt (optional), or to your taste

Wash the rice in 3 to 4 changes of water, stirring lightly with your fingers, until the water runs almost clear. Soak it in the 3¾ cups water for 30 minutes or longer.

Place the rice and water in a large, nonstick saucepan, mix in the salt, and bring to a boil over high heat. Reduce the heat to very low, cover the pan (partially at first, until the foam subsides, then snugly), and cook until all the water is absorbed and the grains are tender, 10 to 15 minutes. Transfer to a serving platter and serve.

Makes 6 to 8 servings

SERVING IDEAS:
Present whenever steamed rice is called for, with curries, dals (lentils, peas, and beans), saucy vegetable dishes, stir-fries, and stews.

DO AHEAD:
See page 268. To make last-minute cooking easy, I soak the rice in the pan in which it will be cooked.

Simply Cumin Basmati

Makes 6 to 8 servings

SERVING IDEAS:

Partner with curries or stews, pair with stir-fried dishes, or present with baked casseroles.

DO AHEAD:

If making in advance, do not soak the rice. Cook the cumin seeds and mix in the rice and water. Then remove from the stove and set aside for up to 8 hours. Finish cooking it about ½ hour before serving. Or cook the rice, transfer to a serving casserole, and set aside for up to 8 hours. Reheat in the microwave for 3 minutes on high power or sprinkle with about 1 tablespoon water and heat in a preheated 375°F oven for 15 to 20 minutes.

CUMIN SEEDS ARE TO basmati rice what basil is to the tomato—the most fragrant life partner. Try this recipe and you'll see what I mean.

2 cups basmati rice, picked over
3¾ cups water
2 tablespoons canola oil
1 tablespoon cumin seeds
1 teaspoon salt, or to your taste
Chopped fresh herbs for garnish (such as mint, basil, cilantro, parsley)

Wash the rice in 3 to 4 changes of water, stirring lightly with your fingers, until the water runs almost clear. Soak it in the 3¾ cups water for 30 minutes or longer.

In a large saucepan, heat the oil over moderately high heat and stir in the cumin seeds, which should sizzle upon contact with the hot oil. Immediately add the rice and its soaking water. Mix in the salt, raise the heat to high, and bring to a boil. Reduce the heat to very low, cover the pan (partially at first, until the foam subsides, then snugly), and cook until all the water is absorbed and the rice grains are tender, 10 to 15 minutes.

Transfer to a serving platter, garnish with the chopped herbs, and serve.

VARIATION: To make this a little more elaborate, top with some sautéed or grilled vegetables or meats just before serving, or mix in some lightly steamed grated carrots for a saffron-added look.

Herbal Basmati

EAST MEETS WEST IN this mouthwatering potpourri of Indian basmati rice and spices and herbs from the Western world.

2 cups basmati rice, picked over
3¾ cups water
2 tablespoons canola oil
One 3-inch stick cinnamon
5 black cardamom pods, pounded lightly to break the skins
2 teaspoons cumin seeds
1 tablespoon mixed dried Italian herbs
1 teaspoon dried fenugreek leaves
1 teaspoon salt, or to your taste
Finely chopped fresh herbs of your choice, for garnish

Wash the rice in 3 to 4 changes of water, stirring lightly with your fingers until the water runs almost clear. Soak it in the 3¾ cups water for 30 minutes or longer.

In a large saucepan, heat the oil over moderately high heat and cook the cinnamon and cardamom pods, stirring, for a few seconds. Stir in the cumin seeds, which should sizzle upon contact with the hot oil. Immediately stir in the dried herbs and fenugreek leaves, and add the rice and its soaking water. Mix in the salt, raise the heat to high, and bring to a boil. Reduce the heat to very low, cover the pan (partially at first, until the foam subsides, then snugly), and cook until all the water has been absorbed and the rice grains are tender, 10 to 15 minutes.

Transfer to a serving platter, garnish with chopped herbs, and serve.

Makes 6 to 8 servings

SERVING IDEAS:
This versatile preparation complements menus from all over the world—just change the herbs and present it with a new dish every day.

DO AHEAD:
See Simply Cumin Basmati, page 270.

Savory Saffron Rice with Nuts, Raisins, and Silver Leaves

Makes 6 to 8 servings

THIS IS A BANQUET rice dish par excellence. For added color, sprinkle on some finely diced red bell peppers and chopped cilantro.

SERVING IDEAS:

This lavish rice dish is best when teamed with meat, chicken, or seafood curries and yogurt raitas. It is also charming with grilled or roasted fare.

DO AHEAD:

The rice may be cooked up to 8 hours in advance. Reheat as directed on page 268, garnish, and serve.

NOTE:

The stir-fried nuts are added to the dish as a last-minute garnish. If they are cooked with the rice they will absorb moisture and lose their crispy crunch.

2 cups basmati rice, picked over
3¾ cups water
½ teaspoon saffron threads
¼ cup low-fat milk (1 percent or 2 percent), at room temperature
3 tablespoon safflower or vegetable oil
¼ cup blanched almond slivers
¼ cup shelled raw pistachio nuts, halved lengthwise
¼ cup coarsely chopped walnuts
¼ cup pine nuts
½ cup raisins
5 black cardamom pods, pounded lightly to break the skins
One 3-inch stick cinnamon
1 teaspoon black cumin seeds
¾ teaspoon salt, or to your taste
Chopped cilantro (fresh coriander) leaves and four to six 4-inch square silver leaves for garnish

Wash the rice in 3 to 4 changes of water, stirring lightly with your fingers until the water runs almost clear. Soak it in the 3¾ cups water for at least 30 minutes or longer. Soak the saffron in the milk for 30 minutes or longer.

In a large, nonstick saucepan, heat 1 tablespoon of the oil over moderate heat and stir-fry the nuts, until they are golden, 1 to 2 minutes. Remove to a bowl and set aside.

Add the remaining 2 tablespoons oil to the same pan, raise the heat to moderately high, and cook the raisins, cardamom pods, and cinnamon stick, stirring, until the raisins puff up, about 1 minute. Stir in the cumin seeds, which should sizzle upon contact with the hot oil. Mix in the rice and its soaking water and the salt. Raise the heat to high and bring to a boil. Reduce the heat to very low, cover the pan (partially at first, until the foam subsides, then snugly), and cook the rice until all the water is absorbed and the rice grains are tender, 10 to 15 minutes.

Remove from the heat and gently fork in the reserved saffron milk with the saffron threads and let the rice rest for about 5 minutes. (If the rice is stirred too much, the cooked grains will break.) Transfer to a serving platter, garnish with the silver leaves and the reserved nuts, and serve.

Saffron Rice with Spinach, Red Bell Peppers, and Wild Mushrooms

THIS FESTIVE RICE DISH comes with a booster shot of calcium.

Makes 6 to 8 servings

2 cups basmati rice, picked over
½ teaspoon saffron threads
1¾ cups water
2 cups nonfat milk
3 tablespoons peanut or vegetable oil
2 cups finely chopped onions
2 teaspoons minced garlic
1 cup chopped fresh or reconstituted dried wild mushrooms
1 bunch fresh spinach (about ½ pound), trimmed of tough stems, thoroughly washed, and finely chopped
2 large red bell peppers, seeded and cut into ¼-inch dice
3 to 5 jalapeño peppers (optional), to your taste, finely chopped
One 3-inch stick cinnamon
10 green cardamom pods, pounded lightly to break the skins
1 teaspoon black cumin seeds
¾ teaspoon salt, or to your taste
Garam masala for garnish

Wash the rice in 3 to 4 changes of water, stirring lightly with your fingers until the water runs almost clear. Place it in a large bowl and mix in the saffron threads. Add the water and milk and let the rice soak for 30 minutes or longer.

In a large, nonstick skillet, heat 2 tablespoons of the oil over moderately high heat and cook the onions, stirring, until they are dark brown, 7 to 10 minutes. Add the garlic and mushrooms and cook, stirring, for 1 to 2 minutes. Remove everything to a bowl. Add the spinach to the same skillet and cook, stirring occasionally, until it wilts, 3 to 4 minutes. Mix in the peppers and cook, stirring, for another 2 to 3 minutes. Transfer to the bowl with the onions and mushrooms and set aside.

In a large saucepan, heat the remaining tablespoon oil over moderately high heat and cook the cinnamon and cardamom, stirring, for a few seconds. Add the cumin seeds. Quickly add the rice and its soaking liquid. Mix in the salt, raise the heat to high, and bring to a boil. Reduce the heat to very low, cover the pan (partially at first, until the foam subsides, then snugly), and continue to cook until all the liquid is absorbed and the rice grains are tender, 10 to 15 minutes.

Let the rice rest for 5 to 7 minutes, transfer to a platter, top with the reserved cooked spinach and bell peppers, garnish, and serve.

SERVING IDEAS:

Perfect as a vegetarian one-dish meal with a yogurt raita and Italian Parsley and Mango Chutney (page 260).

DO AHEAD:

The vegetables and the rice may be cooked up to 8 hours in advance and stored separately. Reheat as directed on page 268, garnish, and serve.

VARIATION:

To make a nonvegetarian version, cook the onions until golden, then add some diced chicken tenders or shrimp, and sauté until they become golden. Then proceed with the recipe.

NOTE:

Cumin seeds will sizzle upon contact with the hot oil.

Basmati Rice with Lobster Mushrooms and Peas

Makes 6 to 8 servings

SERVING IDEAS:

This is best when served with a simple yogurt raita and Green Cilantro Chutney (page 257). As part of a larger buffet it is lovely with a selection of curries and bean entrées.

DO AHEAD:

Can be made up to 8 hours in advance and reheated as directed on page 268.

THIS PURELY VEGETARIAN DISH is made with a rare variety of mushrooms called lobster mushrooms, which are akin to real lobsters both in color and flavor. They are sporadically available from September to November. If you can't find them, use chanterelle, portobello, shiitake, morel, or regular mushrooms instead.

2 cups basmati rice, picked over
3¾ cups water
1 tablespoon olive oil
One 3-inch stick cinnamon
1 teaspoon cumin seeds
1 cup halved and thinly sliced onions
2 teaspoons minced garlic
¾ to 1 cup diced fresh lobster mushroom caps, to your taste
1 cup green peas, preferably fresh
Garam masala for garnish

Wash the rice in 3 to 4 changes of water, stirring lightly with your fingers until the water runs almost clear. Soak it in the 3¾ cups water for at least 30 minutes or longer.

In a large, nonstick saucepan, heat the oil over moderately high heat and cook the cinnamon and cumin seeds, stirring, until they sizzle, 15 to 30 seconds. Add the onions and cook, stirring, until they turn golden, 4 to 5 minutes. Add the garlic and mushrooms. Continue to cook, stirring occasionally, for 2 to 3 minutes, then add the peas and cook for another minute.

Mix in the rice and its soaking water, raise the heat to high, and bring to a boil. Reduce the heat to very low, cover the pan (partially at first, until the foam subsides, then snugly), and cook until all the water is absorbed and the rice grains are tender, 10 to 15 minutes.

Transfer to a serving platter, garnish with the garam masala, and serve.

Curried Rice with Roasted and Sautéed Vegetables

TRY THIS DYNAMIC PREPARATION when you have a little extra time on your hands. This combination dish is essentially two different recipes presented as one. Serve them separately, if you wish.

The partial flame roasting of the zucchinis and bell peppers adds a whiff of smoke to this recipe.

For the rice:

2 cups basmati rice, picked over

3¾ cups water

1 tablespoon peanut oil

1 teaspoon cumin seeds

2 teaspoons minced garlic

1 tablespoon peeled and minced fresh ginger

1 teaspoon curry powder

½ teaspoon garam masala

1 teaspoon salt, or to your taste

1 cup finely chopped vine-ripened tomatoes (1 large tomato)

½ cup firmly packed finely chopped cilantro (fresh coriander) leaves, soft stems included

For the vegetables:

Six 1 × 6-inch-long baby green and yellow zucchinis

3 large bell peppers (1 each red, yellow, and orange)

1 to 2 tablespoons peanut oil

1 small red onion, cut in half lengthwise and thinly sliced

2 to 4 small purple potatoes boiled in lightly salted water to cover until tender, drained, cut in half lengthwise, and sliced ¼ inch thick

1 tablespoon minced garlic

1 tablespoon ground coriander

½ teaspoon salt, or to your taste

½ teaspoon freshly ground black pepper, or to your taste

Garam masala and chopped cilantro leaves for garnish

Makes 6 to 8 servings

SERVING IDEAS:

Stunning as a one-dish meal with a yogurt raita and a tall glass of iced tea or fresh lemonade.

DO AHEAD:

Make the rice and the vegetables up to 8 hours in advance and store separately. Reheat the rice as directed on page 268, then top with the vegetables. Some juices may accumulate in the vegetable bowl; drizzle them over the rice also.

continued

Wash the rice in 3 to 4 changes of water, stirring lightly with your fingers until the water runs almost clear. Soak it in the 3¾ cups water for 30 minutes or longer.

In a large saucepan, heat the oil over moderately high heat and cook the cumin seeds, stirring; they will sizzle upon contact with the hot oil. Quickly add the garlic, ginger, curry powder, garam masala, and salt and cook, stirring, for about 1 minute. Mix in the tomatoes and cilantro and cook, stirring, until the juices from the tomatoes completely evaporate, 2 to 4 minutes.

Add the rice and its soaking water. Raise the heat to high and bring to a boil. Reduce the heat to very low, cover the pan (partially at first, until the foam subsides, then snugly), and continue to cook until all the water is absorbed and the rice grains are tender, 10 to 15 minutes.

Meanwhile, roast the zucchini and bell peppers. Using a long-handled fork, place each one over a direct flame and roast, turning frequently, until they are spotted on all sides but still firm. (You can also do this under a broiler). Remove from the flame and slice the zucchinis diagonally into ¼-inch-thick ovals and the peppers into 1-inch cubes. Set aside.

In a large grilling pan with a ridged bottom (or a nonstick skillet), heat the oil over moderately high heat and cook the onion, stirring, until medium brown, 4 to 5 minutes. Add the potatoes and cook, turning occasionally, until they are golden on both sides, 2 to 4 minutes. Mix in the zucchini and peppers, and add the garlic, coriander, salt, and black pepper and cook, turning carefully, for 3 to 5 minutes.

Transfer the rice to a platter and fluff with a fork. Top with the vegetables, garnish with the garam masala and cilantro, and serve hot.

Stir-fried Basmati with Tomato, Spinach, Yellow Zucchini, and Italian Herbs

YEARS AGO, WHENEVER I cooked basmati rice, I automatically reached out for my Indian herbs and spices, only because I was familiar with them. But once I swerved toward other seasonings, there was no looking back. Today, I make my basmati rice with Italian, American, Mexican, and Chinese seasonings. And they are all wonderful.

2 tablespoons extra-virgin olive oil
2 teaspoons black cumin seeds
1 tablespoon dried mixed Italian herbs, or more to your taste
1 tablespoon minced garlic
2 cups coarsely chopped vine-ripened tomatoes (2 large tomatoes)
3 cups firmly packed finely chopped fresh spinach leaves, trimmed of tough stems and thoroughly washed
2 cups finely diced yellow zucchini or yellow pattypan squash (4 to 5 medium size)
1 recipe Steamed Basmati Rice (page 269)
1 teaspoon garam masala

In a large, nonstick skillet, heat the oil over moderately high heat. Tilt the skillet to one side so that the oil gathers in one small area and stir-fry the cumin seeds and Italian herbs for a few seconds; The cumin seeds should sizzle upon contact with the hot oil. Add the garlic and tomatoes and cook, stirring, for 1 to 2 minutes. Add the spinach and stir-fry until it wilts, 2 to 3 minutes, and add the zucchini and stir-fry 3 to 4 minutes more. Mix in the cooked rice and garam masala and stir-fry very carefully for another 3 to 4 minutes to blend the flavors. Transfer to a platter and serve.

Makes 6 to 8 servings

SERVING IDEAS:
Accompany with a chicken curry or eggplant Parmesan and a salad. Or present it as a salad at room temperature.

DO AHEAD:
Can be made up to 2 days in advance and refrigerated. Reheat as directed on page 268 or serve chilled or at room temperature.

Mexican-Style Basmati Rice

Makes 6 to 8 servings

SERVING IDEAS:

An excellent rice to partner with Indo-Mexican Black Beans or Curried Red Beans (page 173 or 174) and a yogurt raita.

DO AHEAD:

Can be made 3 to 5 days in advance and reheated as directed on page 268.

NOTE:

Cumin seeds will sizzle upon contact with the hot oil.

USUALLY MADE WITH LONG-grained rice, this dish is even better made with basmati rice.

2 cups basmati rice, picked over
One 1½-inch piece fresh ginger, peeled and cut into thin slices
2 large cloves garlic, peeled
1 to 4 serrano peppers, to your taste, stems removed
3 tablespoons fresh lemon juice
1 large, vine-ripened tomato, coarsely chopped
½ cup firmly packed cilantro (fresh coriander) leaves, soft stems included
2 tablespoons olive oil
1½ cups finely chopped onions
1½ teaspoons cumin seeds
1 teaspoon ground cumin
1 teaspoon paprika
2 teaspoon dried oregano
½ teaspoon garam masala
1 teaspoon salt, or to your taste
½ cup each finely chopped carrots, green beans, mushrooms, and fresh or thawed
   frozen peas
2¾ cups water
Chopped cilantro for garnish

Wash the rice in 3 to 4 changes of water, stirring lightly with your fingers until the water runs almost clear. Drain and set aside.

In the work bowl of a food processor fitted with a metal S-blade and the motor running, process the ginger, garlic, and peppers until minced by dropping them through the feed tube. Add the lemon juice, tomato, and cilantro and process until everything is smooth. Set aside.

In a large nonstick saucepan, heat the oil over moderately high heat and cook the onions, stirring, until golden, 3 to 4 minutes. Stir in the cumin seeds, ground cumin, paprika, oregano, garam masala, and salt. Mix in the rice and stir-fry very carefully until the rice turns golden, 3 to 4 minutes. Add the vegetables and cook for another 3 to 4 minutes. Mix in the tomato puree and water, raise the heat to high, and bring to a boil. Reduce the heat to very low, cover (partially at first, until the foam subsides, then snugly), and continue to cook until all the water has evaporated and the rice grains are tender, 10 to 15 minutes. Transfer to a platter, garnish, and serve.

Chinese Egg-Fried Basmati

YEARS AGO, I TOOK some Chinese ingredients to my family in India. On my last visit, I noticed they were still lying in the refrigerator, unopened and untouched. So I showed them this (and a few other) quick and easy recipe. Now I have standing orders from Veena and Amita, my sisters-in-law, to keep their pantries well stocked.

Basmati rice and ground coriander give this traditional Chinese recipe a charming twist.

1 recipe Simply Cumin Basmati or Steamed Basmati Rice (page 270 or 269)
2 cups mixed vegetables (choose from finely diced fresh carrots, green or yellow beans, celery, and zucchini; thinly sliced mushrooms; thawed frozen peas and corn; and broccoli and cauliflower, chopped into 1-inch florets)
2 tablespoons peanut oil
3 extra-large eggs, lightly beaten
2 teaspoons minced garlic
1 tablespoon peeled and minced fresh ginger
1 tablespoon ground coriander
½ teaspoon coarsely crushed Szechuan peppercorns
1 to 2 cups thoroughly washed, finely chopped mustard greens or bok choy, to your taste, stems included
½ cup finely sliced scallion greens
½ cup loosely packed finely chopped cilantro (fresh coriander) leaves, soft stems included
1 teaspoon sesame oil
¼ cup dark soy sauce, or more to your taste
Salt and freshly ground black pepper, to taste
2 tablespoons sesame seeds, toasted (page 294), for garnish

Place the vegetables in a microwaveable dish, cover, and cook on high heat in the microwave until crisp-tender, 2 to 3 minutes. Set aside. Or place in a small saucepan with ¼ cup water and cook over moderate heat until tender-crisp, 4 to 5 minutes. Drain and set aside.

In a large, nonstick skillet or wok, heat 1 tablespoon of the oil over moderately high heat and stir-fry the eggs until set, about 1 minute. Remove to a bowl and set aside.

Add the remaining tablespoon oil to the skillet and stir-fry the garlic and ginger until golden, 1 to 2 minutes. Add the coriander and Szechuan peppercorns,

Makes 6 to 8 servings

SERVING IDEAS:
Can be served hot, cold, or at room temperature, which makes it perfect for bagged lunches and picnics.

DO AHEAD:
Can be made up to 2 days in advance and refrigerated.

and mix in the mustard greens and stir-fry until wilted, 1 to 2 minutes. Add the cooked vegetables (plus any juices that may have accumulated in the bowl) and stir for another minute, until all the juices evaporate.

Add the cooked rice, eggs, scallions, and cilantro, and stir in the sesame oil and soy sauce. Cook, stirring, for a minute or two to blend flavors. Taste and add some salt and pepper, if needed. Transfer to a serving platter, garnish with the sesame seeds, and serve.

Layered Chicken Curry and Basmati Rice Biryani Pilaf

MY DAUGHTERS, SUMITA AND Supriya, are in heaven when I pack this dish for them to take back to college. It freezes very well and reheats in the microwave oven. For added health benefits, I sometimes throw in a cup or two of chopped spinach (after browning the onions) in the chicken. Or make it with brown basmati rice.

For the chicken:

2 to 3 tablespoons peanut oil

1½ cups finely chopped onions

2 teaspoons minced garlic

1 tablespoon peeled and minced fresh ginger

1 tablespoon ground coriander

1½ teaspoon garam masala

2 cups finely chopped vine-ripened tomatoes (2 large tomatoes)

1½ cups nonfat plain yogurt, whisked until smooth

2 pounds boneless, skinless chicken tenders, tendons removed and each cut into 2 to 3 pieces

½ cup firmly packed finely chopped cilantro (fresh coriander) leaves, soft stems included

¾ teaspoon salt

For the rice:

2 cups basmati rice, picked over

3¾ cups water

1 tablespoon peanut oil

One 3-inch stick cinnamon

4 bay leaves

5 black cardamom pods, pounded lightly to break the skins

1 teaspoon black cumin seeds

1 teaspoon minced garlic

¾ teaspoon salt, or to your taste

¼ cup almond slivers, toasted (page 34), for garnish

SERVING IDEAS:

Present with a green mint or cilantro chutney and nonfat plain yogurt. Chilled fresh seasonal fruits are an ideal ending to this one-pot meal.

DO AHEAD:

Assemble up to a day in advance and store in the refrigerator until ready to bake.

continued

In a large saucepan, heat the oil over moderately high heat and cook the onions, stirring, until dark brown, 7 to 10 minutes. Add the garlic, ginger, coriander, and garam masala, then mix in the tomatoes and cook, stirring as necessary, until most of the liquid evaporates, 3 to 5 minutes. Add all of the yogurt a little at a time, stirring constantly to prevent it from curdling. Mix in the chicken pieces, cilantro, and salt, cover the pan, raise the heat to high, and cook over high heat for the first 2 to 3 minutes. Reduce the heat to moderate and continue to cook, stirring occasionally, until the chicken is cooked through and the sauce is very thick, 10 to 15 minutes. Set aside.

Wash the rice in 3 to 4 changes of water, stirring lightly with your fingers until the water runs almost clear. Soak the rice in the 3¾ cups water for 30 minutes or longer.

In a large saucepan, heat the oil over moderately high heat and cook the cinnamon, bay leaves, and cardamom pods, stirring, for a few seconds. Stir in the cumin seeds, which should sizzle upon contact with the hot oil. Quickly add the garlic and the rice and its soaking water. Mix in the salt, raise the heat to high, and bring to a boil. Reduce the heat to very low, cover the pan (partially at first, until the foam subsides, then snugly), and continue to cook until all the water has been absorbed by the rice and the rice is almost done, 8 to 10 minutes.

Preheat the oven to 300°F. To assemble the dish, layer the rice and the chicken in a large ovenproof casserole that will fit your oven starting with the rice and ending with the chicken. Cover with a sheet of aluminum foil and bake for 10 to 15 minutes. (Turn the oven off and the dish can stay in the warm oven up to 1 hour, if need be.) Garnish with toasted almond slivers and serve.

Basmati Pilaf with Stir-fried Shrimp and Asparagus

THIS SNOWY-WHITE PILAF, enriched with juicy pink-red shrimp and tender green asparagus, is a kaleidoscope of colors. And it reveals basmati rice at its nutritional best.

For the shrimp:

1 pound medium-large shrimp with tails on (30 to 35 per pound), shelled and deveined

3 to 4 tablespoons fresh lime or lemon juice, to your taste

2 teaspoons minced garlic

1 tablespoon crushed dried oregano

¾ teaspoon garam masala

1 teaspoon paprika

½ teaspoon salt, or to your taste

For the rice:

2 cups basmati rice, picked over

3¾ cups water

3 tablespoons safflower oil

1 bunch asparagus, tough bottoms snapped off and tops cut into 1-inch pieces

1 cup finely chopped onions

1 teaspoon minced garlic

1 tablespoon crushed dried oregano

1 teaspoon garam masala

¾ teaspoon salt, or to your taste

½ cup seeded and minced red bell peppers for garnish

Put the shrimp in a large bowl. Combine the lime juice, garlic, oregano, garam masala, paprika, and salt, add to the bowl, and toss until the shrimp are fully coated with the mixture. Cover with plastic wrap and marinate the shrimp for at least 2 and up to 24 hours in the refrigerator.

Wash the rice in 3 to 4 changes of water, stirring lightly with your fingers until the water runs almost clear. Then soak it in the 3¾ cups water for 30 minutes or longer.

continued

SERVING IDEAS:
  This gorgeous party dish pairs well with a bowl of Chilled Roasted Tomato and Red Bell Pepper Soup or Gingered Tomato Soup (24 or 22) and a tossed green salad.

DO AHEAD:
  Can be made up to 8 hours in advance. Do not add the shrimp until ready to serve; the shrimp should not remain at room temperature for longer than an hour.

In a large, nonstick saucepan, heat 1½ tablespoons of the oil over moderately high heat and cook the shrimp with their marinade until golden on both sides, 4 to 5 minutes. Remove to a bowl, cover, and set aside.

Add another ½ tablespoon of the oil to the same pan and cook the asparagus, stirring, until crisp-tender, 2 to 4 minutes. Remove to the bowl with the shrimp.

Add the remaining tablespoon oil to the same pan and cook the onions, stirring, until golden, 3 to 4 minutes. Mix in the garlic, oregano, garam masala, and salt, and cook, stirring, for 1 to 2 minutes. Add the rice and its soaking water, raise the heat to high, and bring to a boil. Reduce the heat to very low, cover the pan (partially at first, until the foam subsides, then snugly), and continue to cook until all the water has been absorbed and the rice grains are tender, 10 to 15 minutes.

Remove to a platter, add the shrimp and asparagus, garnish with the minced red bell peppers, and serve.

Basic Wild Rice Pilaf

WILD RICE IS NOT a true rice, but a long-grain aquatic grass seed. And it is not wild, as the name suggests. It is cultivated in paddies. Nutritionally speaking, wild rice compares to brown rice and is rich in protein and vitamin B.

1½ cups wild rice
2 tablespoons olive oil
4 bay leaves
2 teaspoons cumin seeds
1 cup thoroughly washed, finely chopped leek whites
1 teaspoon minced garlic
4½ cups water
¾ teaspoon salt, or to your taste
Chopped cilantro (fresh coriander) or parsley leaves for garnish

Put the rice in a large sieve and wash thoroughly under running water. Set aside.

In a large saucepan, heat the oil over moderately high heat and cook the bay leaves, stirring, for a few seconds. Stir in the cumin seeds, which should sizzle upon contact with the hot oil. Stir in the leeks and cook, stirring as necessary until they turn golden, 2 to 3 minutes. Add the rice, garlic, water, and salt, raise the heat to high, and boil for 2 to 3 minutes. Cover the pan, reduce the heat to low, and cook until all the water is absorbed and the rice is soft, 50 to 60 minutes.

Remove to a platter, garnish with chopped cilantro, and serve.

Makes 6 to 8 servings

SERVING IDEAS:
Especially good with curries and casseroles. Often I mix in equal portions of basmati rice and serve it with grilled fare and a yogurt raita.

DO AHEAD:
Can be made 3 to 5 days in advance and refrigerated; serve hot, cold, or at room temperature.

Basmati and Wild Rice Pilaf with Tofu, Snow Peas, and Shiitake Mushrooms

Makes 4 to 6 servings

SERVING IDEAS:
Present with Chicken Salad with Pineapple and Orange (page 38), or pair with grilled meats.

DO AHEAD:
Can be made 3 to 5 days in advance and refrigerated; serve hot, cold, or at room temperature.

NOTE:
Both the rices should be cooked ahead of time, cooled, and then mixed together. If handled while it is still hot, freshly cooked basmati rice breaks easily and the visual appeal of the finished dish suffers. The taste, however, remains unaltered.

THIS EXCITING MIXTURE OF white basmati rice and black wild rice becomes even more enticing when we embellish it with stir-fried tofu and some exotic vegetables.

3 cups Simply Cumin Basmati (page 270), at room temperature
3 cups Basic Wild Rice Pilaf (page 285), at room temperature
½ cup finely sliced scallion greens
½ cup loosely packed finely chopped cilantro (fresh coriander) leaves, soft stems included
1 tablespoon canola oil
2 teaspoons minced garlic
2 teaspoons peeled and minced fresh ginger
One 10½-ounce package extra-firm tofu, pressed dry between paper towels and cut into ½-inch cubes
1 cup sliced fresh or reconstituted dried shiitake mushroom caps
15 to 20 young Chinese snow peas
½ teaspoon lemon pepper blend

In a large bowl, using a large slotted spoon or your hands, mix together the basmati and wild rices, carefully breaking apart any clumps that may have formed. Mix in the scallion greens and cilantro. (If you wish to serve this dish hot, reheat it in the microwave oven for 2 to 3 minutes on high power or in a skillet over moderately high heat, turning gently, for 2 to 3 minutes until hot.) Transfer to a serving platter and set aside.

In a large, nonstick skillet, heat the oil over moderately high heat and stir-fry the garlic and ginger until golden, 1 to 2 minutes. Add the tofu and cook, stirring gently as necessary, until it turns golden, 2 to 4 minutes. Push the tofu to one side, add the mushrooms, and stir-fry for 1 to 2 minutes. Slide the mushrooms toward the tofu and stir-fry the snow peas for 1 to 2 minutes. Mix the stir-fried tofu and vegetables together in the skillet and season with the lemon pepper.

Transfer to the rice platter and place the vegetables either as a ring around the rice, over the top as a garnish or gently mix everything together.

Hearty Brown Basmati Pilaf

BROWN BASMATI HAS THE same fragrance as its white counterpart, but is much more nutritious and healthful because it comes with the germ and bran intact. And for that reason, it takes much longer to soften (45 to 50 minutes as opposed to 10 to 15 minutes). But remember, once the rice is on the stove, you just play the waiting game.

Most of the white basmati recipes in this book can be made with brown rice also. Just adjust the cooking time.

2 cups brown basmati rice, picked over
4 cups water
2 tablespoons extra-virgin olive oil
One 3-inch stick cinnamon
5 to 7 black cardamom pods, to your taste, pounded lightly to break the skins
4 bay leaves
1½ teaspoons cumin seeds
1 large onion, cut in half lengthwise and thinly sliced
2 large cloves garlic, coarsely chopped
1 tablespoon peeled and minced fresh ginger
1 teaspoon salt, or to your taste
1 to 2 tablespoon fresh lime or lemon juice, to your taste
¼ cup firmly packed finely chopped cilantro (fresh coriander) leaves, soft stems
*   included*
Garam masala for garnish

Put the rice in a large sieve and wash thoroughly under cold running water until the water runs clean. Soak it in the 4 cups water for an hour or longer.

In a large saucepan, heat the oil over moderately high heat and stir-fry the cinnamon, cardamom pods, and bay leaves for about 1 minute. Stir in the cumin seeds, which should sizzle upon contact with the hot oil. Add the onion, garlic, and ginger. Cook, stirring, until the onion is golden, 5 to 7 minutes. Mix in the rice and its soaking water, add the salt, raise the heat to high, and bring to a boil. Reduce the heat to low, cover the pan, and cook until the rice is soft, 45 to 50 minutes.

Let the rice rest for 5 to 7 minutes and transfer to a serving platter. Gently mix in the lime juice and cilantro, garnish with the garam masala, and serve.

Makes 6 to 8 servings

SERVING IDEAS:
  Team with fragrant meat and chicken curries. On the side, serve dry-cooked vegetables, yogurt raita, and chutneys and pickles.

DO AHEAD:
  Once it is cooked, treat this rice like white basmati. To reheat, follow the directions on page 268.

Couscous Pilaf with Cilantro-Glazed Cherry Tomatoes

Makes 4 servings

SERVING IDEAS:

Great by itself as a warm or cold salad with a hot soup, or team with roasted chicken or seafood and some sautéed mixed vegetables.

DO AHEAD:

Stays fresh for 3 to 5 days in the refrigerator; serve hot, cold, or at room temperature.

COUSCOUS IS A GRANULAR Moroccan pasta made from semolina and is available precooked. It cooks very quickly and effortlessly and, like rice, it can be used to make both savory and sweet dishes.

For optimum presentation, use only the very small red, orange, or yellow cherry tomatoes or the colorful pear-shaped tomatoes.

1⅔ cups water
¼ teaspoon salt, or to your taste
1 cup couscous
1 tablespoon olive oil
5 large cloves garlic, coarsely chopped
2 to 4 red serrano peppers, to your taste, finely chopped, or ¼ cup seeded and finely diced red bell pepper
2 teaspoons mixed dried Italian herbs
1 tablespoon fresh lime or lemon juice
½ cup finely diced scallion greens
15 to 20 small cherry tomatoes
½ cup firmly packed finely chopped cilantro (fresh coriander) leaves, soft stems included
Freshly ground black pepper or garam masala for garnish

In a medium saucepan over high heat, bring the water and salt to a boil. Remove from the heat and add the couscous. Stir gently to mix. Cover the pan and let stand until all the water has been absorbed, 8 to 10 minutes.

In a large nonstick skillet, heat the oil over moderate heat and cook the garlic and peppers, stirring, until barely golden, 1 to 2 minutes. Mix in the Italian herbs, add the couscous, lime juice, and scallion greens, and stir gently to mix. Cook, stirring, for a minute or two. Remove to a serving platter.

Add the cherry tomatoes and cilantro to the same skillet and cook, shaking the skillet, over moderately high heat until the tomatoes just start to soften, 2 to 3 minutes. Transfer to the couscous platter and mix lightly. Garnish with black pepper or garam masala and serve.

Savory Yellow Couscous Pilaf with Potato Wedges

HERE I USE COUSCOUS to make a popular Indian snack pilaf called *pooha*. Authentic *pooha* is made with pounded rice, but I find that couscous works beautifully.

1⅔ cups water
¼ teaspoon salt, or to your taste
1 cup couscous
1 tablespoon olive oil
12 to 15 curry leaves, to your taste
1 teaspoon black mustard seeds
¼ teaspoon asafetida
3 to 5 jalapeño peppers, to your taste, skins punctured to prevent them from bursting, or 1 jalapeño pepper, minced
¾ cup finely chopped onions
2 small russet potatoes, boiled in lightly salted water to cover until tender, drained, peeled, and cut into ¾-inch dice
1 cup frozen peas, thawed
¼ teaspoon ground turmeric
1 teaspoon ground coriander
½ teaspoon salt
2 tablespoons fresh lime or lemon juice

Makes 4 to 6 servings

SERVING IDEAS:
  Present as a savory cereal hot, cold, or at room temperature for breakfast, brunch, or in the afternoon with a fruity yogurt shake, caffé latté, or spicy Indian tea. Or place over a bed of chopped greens and serve as a salad with any meal.

DO AHEAD:
  Can be made 3 to 5 days in advance and refrigerated.

NOTES:
  Diced carrots, broccoli and cauliflower florets, mushrooms, and other vegetables can be added along with, or instead of, the potatoes and peas.

In a medium saucepan, bring the water and salt to a boil over high heat. Remove from the heat and add the couscous. Stir gently to mix. Cover the pan and let stand until all the water has been absorbed, 8 to 10 minutes.

In a large, nonstick skillet, heat the oil over moderately high heat and cook the curry leaves, stirring, for about 30 seconds. Add the mustard seeds, cover the skillet (to prevent the seeds from flying out), and cook, shaking the skillet, until they start to pop, about 30 seconds. When the popping subsides, add the asafetida, peppers, and onions and cook, stirring, until the onion turns golden, 3 to 5 minutes. Add the potatoes and peas and cook, stirring, until the potatoes turn golden, 3 to 5 minutes. Mix in the turmeric, coriander, and salt, and add the couscous and lime juice and cook, stirring gently, for 2 to 4 minutes.

Transfer to a platter or individual salad plates and serve.

To End It All . . . Desserts

DESSERTS—HOW WE LOVE them and how we fear the hidden calories that come with them. Yet every time a luscious dessert is placed in front of us, all our resolutions and willpower go to Hawaii, we succumb to temptation, and dig in. And why shouldn't we—a meal is complete only when the last bite is sweet.

So let's give into our cravings and make our last course as sweet and enticing as we possibly can— not with desserts that are sugary sweet and loaded with unnecessary fat and calories, but with delicate flavors that stay with us long after the conclusion of the meal.

Since most of the milk-based Indian desserts are truly an acquired taste (besides being laborious and time-consuming to prepare), my biggest challenge here is to offer simple, easy, and (mostly) low-calorie desserts that are "Indian" yet familiar enough to be enjoyed by people all over the world.

Fruit ice creams, custards, puddings, and mousses have a new identity when combined with Indian garnishes and flavors. Popular Indian desserts also undergo instant transformation when presented with fresh-fruit purees and dessert sauces. Prepare some of these sumptuous desserts, present them with a cup of hot espresso, cappuccino, Darjeeling tea, or *masala chai* (spicy tea), and keep all the dessert lovers happy and contented.

Punjabi Tapioca Pudding

Makes 8 servings

DO AHEAD:

Stays fresh 4 to 6 days in the refrigerator. Garnish and serve.

NOTE:

Don't make the pudding too thick because it will thicken as it cools. If that happens, just stir in some more milk and serve.

THIS EGGLESS VERSION OF tapioca pudding made with low-fat milk is very refreshing and light. It is popularly made during Nav Ratri—the nine days of religious festivities that fall at the change of the seasons twice a year. This is the time to worship Vaishno Devi Mata (the goddess who grants us our innermost wishes) and to cleanse our bodies of toxins. This is done by fasting and eating fruits and root vegetables only. (Tapioca is a product made from cassava root.)

1 cup small pearl tapioca
2 cups water
¼ cup shelled raw pistachios
5½ to 6 cups low-fat milk (1 percent or 2 percent)
¾ cup sugar, or to your taste
Coarsely ground seeds from 6 to 8 green cardamom pods, to your taste
1 teaspoon rose water or 1 to 2 drops rose essence
Four to six 4-inch squares silver leaves and 1 tablespoon ground pistachios for
   garnish

Soak the tapioca in the water for 3 to 4 hours; the tapioca will absorb all the water. Cut the pistachios into thin slivers (or chop or grind finely). Set aside.

Put the milk in a large, heavy wok or saucepan and bring to a boil over high heat. Reduce the heat to moderate and simmer 3 to 4 minutes. (Keep stirring and watch that the milk doesn't boil over.) Add the tapioca and pistachios and continue to cook until the tapioca is soft and the pudding creamy, 15 to 20 minutes. Stir in the sugar and ground cardamom, cook for about 5 minutes, then remove from the heat. Keep stirring and scraping the bottom and sides of the pan—the pudding tends to stick to the pan if not stirred properly.

Transfer to a serving bowl and mix in the rose essence. Cover with plastic wrap (to prevent the formation of a dry crust) and cool to room temperature. Chill in the refrigerator for 6 to 8 hours before serving. Garnish with the silver leaves and ground pistachios and serve.

VARIATION: For added interest, top with pureed berries (any one type or mixed) instead of the silver leaves and ground pistachios. Or place individual servings of the pudding in glass bowls or champagne cups and lightly swirl about 1 tablespoon pureed berries into each one. Garnish with a mint sprig or leaf and 1 or 2 small berries. Sprinkle with some ground pistachios and serve.

Bread Pudding à la Punjab

I LOVE THESE LITTLE squares of deep-fried bread, layered with *rabdi*—a cardamom-laced sweetened milk sauce of a thin custardlike consistency that soaks into the pieces and imparts a flavor that lingers long after the last bite.

Makes 28 pieces; 6 to 8 servings

DO AHEAD:
  You can make this 4 to 6 days in advance and refrigerate.

6 to 10 green cardamom pods, to your taste
¼ cup shelled raw pistachios
¼ cup blanched almond slivers
1 quart half-and-half
1 cup sugar, or to your taste
1 tablespoon rose water or 2 drops rose essence
Twenty-one 4- to 5-inch slices white sandwich bread
2 to 3 cups peanut oil for deep-frying

Grind the whole cardamom pods, pistachios, and almond slivers together in a spice or coffee grinder into a fine powder. Set aside.

In a large, heavy aluminum wok or saucepan, bring the half-and-half to a boil over moderately high heat. Reduce the heat to moderate and simmer, stirring and scraping the sides often, until reduced to about half, 25 to 35 minutes. Watch carefully and adjust the heat to prevent accidental spills. Mix in the sugar, rose water, and most of the ground nuts (save some for garnish) and remove from the heat.

Meanwhile, remove the crusts from the bread and cut each slice into 4 squares. Heat the oil in another large, heavy aluminum wok or skillet over moderately high heat to 350° to 375°F. (The oil is ready when a small piece of bread added to the hot oil immediately bubbles and rises to the top.) Add the bread squares to the hot oil, as many as the wok can hold without overcrowding, and fry, turning once until golden. (This happens very quickly, about 1 minute.) Remove to paper towels to drain.

Arrange 28 fried bread pieces in a single layer (almost touching each other) in a large casserole dish. Spoon a little of the thickened half-and-half over each piece. Cover each piece with another piece of fried bread and top with half-and-half once again. Repeat one more time, using up all the bread and half-and-half. (There should be a total of 3 layers.) Pour leftover half-and-half over the pudding. The pudding may seem a little watery at first, but the bread will absorb all the sauce as it cools down, and you will be able to serve the pudding piece by piece.

Garnish with the reserved ground-nut mixture and refrigerate until chilled, 8 to 10 hours at least. Serve straight from the casserole dish or remove the pieces, stack by stack, and arrange them on platter over a bed of chocolate shavings.

Rice Custard with Saffron and Toasted Nuts

Makes 8 to 10 servings

DO AHEAD:
Can be made 4 to 6 days in advance and refrigerated. Garnish just prior to serving.

FRAGRANT WITH SAFFRON AND cardamom seeds, enriched with lightly toasted nuts, and garnished with pure silver leaves, this celebrated dessert is popularly served in terra-cotta bowls at weddings and formal banquets.

A simple version of this dessert can be made with ground rice. Dissolve some rice flour in milk (like cornstarch), then stir it into boiling milk. The milk should thicken almost immediately. Add the sugar and flavorings, chill, and serve.

1 cup basmati rice, picked over
2 cups water
¼ to ½ teaspoon saffron threads, to your taste
½ gallon plus ¾ cup low-fat milk (1 percent or 2 percent)
2 tablespoons shelled raw pistachios
1 tablespoon blanched almond slivers
Seeds from 6 to 8 green cardamom pods, to your taste
¾ cup sugar, or to your taste
Four 4-inch squares silver leaves (optional), or more to your taste, for garnish

Wash the rice in 3 to 4 changes of water, stirring lightly with your fingertips until the water runs almost clear. Soak it in another change of water to cover for 8 to 10 hours or overnight.

In a small skillet, lightly toast the saffron threads over moderate heat for 40 to 60 seconds, then soak them in 1 tablespoon of the milk and set aside.

Put the pistachios, almonds, and cardamom seeds in a small nonstick skillet and toast lightly over moderate heat until golden, 1½ to 2 minutes. Cool slightly and grind in a small spice or coffee grinder into a fine powder. Set aside.

In a large, heavy aluminum wok or saucepan, bring the ½ gallon milk to a boil over high heat. (Keep stirring and watch that the milk doesn't boil over.) Reduce the heat to moderate and simmer 5 to 7 minutes, stirring constantly with a large slotted spoon.

Meanwhile, drain and place the rice in a blender (it can be done in a food processor, but the blender makes the rice smoother), with the ¾ cup milk and grind until it has an almost smooth, batterlike consistency; some texture will remain. Add the ground-rice mixture to the milk in a slow stream, stirring constantly to prevent the formation of lumps. (If lumps develop, process in a blender until smooth, then return everything to the pan.) Cook over moderate heat for another 5 minutes, stirring constantly and scraping the bottom and sides of the pan. Add the sugar and three quarters of the ground pistachios, almonds, and cardamom. Cook 2 to 4 minutes over low heat, and remove from the heat.

This custard should be of a medium consistency, as it will thicken as it cools down. (If it thickens too much while cooking, add some more milk.) While it is still hot, transfer to a serving bowl. Gently stir in the saffron so some threads show on top. Cover with plastic wrap to prevent the formation of a crust and cool to room temperature. Chill for 8 to 10 hours or longer. Garnish with the silver leaves and the remaining nuts and serve.

Sweet Saffron Rice

DO AHEAD:

Can be made a few hours in advance. Reheat with a sprinkling of water. Leftovers stay fresh, refrigerated, for about 5 days.

AT MY REQUEST, RAKSHA Bhatia and her sister, Smriti Chadda (who was visiting from India), made this old-fashioned Indian dessert especially for me. In my grandmother's day this dish was customarily served only on special occasions, because it was enriched with saffron—the most expensive spice in the world.

1½ cups basmati rice, picked over
1½ cups water
½ teaspoon saffron threads, coarsely ground
¼ cup nonfat milk
2 tablespoons unsalted butter
6 green cardamom pods
8 to 10 cloves, to your taste
One 1-inch stick cinnamon
¾ cup sugar, or to your taste
20 to 25 raisins, to your taste
2 teaspoons blanched almond slivers
Four 4-inch squares silver leaves for garnish
Coarsely ground almonds and pistachios for garnish

Wash the rice in 3 to 4 changes of water, stirring lightly with your fingertips until the water runs almost clear. Soak it in 1½ cups water for 30 minutes or longer. Soak the saffron in the milk for 30 minutes or longer.

In a large, nonstick saucepan, heat the butter over moderate heat and cook the cardamom pods, cloves, and cinnamon, stirring, until fragrant, 1 to 2 minutes. Mix in the rice and its soaking water, raise the heat to high, and bring to a boil. Reduce the heat to low, add the saffron and milk, cover the pan, and cook until most of the liquid is absorbed into the rice, 7 to 10 minutes.

Preheat the oven to 200°F. Transfer to a baking dish, gently stir in the sugar, raisins, and almonds with a fork (a spoon will break the rice grains), cover the dish with a sheet of aluminum foil, and place in the oven for 15 to 20 minutes. (Or leave the rice in the pan, add the sugar, raisins, and almonds, and cook over very low heat for 15 to 20 minutes.) Stir occasionally to prevent the sugar from sinking to the bottom of the pan and caramelizing.

Remove from the oven, garnish with the silver paper and ground nuts, and serve it hot or at room temperature.

Saffron Mousse

IN INDIA WE CALL this *shrikhand*. It is made with yogurt cheese and exotic flavorings. Extremely light in calories and loaded with nutrients, this is the one dessert we can eat that is actually good for us.

½ teaspoon saffron threads
1 cup low-fat milk (1 percent or 2 percent)
1 tablespoon blanched almond slivers
1 tablespoon shelled raw pistachio nuts
Seeds from 6 to 8 green cardamom pods, to your taste
2 cups yogurt cheese (page 79)
¾ cup sugar, or to your taste
½ teaspoon ground ginger

Mix the saffron with the milk and set aside for 30 to 60 minutes. Grind the almonds, pistachios, and cardamom pods together in a spice or coffee grinder into a fine powder and set aside.

In a large bowl, with a handheld electric mixer, beat together the yogurt cheese and sugar at medium speed until smooth. Add the saffron milk, three-quarters of the nut mixture, and the ginger, and mix well.

Remove to a serving bowl, garnish with the remaining nut mixture, and serve chilled.

Minty Ricotta Cheese and Chocolate Bonbons

Makes 30 to 35 bonbons

Do Ahead:

The bonbons stay fresh in the refrigerator for about 15 days and in the freezer for about 3 months.

Variation:

To make pistachio bonbons, roll the round balls in finely ground raw pistachio nuts. You can experiment with other nuts also.

VERY CHOCOLATY, LIGHTLY MINTY, with the extra goodness of nonfat ricotta cheese.

3 tablespoons unsalted butter
2 cups nonfat ricotta cheese
½ cup sweetened condensed milk
1 teaspoon pure vanilla extract
½ cup semisweet chocolate chips
¼ cup nonfat chocolate mint syrup
Four to six 4-inch squares silver leaves

In a large wok or saucepan, melt the butter over moderately high heat. Add the ricotta cheese and cook, stirring and scraping the sides of the wok constantly with a large round or triangular slotted spatula, until all the liquid from the cheese evaporates, 10 to 12 minutes. Mix in the condensed milk and vanilla and continue to cook, stirring and scraping the sides of the wok, until the liquid dries up once again, 4 to 5 minutes. Add the chocolate chips and syrup, cook, stirring and scraping, until the chocolate chips melt and everything becomes smooth, 3 to 4 minutes. Remove from the heat, bring to room temperature, about 1 hour, then chill for about another hour.

Make thirty to thirty-five 1-inch balls from the chilled mixture and set aside. Garnish with silver leaves and place in paper candy cups. Transfer to a serving dish and serve.

Strawberry and Vanilla Ice Cream with Fresh Fruits and Chocolate Syrup

SOMETIMES ELABORATE MEALS CALL for simple desserts. Here is a charming one to try. Made with scoops of store-bought pink and white ice cream dressed with lots of colorful fresh fruits and topped with nuts and cardamom seeds, this dessert showcases how, with a dash of Indian spice, we can transform an old concept into something new.

Strawberry essence, a concentrated flavor extract, is available in Indian markets.

Makes 8 to 10 servings

DO AHEAD:

Toast and grind the nuts and cardamom pods and refrigerate up to 2 months ahead. Get the fruits ready a few hours ahead of time. Assemble closer to serving time.

1 tablespoon shelled raw pistachios
1 tablespoon blanched almond slivers
4 to 6 green cardamom pods, to your taste
¾ cup hulled and finely diced fresh strawberries
2 tablespoons sugar
2 to 4 drops strawberry essence, to your taste
3 to 4 medium-size ripe bananas, peeled and diced or sliced, to your taste
3 tablespoons fresh lemon or lime juice
¾ cup canned crushed pineapple
¼ gallon strawberry ice cream
¼ gallon vanilla ice cream
Chocolate syrup or sauce to taste
Sprigs of fresh mint for garnish

Put the pistachios, almonds, and cardamom pods in a small, nonstick skillet and toast lightly, shaking the pan, over moderate heat, until golden and fragrant, 1½ to 2 minutes. Cool slightly and grind in a small spice or coffee grinder into a fine powder. Set aside for garnish.

In a small bowl, combine the strawberries, sugar, and essence and set aside to macerate for at least 15 to 20 minutes. (May be refrigerated for 6 to 8 hours.) In another bowl, combine the bananas and lemon juice and set aside at room temperature for up to 3 hours. (This is not necessary if you cut the bananas just prior to serving.) Drain out most of the juice and place the pineapple in a third bowl.

Just prior to serving, place rounded scoops of strawberry and vanilla ice cream on a large serving platter. Top with the prepared fruits, then drizzle the chocolate syrup over them. Garnish with the ground nuts and mint sprigs and serve.

Vanilla Ice Cream with Alphonso Mango Sauce

Makes 8 to 10 servings

Do Ahead:

Make the mango sauce up to 8 hours in advance and refrigerate. Assemble the dessert closer to serving time.

INDIA PRODUCES SOME OF the world's best tasting mangoes. Alphonso mangoes, India's most fragrant and sweetest variety, are a spellbinding treat just by themselves or when paired with ice cream and in milk and yogurt shakes. Unfortunately, we cannot find fresh Alphonso mangoes in America, so for this recipe, I use canned Alphonso puree, available in Indian markets. If you can't find canned Alphonso mango pulp, use the most fragrant fresh mangoes and puree them to make a sauce.

Mangoes are ripe when they exude a fragrant, sweet aroma, and "give" slightly to the touch, just like ripe avocados.

1½ cups Alphonso mango pulp
2 large fresh mangoes, peeled, seeded, and cut into ¼-inch dice
½ gallon vanilla ice cream
Sprigs fresh mint for garnish

Put the pureed mango pulp in a medium bowl. Mix in the diced fresh mangoes and refrigerate until needed.

On a large colorful platter or in a serving bowl, place rounded scoops of the ice cream. Top with the mango sauce, garnish with the mint, and serve.

Quick Kulfi Ice Cream with Caramel Sauce

KULFI, THE FRAGRANT ICE cream from India, takes on an international flavor when it is paired with this caramel sauce. Authentic kulfi is made by evaporating and condensing full cream milk on the stove until it is reduced to about a third of its original volume. In this lighter and quicker version, I use canned low-fat evaporated and condensed milks.

Makes 8 servings

DO AHEAD:
Kulfi stays fresh for about 2 months in the freezer, the sauce about 2 months in the refrigerator. Assemble just prior to serving.

For the kulfi ice cream:

Two 12-ounce cans evaporated low-fat milk
Two 14-ounce cans sweetened low-fat condensed milk
1 cup nonfat Cool Whip or melted nonfat vanilla ice cream
2 tablespoons each ground or thinly slivered pistachios, cashews, and blanched
    almonds
1 teaspoon ground green cardamom seeds
2 to 4 drops pure pistachio, lemon, or vanilla extract, to your taste
Fresh berries or diced mangoes for garnish

For the caramel sauce:

½ cup sugar
¼ cup water
½ cup milk
1 to 2 teaspoons fresh lemon juice, to your taste

Put the evaporated and condensed milks and the Cool Whip in a large bowl and stir. Add the ground nuts, cardamom seeds, and flavor extract.

Transfer to one large or two small pie plates. Cover and place in the freezer until completely frozen, at least 4 to 5 hours.

To make the sauce, combine the sugar and water in a medium, heavy-bottomed saucepan and stir to mix. Put on medium heat and cook, stirring as necessary, until it turns dark caramel brown, 10 to 12 minutes. Add the milk (it will immediately bubble up to the brim of the pan, so be careful and remove the pan from the heat if necessary) and continue to cook until the mixture is smooth, 2 to 4 minutes.

To serve, place the kulfi dishes at room temperature for 4 to 5 minutes. Run a knife along the inside surface and invert onto a platter. Pour the caramel sauce over the kulfi, garnish with fresh berries or mango, and serve.

Frozen Saffron Yogurt

Makes 8 servings

DO AHEAD:

Frozen yogurt stays fresh in the freezer for 2 to 3 months.

THIS IS PURCHASED FROZEN nonfat yogurt brought to room temperature and combined with saffron and nuts and refrozen. How can anything be simpler than that?

¾ to 1 teaspoon saffron threads, to your taste
1 tablespoon nonfat milk
½ gallon frozen nonfat vanilla yogurt
½ teaspoon ground green cardamom seeds
¼ cup ground pan-toasted (page 34) mixed nuts—almonds, pistachios, cashews, peanuts, etc.
Fresh pureed ripe peaches, nectarines, apricots, berries, or mangoes for garnish

Soak the saffron threads in the milk for about 1 hour.

Let the frozen yogurt thaw at room temperature until it melts, about 1 hour. Mix in the saffron milk and ground cardamom and transfer to a medium freezer bowl or a fluted cake pan. Freeze until it becomes firm, 2 to 4 hours.

To serve, set at room temperature 5 to 7 minutes (or dip in a bowl full of hot water). Invert onto a platter, remove the pan, garnish with the toasted nuts and fruits, and serve.

Almond and Cashew Biscotti with Fragrant Cardamom Seeds

THIS RECIPE WAS GIVEN to me by Anjana Gadh, my nephew's wife. Anjana loves to experiment with all sorts of new recipes and flavors.

Makes 35 to 40 biscotti

2¼ cups all-purpose flour
1½ teaspoons baking powder
¾ cup blanched almond slivers
¾ cup coarsely chopped cashews
¾ cup sugar
½ cup (1 stick) unsalted butter
2 large eggs
1 teaspoon pure vanilla extract
2 teaspoons grated orange or lemon rind
1 teaspoon fennel seeds
Seeds from 8 to 10 green cardamom pods, to your taste, ground to a powder
1 large egg, whisked until smooth, for egg wash

DO AHEAD:
You can store these at room temperature for 10 to 15 days, in the refrigerator for about 2 months, or freeze for 3 to 4 months. Lightly reheat the refrigerated and frozen biscotti in the oven before serving.

Preheat the oven to 350°F. Grease a heavy baking sheet.

In a large mixing bowl, combine the flour and baking powder and set aside. Place the almonds and cashews in a small skillet and toast over moderate heat until golden and crisp, 5 to 7 minutes. Set aside.

In a large bowl, with a handheld electric mixer, beat the sugar and butter together at medium speed until fluffy and creamy, 2 to 3 minutes (or beat in a heavy-duty mixer fitted with a whisk attachment). Add the 2 eggs, vanilla extract, orange rind, fennel seeds, and cardamom and beat until mixed. Gradually add the flour mixture and toasted almonds and cashews.

With moistened fingers, divide the dough in half and shape each portion into a neat 10 × 2-inch log. Place the logs 2 to 3 inches apart on the cookie sheet. Brush with the egg wash and bake until they are golden and feel firm to the touch, 15 to 20 minutes. Carefully remove the baked logs to a rack to cool, 20 to 25 minutes. Reduce the oven temperature to 275°F.

Transfer the cool biscotti logs to a cutting board and, with a serrated knife, cut each log into diagonal ⅓ to ½-inch-thick slices (18 to 20 slices each). Place the biscotti slices on a cookie sheet and bake until they begin to turn golden, 5 to 7 minutes. Turn the slices over and bake for another 3 to 5 minutes. Remove to a rack and cool completely. Transfer to airtight containers.

Aarti's Cardamom-Almond Cake

Makes one 10-inch cake;
8 to 10 servings

Do Ahead:
Stays fresh for 2 to 3 days at room temperature and 5 to 7 days in the refrigerator.

AARTI, MY THIRTEEN-YEAR-old niece, makes this delicious cake that is very popular in our group of friends. Serve it any time of the day.

Aarti's mother, Asha, sometimes swaps part of the all-purpose flour with whole-wheat flour, 2 eggs with 4 egg whites, and uses yogurt instead of sour cream.

1 tablespoon plus 1 cup sugar
1 tablespoon ground almonds
1 tablespoon ground pistachio nuts
½ teaspoon ground green cardamom seeds
1 cup (2 sticks) unsalted butter, at room temperature
2 large eggs
1 cup nonfat sour cream
1 teaspoon baking powder
1½ teaspoons baking soda
1 teaspoon pure vanilla extract
2 cups all-purpose flour
¾ to 1 cup sliced almonds, to your taste

Preheat the oven to 350°F. Grease and flour one 10-inch bundt pan.

In a small bowl, combine the 1 tablespoon sugar and the ground almonds, pistachio nuts, and cardamom seeds and set aside until needed.

In a food processor or in a large bowl with handheld electric mixer, beat the butter and remaining 1 cup sugar together at moderately high speed until fluffy. Add the eggs, sour cream, baking powder, and vanilla and heat until everything is well mixed. Add the flour and heat once again until a smooth batter forms.

Sprinkle the sliced almonds on the bottom of the prepared bundt pan. Pour half the batter into the pan. Top with sugar-almond mixture, then top with the rest of the batter.

Bake on the center rack of the oven until a toothpick inserted in the center comes out clean, 30 to 40 minutes. Remove from the oven and let cool for at least 30 minutes before transferring it to a serving platter.

Moyne's 22-Carat Cake

MOYNE PURI, A NATIVE of Trinidad and my relative by marriage, makes this loaded with healthful ingredients, devoid of any butter or oil, yet delicious enough to be served any time of the day.

Makes one 10-inch cake;
8 to 10 servings

DO AHEAD:
Stays fresh for 2 to 3 days at room temperature and up to 6 days in the refrigerator.

2 large eggs
1½ cups sugar, or to your taste
2 cups unsweetened applesauce
2 cups grated carrots (4 medium-size carrots)
1 teaspoon baking soda
1 teaspoon baking powder
Pinch of salt
½ teaspoon ground green cardamom seeds
¼ teaspoon ground cinnamon
2 cups all-purpose flour
½ cup chopped walnuts

Preheat the oven to 350°F. Grease and flour one 10-inch bundt pan.

In a large bowl, mix together the eggs, sugar, applesauce, and carrots with a spatula. Add the baking soda and powder, salt, cardamom, cinnamon, and flour in that order, and stir to mix well.

Set aside 2 tablespoons of the walnuts and add the rest to the flour mixture.

Sprinkle the reserved walnuts over the bottom of the prepared cake pan. Pour the cake batter into the pan. Bake on the center rack of the oven until a toothpick inserted in the center comes out clean, 55 to 60 minutes.

Remove from the oven and let cool for at least 15 to 20 minutes before transferring to a serving platter. (As the cake cools, it shrinks slightly and is easier to remove from the pan.)

Mail-Order Sources

Bharat Bazar
11510 W. Washington Blvd.
Los Angeles, CA 90066
(301) 398-6766

Khalsa Fabric Plus
2021 W. Capitol Ave.
W. Sacramento, CA 95691
(916) 372-4643

New Delhi Imports
4025 Satilite Blvd., Suite D
Duluth, GA 30093
(404) 623-9560

Sona Imports
2D 1248 Clairmont Rd.
Decatur, GA 30030
(404) 636-7979

Kamdar Plaza
2646 West Devon Ave.
Chicago, IL 60659
(773) 338-8100

Patel Bros
2610 West Devon Ave.
Chicago, IL 60659
(773) 262-7777

East West Foods
Lamplighter Square
South Nashua, NH 03062
(603) 888-7521

India Grocery
199 Concord St.
Framingham, MA 01701
(508) 872-6120

India Grocers
15 Richardson Heights North
Richardson, TX 75080
(214) 234-8051

House of Spices (India) Inc.
Keystone Park Shopping Center
13929 N. Central Expwy., Suite 419
Dallas, TX 75243
(214) 783-7544

Index